T0114089

Jim Noble has written the book I wish I had read as a beginning teacher over 40 years ago. He reminds us that it is okay to see teaching as a joy, as something that makes us want to get up in the morning. He also reminds us that sharing mathematics with young learners is at the heart of this joy. As I read the book, I enjoyed working on the mathematics that Jim shared, I valued hearing the personal contexts from which these activities and thus the lessons had arisen and most of all, I enjoyed thinking which learners I would most like to work on this mathematics with. I have agreed to work in my grandsons' school next year. They will be 5 and 10. This will be my handbook. It will also follow them into secondary school where we will develop the ideas in more depth.

Tony Cotton, Editor: *Mathematics Teaching*, July 2022

It is a real privilege to read about the favourite lessons of a friend and colleague, who my own children were lucky enough to have as their Maths teacher. Jim's creative lessons breathe joy and connect disciplines and span grade levels. As an Early Years teacher I made lots of connections, especially with the playful approach, the use of Maths to explore and understand the world and Jim's use of questioning with his students. His 20 lessons are based on building mathematical behaviours, strong connections and deep understandings – not forgetting a generous sprinkling of fun. Jim's writing is highly readable using strong stories that hook in the reader and eclectic references to resources that anchor, enrich and extend our understanding of Jim's ideas. The layout too, with clever use of summaries and bullet points to pick out key ideas and themes, supports the busy teacher and means that this book can be dipped into even during hectic term-time. No doubt all readers will also appreciate the honesty and humour with which Jim writes about his teaching experiences. An inspiring read.

Estelle Ash, International School of Toulouse, July 2022

Jim Noble's new book *Mathematics Lessons to Look Forward To!* fills a slot on the book shelf that, for me, has been empty until now. The premise is simple: just what it says on the cover. But this isn't a photocopy-and-hand-out kind of book at all. The tone is conversational, informal. The mood is reflective, contemplative even. The lessons and their impact are things that Jim Noble has clearly trialled in many forms (as a friend and colleague, I've been lucky enough to see some of them in real life!) and then regarded from many angles, sifting, pondering, tweaking. He wants us to examine them with us, and if we're so inclined, for us to make them our own. He takes a philosophical turn too, looking at what the lessons have to say about distinctively mathematical ways of knowing. It's great to see the joy and questioning approach that are the hallmark of his teaching come through on the page here. And, as a primary teacher, I find so much to think about in this book. In fact, many of the lessons could easily be adapted for primary classes of all ages.

Simon Gregg, International School of Toulouse, July 2022

MATHEMATICS LESSONS TO LOOK FORWARD TO!

This book is essential for anyone involved or thinking about being involved in teaching and learning mathematics at school. It is packed full of practical and fun lesson ideas and activities, combining the author's infectious enthusiasm for school mathematics with the relentless challenge of engaging students with the nature of the subject. Using humour, enthusiasm and years of teaching expertise, Jim Noble presents the features and potential of ideas and experiments he has used in his classroom. He draws on his extensive experience of using these activities to demonstrate their pros and cons, what you might expect and where they might lead.

In a humorous and engaging account, alongside noting successes the author also includes the moments where things have gone slightly awry. These experiences and the context are used as a vehicle for thinking about the broader goals and issues of mathematics education and challenging some of the stereotypical misunderstandings. Each chapter draws out an important idea for teachers to think about, following a basic three-part structure:

- The lesson and how it works
- What happens and why it matters
- How could it be different? Variations and similar tasks.

Without preaching anything other than the joy of mathematics, this intelligent, humorous and practical book will act as a catalyst and inspiration for teachers looking to develop their own understanding and practice.

Jim Noble is a teacher, workshop leader and author. He has been teaching secondary mathematics since 1999 and working with teachers since 2010. Jim trained in the UK and has worked extensively with the International Baccalaureate. He lives and teaches near Toulouse with his family.

MATHEMATICS LESSONS TO LOOK FORWARD TO!

20 Favourite Activities and Themes for Teaching Ages 9 to 16

Jim Noble

 Routledge
Taylor & Francis Group

LONDON AND NEW YORK

Designed cover image: Pierre Claverie

First edition published 2023
by Routledge
4 Park Square, Milton Park, Abingdon, Oxon, OX14 4RN

and by Routledge
605 Third Avenue, New York, NY 10158

Routledge is an imprint of the Taylor & Francis Group, an informa business

© 2023 Jim Noble

The right of Jim Noble to be identified as author of this work has been asserted in accordance with sections 77 and 78 of the Copyright, Designs and Patents Act 1988.

All rights reserved. No part of this book may be reprinted or reproduced or utilised in any form or by any electronic, mechanical, or other means, now known or hereafter invented, including photocopying and recording, or in any information storage or retrieval system, without permission in writing from the publishers.

Trademark notice: Product or corporate names may be trademarks or registered trademarks, and are used only for identification and explanation without intent to infringe.

British Library Cataloguing-in-Publication Data
A catalogue record for this book is available from the British Library

ISBN: 978-1-032-21047-6 (hbk)
ISBN: 978-1-032-21049-0 (pbk)
ISBN: 978-1-003-26650-1 (ebk)

DOI: 10.4324/9781003266501

Typeset in Interstate
by Apex CoVantage, LLC

Access the Support Material: https://noblegoals.net/books/

CONTENTS

FOREWORD

Jim has been teaching real adolescents in real classrooms for nearly 25 years, and for all that time he has also been thinking, attending conferences, working with colleagues, trying things out, reading (books, articles, papers), watching (learners, films, videos) and also doing mathematics for himself, alone or with peers or with his students. Much of the seed corn of the ideas in this book has been around for all that time, but Jim continues to craft his teaching in the light of experience. In this book you get the naked story of his thinking and the sources that inform his thinking and practice. But this book is much more than one person's teaching journey. It is an engaging, profound and stimulating record of how secondary mathematics is taught and learnt in ways that resonate with how learners think, how they explore and reason mathematically, harnessing their curiosity as well as their concerns about truth, possibilities and the future. As such, it sits somewhere alongside Francis Su's *Mathematics for Human Flourishing* and the work of those who strive to teach mathematics with and for social justice. It has the added authenticity of 20 years' successful practice in one school.

But there is more – it is also mathematically challenging. It cannot be fully read without a pen and paper to test predictions and conjectures. Excitement about mathematical realisations leaps out of his writing: somewhere unexpected the sum of some irrationals turns out to be rational; somewhere the pouring of rice creates cones (what cones?); somewhere a drain cover exhibits prime factor decomposition. It would be hard to read it without some physical activity. He engages sight, sound, movement, observation, emotion and social conscience – all of what it means to be human – in mathematical activity and also in his own planning and development of teaching.

In an age when efficiency and optimisation seem to have become educational 'must haves', Jim's view is refreshing: "No, I can't tell you specifically what mathematics was learned. . . . No, I can't provide evidence that every child involved was thinking non-stop about the exercise. . . . It's up to you to decide". But it is clear that mathematics *is* learned in his classrooms, because it is unavoidable. Technical content about ratio and proportion comes from comparing unequal quantities in contexts where fairness matters to the learners; technical content about some aspects of measurement comes from trying to make a conical hat; algebraic competence is practised in the context of modelling situations that matter.

"Mostly what happens", he says, "is that students exhibit mathematical behaviour intuitively and learn stuff". Mathematical behaviour comes first; learning 'stuff' follows. Purpose makes practice rather than letting purposeless practice flounder around trying to find a home.

As is clear in the book, I have known Jim a long time. I admire his thinking and am humbled by his energetic devotion to his students and to mathematics. More recently, this devotion extends internationally to the profession of mathematics teaching. We must not lose experience such as his in a mistaken rush for uniformity or mechanistic recipes that deny the importance of exploration. His students explore mathematics mathematically. He still enjoys teaching and shows us moments of his own delight as well as theirs.

Anne Watson, University of Oxford, July 2022

PROLOGUE

Lessons to look forward to . . .

I get that mornings can be wonderful. Sunrises, the birds' morning chorus and the lovely peaceful light. I have even experienced the rush of an early morning run and the self-satisfied feeling of accomplishing before breakfast. On balance though, I was not made for early mornings. A 6.15 am alarm on a Thursday morning is rarely welcome, but put it on a school day deep into term when accumulated fatigue has a firm grip on you and there is genuine resentment at the disruption to much-needed rest that can make you forget how lucky you are to have a job you enjoy so much. Maybe I had parents' meetings yesterday – productive but tiring. Maybe I was helping my colleague with the school production this week and things have gotten away from me. Maybe there was one of those unpredictable school events yesterday that sucked me into a vortex of communication I had not allowed for in my planning. Maybe I even did something crazy like an extracurricular activity for myself that kept me up past 11 last night. Any of the above may contribute to that irrational anger at being forced to get out of bed. Maybe I am just not made for mornings. As the first wave of resentment passes and I begin to accept my reality and wake up, I begin to focus on the day ahead. I remember who I am teaching today and what I have planned (of course I am always planned!). I don't mean to sound overly dramatic, but this really is the pivotal moment in the day. There are days when this is accompanied by doubt and uncertainty – *I am not really sure how that is going to go* or *I still haven't got that quite right* – and so the day begins with trepidation. On other days though, remembering what you have planned is just the tonic you need to put a spring in your step. It uplifts you because you know you are going to enjoy your job and create the circumstances that allow you to do it well. These days are priceless and whilst there are clearly a number of factors to build in here, it has been a central goal of my career to wake up to more of these mornings. These are the lessons I look forward to!

INTRODUCTION

What, who and why

I am a mathematics teacher. There, I said it, I confessed. I fill my working days thinking about and trying to help children explore, understand, engage, enjoy and feel confident with mathematical ideas. For better or worse, it has been so much more than a job and has definitely intersected with hobby, obsession, passion, calling and probably more. I imagine that there are others that feel similarly about their work, but I can really only talk about teaching. My own experiences and those of teachers I have known and worked with convinces me that teachers do tend to lead these all-consuming lives caught in perennial pursuit of optimisation, only coming up for air during holidays. The holidays when your friend Ben (everyone has this friend), with a real job, sneers with envy at how good you've got it. When you try and convince them you'll be busy thinking about and planning for next year, they offer mock confusion and say something like *"Aren't you just going to do the same thing you did last year?"* You sigh while your face speaks volumes and try to decide if you want to explain or just laugh it off and change the subject. Later that evening you are hit with a sobering epiphany: *OMG – why don't I just do the same thing I did last year?*

Maybe I should just stop there and leave that pivotal question hanging. Maybe that's the answer: maybe *all* I have to do is get approximately 800 perfectly packaged lessons absolutely nailed down and just churn them out on autopilot year after year. Really, maybe I should! Of course, I would guess that most of us actually do, in a sense that teaching experience helps us to accumulate a repertoire of resources, activities, questions, answers and understanding that does increasingly allow us to rely on many things we have done, developed and learned in the past. Any given year, though, is likely to provide experiences that we definitely do not want to repeat as well. The sheer number of variables in our profession compound to mean that repetition alone is simply not an option. A different class, a different day, a different time of day, something that happened last lesson, something that just happened, a syllabus change, a new directive and a number of similar changing variables will all have knock-on effects. More significant is the very nature of optimisation: how likely is it at any point that we have found 'the best way' of doing something? A new idea, a new shared experience, a new book or blog or professional development session will always offer hope for new, better experiences for us and our students. It is at once the thrill and the frustration of our jobs that there is always the potential for more, different and better.

None of this pays enough attention to the human nature of our profession. Our products are people, not things. Individuals with their own thoughts, ideas, strengths and barriers, problems and dreams. Bringing any semblance of order to all this does indeed seem a *tall* order. I'd love to hit Ben with the perfect analogy here, something about sport, or maybe space exploration, but each attempt fails on some level or another and invites an often fruitless debate about the analogy instead. The best I can do is to consider humankind's quest for knowledge over our time to date and how our body of knowledge has evolved over that time; how what we know depends so much on why we needed to know it or went looking for it. Some knowledge accumulates whilst other knowledge is subject to paradigm shift, some endures and some evolves. Knowledge and how we produce it, acquire it, share it and use it is such an incredible and complex beast. As such, teaching and learning is a deeply reflective experience in general. Teaching and learning mathematics is a vast and absorbing subset on its own. It centres on developing understanding of the very nature of mathematics as a subject, its beauty, fascination and purpose, its possibility and methodologies and the journey we all go on as we do so. So yes, Ben, I'll do a fair bit of what I did last year. A lot happened, I noticed a lot, I read a lot, some things went better than others and I want to develop some of it to make more progress as well as to account for some changing variables. Each year needs to build in some way on the last, at least a little! (Ben says, *"OK Jim"*, and walks off to say hello to someone else.)

My own journey to date has been such a thrill and driven by a potent mix of reflecting on my own practice, noticing what happens in my classroom and the books, blogs, conferences, training and input I have had from so many others. These are the educators who have trained me at university, the colleagues I have worked and shared classrooms with, the professionals on social media, the teachers I have been lucky enough to attend and run workshops with and those who have taken the time to write and talk about their experiences, ideas and reflections. I have barely scratched the surface of what is out there.

So the chief goal of this book is to share some of my experiences, ideas, reflections and activities so I can contribute to this growing body of knowledge for mathematics educators in my own way. Maybe you are just starting out with teaching, maybe you are one of the heroic primary all-rounders who wants to think a bit more about mathematics teaching or maybe you are a seasoned professional. In any case I'll offer stacks of ideas that provide you with practical inspiration for your classroom and ideas for what you might develop next year that you can tell your friend Ben about as well as lots of provocation for thought and discussion (probably not with Ben). The book runs, ostensibly, through '20 of the lessons I look forward to that I'll probably do again next year'. In each case I'll share a lesson idea with you along with my experiences of using it in different ways over the years. I'll share my reflections on why we might want to teach these topics and I'll dwell on the key features and potential of the activity and its type. Then we will look at variations and similar ideas. Through all of this I hope it becomes apparent that these are all lessons that my students, too, might look forward to. I tell classroom stories throughout, which I hope helps to keep you engaged and remember the setting. Our job is serious, but a little lightness is important to keep things in perspective and make us smile! I am acutely aware of the potential for fallacy in anecdotes and the wider debate about mathematics education. What I am offering is here for you to take, think about, throw around, interrogate, agree with, disagree and to fuel thought. I certainly don't set out to offer a pedagogical 'right' (in any sense of the word) or any kind of silver bullet, and I definitely aim to avoid preaching anything other than the wonder of mathematics.

About me

It is reasonable to think that readers might want to know a little bit about who I am and why I might be qualified to write any kind of book about mathematics education. So here goes. . . . I am well into my third decade of teaching secondary mathematics. I grew up in a somewhat nomadic family, attending 8 different schools in three different countries. I trained at Nottingham and Oxford Universities under Tony Cotton and Anne Watson, respectively. After working in the English state system for 5 years, I have been teaching mathematics at the International School of Toulouse since 2004 where I have done lots of work with the International Baccalaureate (IB). For the last 10 years, alongside teaching, I have been running teacher workshops on all manner of things in all sorts of wonderful places around the world. I have done school visits where I work with departments and offer enrichment talks for students and parents. I have been involved with curriculum design and examining and I author successful websites for teachers and students. (That's what I actually do in my holidays, Ben.) In addition, I have also been teaching the compulsory Theory of Knowledge element of the IB's 16-18 diploma program for the last 10 years. I am often given to saying that of all the things that have impacted my thinking about teaching and learning mathematics, this has been the most profound and far-reaching, for better or worse! There you go – credentials?

If I am honest, experience has made me increasingly aware of the aspects of my own practice that could be developed (appraisal-speak). I have played to my strengths over the years in the hope that they compensate for my weaknesses. I wonder if I knew at the start that I was getting into a profession I would probably never master. The relationship between experience and expertise is a complex one and hopefully, but not necessarily, at least some kind of proportional. I love to think about it all. Probably the most significant outcome of all the things I have been lucky enough to do is that I have learned that teachers have such a broad range of strengths and things to offer that it is rare for any of us to have the full range of experiences and the full picture. Although I confess to having met some whose array of strengths has caused envy.

The thing I have enjoyed most about all the aspects of my experience is the challenge of trying to communicate what I think I know and have noticed and encouraging others to do the same. That is why I am writing. Maybe the credentials are enough to convince you; if they are not, then I hope you are convinced by my interest in sharing some of the things I have found most exciting and inspiring.

Originality and the lost bone

Cryptic, eh? In my first year of teaching I was given a photocopy of an activity called 'The lost bone'. On one side was a scale map of a garden with all its features and on the other was the story of the long-suffering 'Bonzo the dog'. A remarkable dog for many reasons. You see, poor hungry Bonzo buried his bone somewhere in this garden but sadly cannot remember where. The dog is remarkable because, despite forgetting the location of the bone, he remembers that he buried it at least 1 m from the garden path, not within 2 m of the garden shed, not under the sweep of the gate, and in a place where he could see it from his favourite spot – along with many other similarly unlikely tricks of dog memory. It was clearly originally made with a typewriter and the map of the garden is hand-drawn. There are the noisy black marks of repeated photocopying and the text and drawings are slightly crooked for the same reason.

You'll get the idea by now – students are expected to use a pencil, compass and ruler to narrow down the location of the bone for the legendary Bonzo. We could get stuck in all the stuff about use of context here and despair at how ridiculous it is that Bonzo remembers all these very specific and precise details but not where the bone is and so on, but let's not – it's a puzzle. This version of an activity I am sure you have all seen before is really well made. If you are not really accurate with your constructions, you won't reveal the tiny patch of garden where the bone is and all the satisfaction that comes with it.

I don't have a digital version of this, but I do have a plastic box on my shelf where I know I will always find it. Once a year I go straight to it and make a bunch of photocopies, and now, my poor students are subjected to the arguably irrelevant story of 'the lost bone' and how I have no idea where it originally came from, how far it has travelled and how many willing students have helped feed Bonzo over the years.

I'd love to be able to trace this back to its origins and see who took the time to create the puzzle, type out the details and hand-draw the scale map. Even then

I am unlikely to find the person who originally had such an idea. Yes, I'd find the creator of the lost bone, but they would almost certainly have been developing something they had seen before. Perhaps they put their own original twist on it; perhaps many, many teachers have done so since. For 20-plus years I have promised myself I would, but keep going back to the lost bone because it is so well done. If I could trace it back, I would owe a lot of gratitude.

I wanted to write something early about originality. It would be bold, and probably just wrong, to claim that there are no original ideas left in teaching. Maybe even a bit depressing. That said, it would be equally wrong to imagine that any of the ideas I share in this book are completely original. Some are not at all, and I have credited sources and inspiration where I can. In some cases, ideas are original to us because we have never seen them before, but it is quite likely that others have had the same idea in some other place. In many cases, new ideas are development, evolution or twists on ideas we have seen in other places. I suppose I wanted to make a disclaimer about the originality of the ideas in the book. More significantly, whilst ideas, tasks and inspiration are key ingredients, the when, how and why of their introduction and use is of equal importance.

If you are paying attention so far, I have been at pains to point out that (a) I am no expert and (b) I don't really have any original ideas. Good so far, isn't it? On that note, please find 'The lost bone' that I have clearly taken from someone else at this address noblegoals.net/books.

ON MATHEMATICS EDUCATION

One of the great fears I have about writing this book is putting my head above the parapet and opening myself up to scrutiny! Even writing that down makes me want to stop. The attention I have been able to pay to past and current debates about maths education tells me some useful things. Firstly, there are a lot of committed, hardworking and intelligent people in our field who have done some amazing work. Secondly, the best debates are ones where people learn from each other as opposed to compete. Thirdly, that no, one, considered, school of thought is likely to be entirely right and none entirely wrong. Generally speaking, if people have put time, thought and research into their thinking they should probably be heard. I am skilfully avoiding committing to a school of thought in this book. It's about my experiences teaching and learning maths and I hope to acknowledge different schools of thought along the way. It's not that I want to avoid the debate – actually it is that I want to avoid the debate! You can read all that somewhere else and probably have already.

The joy of maths

Although I am generally quite comfortable on the fence, I don't expect to be able to hide my preferences and views along the way, so I won't; I just don't expect everyone to feel the same way or to successfully argue that I am right about them. What I will do is lay down a marker right here. It's nothing revolutionary, but probably important. I love mathematics and I love doing mathematics. I see it as a joyful, playful pursuit as well as an incredibly powerful tool for understanding the world we live in. I understand mathematics as an area of knowledge and its place amongst others and how they work together. I think children have the capacity to think and behave mathematically and I think they should all have the opportunity to develop that as far as they can.

I rail against the idea that 'real mathematics is cool, and if you can just survive the seemingly meaningless school mathematics experience then you'll be able to do real mathematics'. I think school mathematics is real and it is cool, and I can't think of a single reason why we wouldn't want to give all our children the opportunity to experience that.

I also think that teaching and learning mathematics can be quite hard and that practical constraints can make it harder. That's why tasks, activities and approaches that facilitate spreading the joy and power are so important.

Why on earth?

Ah, the eternal question – why on earth are we doing any of this? It's the unerr-ingly, real clichéd cry of the student who probably wants to be doing something else. Of course it may just be a curious mind, you know. I have noticed though, through conversations with students, parents and teachers of other subjects (I know – quite a group) that this is a prevailing question and that it is widely assumed that the best we can come up with are some tenuous contextual links, wafty philosophical claims or wild stories of crazy mathematicians past. It's a tough question, it's not a surprise that it's hard to answer and so it's not a sur-prise that people ask it.

Wouldn't it be so wonderfully neat if, for each of my roughly 800 perfectly packaged lessons (I hope I have been clear that these don't actually exist) I had a straight, crystal clear answer to this question. I simply start each lesson by telling my students what we are going to do and then explaining exactly why. The students would nod in appreciation and instant understanding, offering con-firmatory glances at each other and me, and the world is good! No progress without purpose.

As a teacher I have followed what I imagine is a fairly common trajectory of offering answers. I began with a fervent belief that I could not expect my stu-dents to engage successfully with learning if they didn't know why they were doing it. Actually, I think I still feel the same way, I have just changed the way I think about the why. I used to be pretty keen on a utilitarian notion that I had to demonstrate to students the practical use of everything we did. Don't get me wrong, I am not going to go down the path of beating up my naive, younger classroom self. There are many aspects of that teacher I wish I still had, but have lost. Like the pursuit of knowledge I discussed earlier, some things have endured, some have evolved and some have been replaced. I have probably since been to the other extreme and got all philosophical with students about the bigger picture of the human thirst for knowledge over time. Bits of this will have been equally unconvincing to many in my classes. It would be a great story if I now told you about how exactly I have got this right in a single sentence. Sorry. Not that kind of book.

I suppose that, like many, I come down on the side of the bigger picture. The danger is that students are conditioned to expect instant answers to such ques-tions that risk offering shallow, tenuous and unconvincing answers. Students have to know the truth about the subject and its nature. We will deal with the abstract and much of what we do is part of a bigger picture of understanding the subject and its methodologies. Much of what we do is about thinking and behaving mathematically. If this comes across as *I can't really explain just now, but trust me, it will make sense in the future*, then this will be understandably deflating and we need to do better than that. It is often my goal to culture an environment where students don't ask the question. I don't want you to imagine that I have a 'Forbidden to ask me why we are doing this' notice on my wall or that I am afraid of the question. 'Why?' is a wonderful question. No, the thinking is that the task or activity relegates the question to a lower priority for students. That engaging with the task at hand is what they want to do, and they are asking why about something else. Then over time I am able to drip-feed the bigger picture stuff.

All of this is to say that for each of the examples that follow, I am not about to provide you with a 'top 10 reasons why students need to know about this' list, but rather a broader philosophical emphasis on the bigger picture. Of course, we won't miss the obvious opportunities either.

HOW TO ENGAGE WITH THIS BOOK

OK, so I am hoping that this will be fairly obvious. I have already said that I want to share some of my favourite activities and my experiences of using them and use that as a basis for provoking thoughts about making and using tasks. Each of the chapters can stand alone, although there will be threads that run through them, but nothing that stops this being a one chapter at a time book. The key thing for you to think about is how much of the tasks you might want to do - this offers a different experience.

I said earlier that I love mathematics and I love doing mathematics, and I see the difference as important. My favourite training sessions or meetings are the ones where I get to (not have to) actually do some mathematics. As a result, my own workshops with teachers have a similar focus. Always doing mathematics first so we have some experiences to think and talk about. Sure, teachers have a different starting point, but it is really valuable to have a go and, more importantly, to notice what happens to you as you do. The following is a list of questions that I ask teachers to have in their mind as they are working on tasks.

- What happened to you? What was your first reaction?
- What questions did you ask? What decisions did you make about how to approach it?
- What was clear/unclear? What were any barriers you faced?
- What were the key moments that moved you along? What were the frustrations?
- When did you need/seek/get input? How did it help?
- What do you think some of your students would do?
- How could you present the task differently to elicit different responses or address the barriers/frustrations?

This list is already too long, but it's not exhaustive and it's just designed to provoke people to pay attention and notice.

So one way to engage with the book would be to expect that you will try some tasks as you read. In that sense, each chapter could be the basis of a department meeting or a precious training hour. Even if you just take 20 minutes of your department meeting it will be productive and is so much more inspiring than the admin you have to do. Alternatively, you can just read at will; I just wanted to give you the opportunity to think about it and prepare mentally for doing some mathematics and having some resources at the ready. Doing the tasks and noticing will add more to the experience.

To help, I offer a brief spoiler to each chapter at the beginning to help you get ready for what is coming and a summary at the end that draws out the key points and themes and lists some things you might try.

A note on activities – I will present activities in the contexts that I have used them. This is the most obvious way for me to write about them, but it is important for readers to know that the activities themselves are representative of 'types of activity' that facilitate a particular focus, and that each can be twisted, changed, adapted, transferred to work with different students at different stages and ages. As such, I wouldn't want any reader to feel that a given chapter is not for them because they won't ever have to teach this topic at this level, for example. The accounts are designed to focus on broader issues and, where I can, I will offer some of the variations to stimulate thought.

1 What's in the box

What's in the box?

We open with a great activity that explores key concepts of probability. At least as importantly, it offers an excellent opportunity for us to consider what we mean by evidence, how evidence can be different and how it therefore needs to be used differently. As such, it becomes a great way for us to consider the very nature of mathematics with a simple and revealing activity. In addition, we introduce the value of experimental scenarios as a way to think about mathematics, evidence and different types of reasoning.

The advent of social media has made it harder and harder to avoid spending far too long reading about teaching. So many blogs, so many research papers, so many references to great sources. I am pretty sure it's a good thing on the whole, but it has some downsides. Naturally then, as I am a bit of a Twitter junky, you can imagine that I have read a lot about setting contexts for lessons, for example. I even did an advanced diploma in educational studies (yes that's a real thing - somewhere between Degree and Masters) on the role of context in mathematics lessons. It's also reasonable to assume that I regularly give some thought to how this works in my classroom, as all teachers do. The combined weight of these knowledge quests must give rise to some pretty thoughtful contexts for my lessons, right? As it happens though, it is at once refreshing and frustrating to discover that something as simple as walking into a room with a box in your hand and asking students *"What do you think is in the box?"* can really be all you need.

I am going to tell you a little about my experience using this simple activity, primarily as a vehicle for engaging with the principles of probability with different year groups, but also, latterly as a lesson about acquiring and producing knowledge. I teach Theory of Knowledge to IB diploma students, as I mentioned in the introduction. I know, it's only the first chapter and I am already talking about another subject, but please be patient with me. The reason I chose to open with this is because it is a great vehicle for thinking about and demonstrating the different ways in which we know things that are a really significant part of all education (and beyond, of course) but particularly so with reference to

DOI: 10.4324/9781003266501-1

this book about teaching and learning mathematics. Without overdoing it, it has been really helpful to drip-feed little bits of theory of knowledge into my teaching of mathematics to help students understand the different ways of knowing they are using at different times as well as the pros and cons of doing so. As such, it seemed to be a great place to start that we can refer back to along the way. I am sure that experienced teachers have seen and used some version of this activity themselves over the years. Here is my version and what I notice about it.

So, what is in the box? As I said above, I might typically start this lesson by holding up a box (any kind of box) that I have prepared in advance and simply ask students what they think is in it. Students will usually attempt to answer this question straight away. They may base it on what they know about me, what is feasible etc. It is not really surprising that, eventually, someone will guess that they think the box is filled with multilink cubes – a classic classroom manipulative that I am prone to using. Very few will say directly, "*I don't know*", which is surely the truth, and there are lots of things to notice here already. The human tendency to want to guess or to believe, rightly or wrongly, that they have relevant insight into the scenario; that circumstances might be an indicator. If it was a different teacher holding the box they would likely offer a different answer. Students are happy to accept that there is nothing approaching certainty to their answers here, but the fact that so many submit to a belief that they know is an interesting indicator of what might happen generally when they are presented with questions in my classroom. What is important is that they know that they will have to offer some justification – a pretty fundamental principle.

Typically, a conversation will usually result in someone asking if I will shake the box. It is interesting to reflect that it is rare that anyone asks me to please just tell them what is in the box. "Please shake it" always comes first. Perhaps this indicates a preference for wanting to solve the mystery, or work it out for themselves. Perhaps that is too big a leap, but these are the things I think about. I wonder if you want me just to tell you, too. So I'll shake the box and see how that changes people's views. New evidence will end some theories here and maybe support some others.

In an attempt to get moving, I'll now announce that there are, in fact, 20 'things' in the box. It is at this point that students inadvertently confess the limit of the trust they have for you. "*You know, you are a maths teacher, you do stuff like this to try and trick us all the time*". I feign shock and horror that they think I would lie to them and we laugh – privately I ask myself – do I really do that all the time? It's an important moment though to reflect on when and where we might trust the sources that give us information and exceptionally relevant in the current, information age (I am working really hard not to disappear down that rabbit hole). Naturally, I will defend my credentials and implore them to trust me, but rumours of my dishonesty will persist.

Acknowledging the need for more evidence I agree to pull one object from the box, show it to them and put it back. Sure enough, it is an orange-coloured multilink cube. Kudos to the kid that called it. So now we 'know' that there is, at least, one orange cube in the box. This is hard, factual evidence on which we can build. We have, on trust, that there are 20 objects, and so we leap to a conjecture that there are 20 cubes in the box. Someone says, there could be 19 cubes and one paper clip - I delight in the observation and concur, whilst reminding them they just told me I was lying about the 20 objects. You guess what happens next: I repeat the experiment, pull one out, show it to them and then put it back. A lot. After a few times, I'll ask who remembers what we have seen so far just to draw out the point about actually knowing what the evidence is by recording it as opposed to trying to remember it all and relying on increasingly wobbly memories. So we are collecting evidence and at regular intervals, I'll stop to ask students to predict and we are obviously into that bit of probability where the more evidence we collect the more sure we can be about what is in the box. When we stop for predictions we take the opportunity to explore the thinking and justifications and points that come up. This is often where the conspiracy theories come out: *"I think your box has a secret compartment"*; *"I think some of the cubes are marked with something you can feel so you know which ones you are pulling out"*. Again, this is easily dismissed as a bit of humour, but it is an insight into human thinking. Typical reflection points are . . .

- If I pick out two yellow ones, does that mean there are two yellow ones?
- If I haven't picked out a red one, does that mean there isn't one?
- What is the significance of the different shade of green? What does this tell us?
- If I have picked out 10 things, do I have any real chance of knowing more about what is in the box?
- When will I know enough for the knowledge to be useful?
- When will I approach certainty?
- What are the different types of evidence we are using when we make predictions?

Much depends on the class and the circumstances, and so where you spend your time and what kind of responses you get can of course vary a lot, but my experience is that questions like these will bring out lots of reasoning and draw a focus on important subtleties marking the difference between knowing for sure and nearly knowing.

The big prediction – When the moment is right (time is running out in the lesson if I am honest), I ask students to nail their colours to the mast and make a prediction for what is in the box. . . . This forces them to come to 'the best guess', which is often a real issue with knowledge. At this point it is also nice where there are still people sticking to the unsupported conspiracy theory and having to make a decision about what they think is 'most likely to be true'. Whilst we would all accept that complete certainty will be unattainable here, there is real mathematics to do to work from the evidence collected to a 'best guess'. If a quarter of all the cubes pulled out are red, then your best guess may be that there are 5 red cubes in the box – assuming that you believed me about the total of 20. Each table will wrangle with each other to reach a decision and then, one by one, I will reveal the cubes to great anticipation and we'll see how they all did.

I have to confess that the closet performer in me really enjoys playing to responses during this kind of lesson. Let me say though that I know there to be all kinds of teachers and definitely don't subscribe to the view that teachers have to be performers. I even have sympathy for the view that this kind of teacher performance can be counterproductive and maybe even a little egocentric. So please don't take from this that I think all classes have to be great performances. Some of mine are, for better or worse. Most are not. We all have to know who we are, play to our strengths and keep a balance. I do have fun with my classes when we do this though. More importantly, hidden inside this simple activity about the eventually complex conceptual differences between theory and practice are lots of opportunities to think about how we acquire and use knowledge and then the role that mathematics has in that.

Guessing based on what we know about the teacher, where we are and other 'circumstantial' evidence is, of course, completely relevant and can narrow down possibilities, whilst being a long way from conclusive. This might be a nice example of abductive reasoning. Recognition of circumstance though is quite important in mathematics. A common complaint about mathematics education is that curriculum is too often chopped up into smaller pieces that are treated discretely whilst opportunities to see how they link together are often missed for various reasons. Recognising when similar ideas are being handled can be really helpful. For example, consider solving equations and changing the subject of a formula. They can mean different things but essentially involve the same kind of thinking about working with two expressions that are equal.

It is properly intuitive for students to know that if I have pulled out a yellow cube twice it doesn't mean for certain that there are two yellow ones. Likewise, if I haven't pulled out a red one, that doesn't mean that there isn't one. As we keep collecting evidence it may also be intuitive (depending entirely on previous experience) that the likelihood of there actually being a red one diminishes the longer the evidence collection goes on without us seeing one. If I have pulled out 1000 cubes (a really long lesson) and we haven't seen a red, then this is quite compelling evidence. There are a couple of important reflections here too.

When is it OK to use intuition in mathematics?

A deeply complex question. I can see some saying *"never, mathematics requires indisputable evidence"* and there is something in that. There is more to it than that though; perhaps intuition alone is not enough to conclude, but it can certainly steer us in a productive direction. A key point is to recognise that intuition has to be built on experiences and is not some kind of 'gut feeling' that comes to you from out of the blue, nor a Jedi mind trick. When we have relevant experience, then intuition can be really useful. Of course, it is equally important to recognise when we don't have that experience and, significantly, when we get into the grey territory between having and not having enough relevant experience. Probability exemplifies this nicely. If I roll an ordinary dice, what are the chances I will roll a 6? This is easily answered. Even if experience of studying probability is limited, if presented with a game where you win if you get a 6 and I win if you don't, anyone with knowledge and experience of rolling an ordinary dice will say "that's not fair". If I roll four dice at the same time and the game is I win if I roll at least one 6 and you win if I don't, I would venture to suggest that fewer people can rely on their intuition to respond to that.

When do I have enough evidence to know?

This is a question that gets to the heart of key differences between mathematics and other subjects like sciences for example. There are variations of the following riddle which is fairly odd sounding now that I am writing it down.

> *A scientist and a mathematician are held captive against the wall of a room. The key to escape is hung on the wall on the other side directly opposite them. Their captor tells them that every 30 minutes they may walk exactly half the distance remaining between where they are and the key. The mathematician hangs their head in despair as they understand their eternal fate, destined to remain captive forever in an infinite trap that always leaves them tantalisingly close to escape but never getting there. The scientist jumps for joy and claims they will be out in about two and half hours. The mathematician attempts to explain the unfortunate reality that escape will only come if they are able to take an infinite number of walks across the remaining distance. The scientist laughs and explains how they will be close enough for all practical purposes way before then.*

Notice I called it a riddle and not a joke. I do hope you weren't expecting a funny punchline and secretly prefer the knowledge point here in the riddle. It's important. In the context of a science lesson, overwhelming evidence like 1000 trials and no red cube is reasonable. Using inductive reasoning, we can move on assuming that there are no red cubes. In mathematical context, it is absolutely not reasonable. This is quite a significant difference for children to wrap their heads around as a bell rings and they jump from one classroom to another and the rules (not just the subject rules I might add) change completely. This has all made me think of the beautiful book *Uncle Petros and Goldbach's Conjecture* by Apostolos Doxiadis, which is a fictional tale about a man who devotes his life to proving Goldbach's conjecture that all even numbers bigger than 2 can be expressed as the sum of two prime numbers. Recommended for many reasons, but in this context because of the significance of the proof over the overwhelming evidence and the impact it has on poor old Uncle Petros.

This activity can bring these points out. As it stands, even if we keep pulling out cubes all day, all that will happen is that we will approach a certainty. In that sense it can be quite unsatisfying and seem quite unmathematical. The mathematics might come when we try to work with the evidence we have. From experimental data, we can 'calculate' the most likely outcome, and this can be argued conclusively even though it is not guaranteed to tell us the truth. It can be a troubling juxtaposition that we can calculate theoretical probabilities with certainty but that we can't guarantee that this is how it will play out. For these predictions to have value in application, we have to be in the territory of the scientist and large amounts of evidence.

I think this ends up being one of the most significant features of mathematics that maybe makes it stand out from other subjects. I often reference this quote from Albert Einstein:

> As far as the laws of mathematics refer to reality, they are not certain; and as far as they are certain, they do not refer to reality.

When we think about the implications of this view, It is no real wonder that getting our heads around school mathematics can be tricky! This will come up again throughout the book, but I did want to introduce this early on as a theme. It is of such key importance when thinking about when and how we know things. In the activity above we have observed some justified and unjustified use of intuition as a means of working towards knowledge. We conduct an experiment to gather evidence and reflect on how the quantity of evidence affects its validity and then some logical deduction to arrive at our best guess. I have found that familiarity with these differences, and others, has helped students to understand the nature of mathematics. Doing mathematics and 'being mathematical' also involves understanding how we make steps and the limits of the validity of the methods we use. Making arguments for why our answers are what they are is, for me, as big a part of mathematics as it is of, say, history for example.

To wrap up the chapter I will just go through some details and variations of the task. Let me give you an example of what I might have had in the box. By the way, in order to salvage what might be left of my reputation as an honest teacher, I always have only 20 things in the box. Here is a possible combination:

8 red cubes, 5 blue, 4 green (including 1 of a different shade), 2 pink and 1 white

No great thought has gone into this. The different shade of green thing happened by accident one time and became such a nice talking point that I try to always include this. *"If we have seen two different shades then we know there are at least two"*. Having one white is also quite nice. It is often quite a while before you see it and I have done it once where it never came out at all. It can be fun thinking about how you want to make up the box. Clearly there can be all kinds of variables here, like different objects. I have been wary of this since I would be able to tell which kind of object I had in my hands as I pulled it out. You could have more objects. This ends up being a really fun part of task design. It always takes time, but it can be challenging to think about what different combinations might result in. If I am honest, most of my tasks evolve through iterating because each time I use them I observe something that doesn't quite work, or an opportunity I had missed etc. No substitute for trying it out in a class.

I used to do this with 20 sweets for added anticipation – the closest prediction gets them! You can collect evidence together or let individuals do it. You can think about tying this in with some activity on fractions and proportions because, ultimately, students will have to understand the proportion of the evidence that was a certain colour and work out that proportion of 20 (or whatever number you chose). Perhaps this activity will draw on an intuitive ability to think about and work with proportion in our students that we can build on.

This task can take a quick twist into more complex territory if you start pulling out more than one cube at a time. Imagine pulling out five cubes at a time. Perhaps it becomes more like a 'Mastermind' exercise here, where we might actually be able to deduce a bit more about the contents of the box. This whole activity could easily become more of a logical deduction exercise if some of the cubes are marked in some way so that you can tell them apart (like the different shades of green). We can get to some more sophisticated parts of permutations and probability here. It's a topic that can escalate really quickly.

At the other end, it seems possible that there is potential in something similar with younger students too. Perhaps as a daily activity where each day you return to the box and pull another couple of cubes out. The principles of asking students to use what they know to guess what is in the box could work across the age range, I think.

And then right back at the other end, you can see that the activity might lead nicely into the principles of sampling and hypothesis testing. We know that any two samples taken from a population have potential to differ, but how much can we reasonably expect to see?

We can easily explore this idea in relevant contexts too. I have actually just been searching for a house to rent for some autumn sunshine in southern Spain – stay with me. Looking at the climate online, I get information like 'It typically rains here on four days in October'. Where does that information come from? What is the journey to that knowledge claim? What evidence is being used? Does this mean that if I book for a week I should get at least three dry days of sunshine? Where we live in Toulouse is Airbus country, and we have regularly seen the A380 test-flying above our house and school (not the same place, I hasten to add, although sometimes they both feel like it). A good urban myth I heard about the A380 is that the engines are held on with only four big bolts but they only need one. I am sure the reality is different, but it has helped me to bring up the notions of safety factors, reliability and maintenance and how our understanding of the truth here is based to some extent on experimental probabilities, comparing what should happen to what does happen in aircraft design and testing. Probability is so often seen as the study of games (perhaps in part to games like the one I am describing) but the likelihood of certain events happening is a massive industry that makes probability easy to justify.

I hope that I have demonstrated some ways in which this kind of activity can get into lots of classrooms at lots of different levels in different ways. The hope is also that I have demonstrated how it helps us think about knowledge and mathematics on a number of levels that I anticipate will come up again in the chapters to follow by putting a focus on the very nature of mathematics. Like I said, this is just one example of one type of lesson. It is a fabulous part of teaching that different people will think of twists, variations and approaches that never occurred to you and that all of these will offer something new. For me, I love the simplicity of this task, that I can base a whole lesson on the question about 'What is in the box?' Although so much of what we do is so complex, it is lovely to find some simple things. I always look forward to this one.

From the box to the classroom

Thoughts and themes

- Activities can be beautifully simple and it is often worth looking for the simple version of what you have in mind to reduce the potential for distraction in the details.

- I am suggesting there is value in helping students to reflect on the different types of reasoning they use so that they might recognise the pros and cons in future applications.
- The focus, then, is on the nature of evidence that students have and the impact this has on their conclusions. Abductive reasoning can help with circumstantial evidence, deductive reasoning can be used to generate a 'best guess' and inductive reasoning increases in value as the amount of experimental evidence increases.

Task to try

- Try asking 'What is in the box?' The contents can be as complex or as simple as you like. I suggested 20 different coloured cubes, but clearly the potential is unlimited.
- This can be a one-lesson activity or a regular 5-minute exercise that builds over time.

2 Cones

What's in the box?

This chapter is about properties of cones and a 'one-question lesson' that invites students to explore this wonderful shape by making it. The chapter explores many ways in which this task provokes students to behave mathematically, which sets this up as a running theme through the rest of the book. Then we get to variations of how the idea of physically building a shape is an important way of engaging with its properties and relationships.

Ah the cone – what a wonderful shape. Mathematicians don't find it hard to appreciate the joy of the cone. They would probably go straight to the wonders of conic sections and amazing places we can go from there. There is a lovely exhibit in the subterranean rooms of the Sagrada Famìlia in Barcelona where, amongst other things, Gaudi's love of mathematics and nature comes through. There is a small part on conic sections and how they then manifest themselves in the design of the building. Is that not enough, I ask you – surely you are hooked? The trouble is that you need so much appreciation and understanding of mathematical ideas to get at conic sections and beyond. This is both wonderful and frustrating. Sometimes you just have to wait. So when do students first come across cones? I guess we could all cite examples like ice cream cones, traffic cones etc etc, but when and under what circumstances might we expect anyone to get curious enough about cones to start asking questions?

Try this . . .

Start with an A2 piece of card. You'll only get one. Make a right cone that has a base radius of 10 cm and a perpendicular height of 24 cm. You have at your disposal a pair of scissors, a pair of compasses, a roll of tape, a pencil, a ruler, a few bits of rough paper and a piece of string.

That's it. . . . Remember to pay attention to the list of questions at the end of the introduction about what happens to you as you work. Please feel free to read on, but don't make the mistake of assuming you know what will happen to you when you do this task. I genuinely believe there is no substitute for doing for all of us.

DOI: 10.4324/9781003266501-2

Most of the tasks that I have organised this book around are ones that I have done year on year with students and teachers alike. One of the pleasant side effects of that is that you see and listen to so many different responses. Because this is such a simple lesson to describe, it is often just projected onto the wall or printed on a piece of paper so that there is little or no need for me to say anything. It's a one-question lesson. Many will look a little bemused: *"Seriously? I just have to build a cone?"*, and most make the mistake of assuming it will be easier than it is. We once ran an evening at school called 'So you think you can count'. It was a competition between teams of parents who had to make it around as many of the student-run stalls as they could in the time allowed. Each stall had a task that had to be completed and the students issued points accordingly. One of my classes had a cone stall with this task, and my favourite memory of that evening was watching a group of aircraft engineers who had teamed up, spend the entire evening at that stall and still didn't manage to make the cone! It was hilarious. Anyway, I am now going to go through some of the things I have noticed – not that they always happen or always happen in this order, or will happen to you and your classes, but just because they might.

What is the net of a cone?

Clearly if you have just studied nets of cones with your students, then they will hopefully know. I have always preferred to do this task first. With astounding regularity, many will assume that the net of the curved surface area of a cone is a triangle. The beauty of having done this task on your own is that you don't have to admit anything like that – but all jokes aside, and giving you the benefit of the doubt on this one, you'll likely know that mathematics is full of these little things that are obvious when you know but not so before you do. It's the worst possible thing to experience any kind of embarrassment when this happens. Model for your students that this is behaving mathematically – make a conjecture, test it, justify it. For me this is a magic moment. I watch a student sketch a triangle on rough paper, cut it out and then notice that it does not, in fact, fold into a cone shape at all. OK, I'll come off the fence here – I could have told the student they were doing it wrong and shown them the shape, but I don't think they were doing it wrong. I think they made a conjecture, tested it and showed their conjecture to be wrong. It all took about 5 minutes at best. This is often followed by a bit of speculation between students about what is the correct shape to fold into the curved surface area. Maybe some discussion, maybe some more cutting, but always concluding that it is some kind of 'Pac-Man shape' (an '80s computer game character that is a major sector of a circle; the minor sector is its mouth!). Clearly the role of formal language is important here and so yes I am happy to let students use that description, but yes also, I will want to teach them to describe it as a sector of a circle.

How do I draw a circle if my compass isn't big enough?

A brief but important distraction. A compass is for drawing circles, right? Can I only draw the circles that my compass fits? What is the basic principle of a compass? How can we simulate that another way? I am not arguing that you want to turn this into a big thing, but it is just one of the little things I notice and pay attention to so I can help students pay attention to it too.

Pythagoras

Depending of course on your setting, it's a lovely moment when someone figures out the length of the sloping bit. Apologies if this does not resonate with you, but it has always amused me that in my anglophone education I have learned to refer to this dimension as the 'slant height'. It just doesn't sound very mathematical and sounds much more like it was made up by the same people that want to call the sector a Pac-Man. You know, the slopey bit. After a series of lessons on applying Pythagoras's theorem and hopefully thereafter, it's reasonable to assume that students presented with a 'find the length of the hypotenuse' (see, hypotenuse sounds much better) question will be able to do so easily. In the context of a new problem, recognising that the theorem can help you to deduce missing information that might help you to solve the problem is a whole different thing altogether. Again, hopefully a regular occurrence, but it is easy to miss the significance of this and it's easy to miss opportunities for this to happen in classes. So now we know something more about the Pac-Man, we know that the radius (jaw length?) is 26 cm.

My card isn't big enough

The base of the cone is easy enough, but, in the first instance, many have not paid attention to the significance of the limited resources given. This often results in a circle that is larger than anyone had imagined drawn right in the middle of the piece of card (again, I'll give you the benefit of the doubt here). You have to know about the second piece before you draw. Even after deducing that the second piece will be a Pac-Man - there is a tendency for people to be stuck on the Pac-Man image and assume that the sector must be over 180 degrees (so it still looks like a Pac-Man as opposed to what's left if they could open their mouths more than 180 degrees). We can see clearly that that's not going to fit. I love the instant conclusion that I must have made a mistake and I am lucky enough that they pointed it out to me before it was too late. Hmmm, perhaps this is a reflection of the fact that I do make mistakes (shocking, I know) and therefore it's an angle worth pursuing before breaking into too much of a sweat.

Relationships

So in order to solve the problem of how big (or small, as the case may be) my mutant Pac-Man is, I have more thinking to do. This is a pivotal moment in the activity. Students know they have a circle with a 10 cm radius for the base and they know they have to get a sector with a radius of 26 cm on the same piece of card. The question now is – how big is the sector? Then how do we define how big a sector is? Is it the angle, the area or the arc length? These, of course, are all dependent on each other, but only the arc length is immediately relatable to the base. Part of the deduction involved with this task is making the link that the arc length is the same as the circumference of the base, and this is a crucial link that ties the height and slant height (still doesn't sound right) of the cone to the base. This will come back when we get to deducing formulae.

Measure versus calculate

It has been fascinating over the years to watch the different approaches there are to the next step. Once we know that the arc length of the curved surface area is the same as the base, we know how long it is and can therefore work backwards to calculate the angle of the sector we need to draw. Depending on your class and their experience, of course, this is what some students will do – great! Others though are drawn to the arguably more efficient approach of wrapping a piece of string around the circumference of the base and then mapping this onto the sector so they know how big it has to be. This even happens amongst maths teachers. It's a nice reflection point about the difference between calculating and measuring, which does bring us back to the scientist and the mathematician from chapter 1. Even if you do calculate the angle, you'll still have to measure it to make it. Surely we will be close enough for all practical purposes? (making a mental note to make sure we talk about compounding errors at some point).

Others will work out that the curved surface area doesn't have to be exactly the right size: as long as it is at least big enough, there can be an overlap. It's another important point about practice and theory. We can make all kinds of theoretical calculations, but in practice you are likely to need a bit more, right?

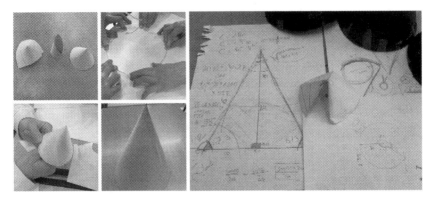

Figure 2.1 Making cones. Some of the various stages of students 'making cones' with a base radius of 10 cm and a perpendicular height of 24 cm.

I guess it depends on the particular application. Having done this, they will draw as much of the sector as they can that fits with the base.

The result of all this is very often a cone that approximately fits the requirements set out at the beginning! Well done, everyone.

Whilst it is simple in one sense for a teacher to get the task running – it's a simple task – the interventions are a tricky business. Listening carefully to conversations and questions and judging inputs well so as to help students keep momentum, without taking all of the opportunity to problem solve out of it. Perhaps I am just a bad student, but I do feel that I have only been able to learn this from paying attention to what happens in my classroom by noticing what happens when I offer certain thoughts.

There are some important observations about the task to summarise. Again, this is one type of task not being held up as how all tasks should be. I promise to stop making this disclaimer. I have just seen too many Twitter threads go out of control when this misinterpretation occurs. I'm just telling you about things I have seen – nothing more. In this case, there is something really powerful about the end goal of producing a physical cone that meets the description from the given material. Sure, there are other times when more openness brings different things to the table, but everyone wants to make the cone and understands what they are working towards. Like what's in the box, it is a simple idea that is carefully charged with lots of possibility and potential.

Also, because of the practical nature, the visual feedback that students get along the way is so helpful. So *often* a teacher needs to observe and point out when students have veered off into unproductive territory. In this case, students can *often* see for themselves. They can test their conjectures and theories easily and learn through iteration. So much depends on when, why and with whom you are using such an activity. As such, the possibility of different approaches is an important feature. All this adds significantly to the accessibility of the task. Mostly I prefer this in its most open form, where I am not trying to control too much the methods that students use because I want to focus on playing with and exploring the properties of the shape before taking a more formal, theoretical look at them. There is something so tangible and profound about actually having to make a shape. It is often not until you try, that you think properly about the various elements and make the significant links.

One of the great tensions in mathematics teaching is the balance between telling, explaining, demonstrating, proving and doing. It is a lovely and important goal that teaching and learning mathematics revolves around understanding. So much discussion is about methods, formulae, algorithms, memory and what order things should get done in. My experience tells me that, not surprisingly, there isn't a definitive answer to this either. There are pros and cons and preferences and maybe I am just indecisive! If I reflect on my own progression through mathematics, I am regularly developing understanding about bits of mathematics that I have known for years and years. This suggests to me that understanding develops over time and that it might be unrealistic to imagine that 'thorough understanding' can somehow be acquired or imparted over a short space of time, but rather that knowledge and understanding can develop symbiotically. Sorry, that's a heavy change of direction, but I want to get to the notion of something like 'the formula for the surface area of a cone'. I know that the base is a circle and so πr^2 and I know that the curved surface area is πrl, where 'l' is my much maligned 'slant height'. Understanding where that comes from though is a different ball game and proving it through algebra and geometry is quite sophisticated. If you have done this activity, then you have drawn the base given the radius of 10 cm. You have used the circumference of this base to deduce the arc length of the curved surface area. You have deduced the slant height based on the perpendicular height and know that it is, in turn, the radius of the sector that makes the curved surface area. As such, you have deduced that the area of the curved surface area will be a function of the base radius, π and the slant height. I know that is not the same as deducing the formula, but at least it is part of the journey. Perhaps, if the class and time is right, you will go on to do the algebra together. Otherwise, perhaps this is just a small bit of understanding that will feed into the bigger picture. I haven't just said 'Hey presto, look, everyone has just discovered the formula for themselves!' – lovely though that may be and even possible in some cases, it is mostly not what happens. Mostly what happens is that students make important links between the different elements of the net of a cone that contributes to their global knowledge and understanding. Mostly what happens is that students exhibit mathematical behaviour intuitively and learn stuff. Its value is its contribution to the bank of mathematical experiences that come into more and more focus over time.

I have used this activity and gone on to show students how we can use this knowledge to prove the formula, which of course depends on a good deal of fluency with algebraic manipulation, whilst also providing an excellent context for using all that knowledge. I would argue though that much younger students could 'Make a cone'. Perhaps the conditions and constraints are different. They are still necessary though. The constraint is often the thing that produces the thinking. The point is that we are talking about a type of task here that can be adapted to different ages, classes and purposes. Thinking about this as a teacher first is the creative part! You could, for example, with a given piece of card or paper ask students to . . .

- Make the tallest cone that you can.
- Make the cone with the biggest volume or biggest base or biggest. . . .
- Make two cubes (or any combination of two shapes) from the same piece of card with a view to having the biggest total volume.
- Pre-cones – Draw and cut two circles out of the piece of paper with the goal that you are trying to use as much of the paper as you can.

Try some – the last one reminds me of the great story of 'Malfatti's Triangles' that David Acheson tells in his book *1089* about how best to pack three circles into any given triangle to maximise the area. Then I am taken to Robert Lang's TED talk about origami and how developments in circle packing gave rise to new possibilities in origami, which in turn led to applications as diverse as folding mirrors to take into space and heart stents that fold small to go in and then expand. I can't do proper justice to either of these – hence the references section – but I wanted to plant a seed ahead of any questions there might be about why we might actually care about any of this. All of them will involve a significant amount of speculating, conjecturing, testing, measuring and problem solving that revolves around the nets, surface and area and volume of 3D shapes.

Prism people

With a massive hat tip to Aisha Miller, who I did my teacher training with, every year when teaching a unit on prisms I hand out a big piece of card and the task is to make a 'prism person'. It could be a robot or an animal, and variations are allowed at the teacher's discretion. I have had all sorts over the years ranging from a detailed pizza to a model of Freddie Mercury holding his hoover in the 'I Want to Break Free' video. The requirements are that there is at least one

Figure 2.2 Prism people. These are images of 'prism people' made by my students that involved them designing and making a variety of different prisms.

cuboid, one triangular prism, one hexagonal prism and one cylinder (I know – now we have to address the relationship between prisms and cylinders). Over the years I have avoided any kind of measurement and calculation and simply recognised that the practice of actually having to design and draw the nets for some of these prisms is a deeply profound experience. Even as a teacher. How do I make the sides meet up with a triangular prism? How do I draw a regular hexagon? What happens if my hexagon is not regular? Prism people are marked on accuracy etc, and bonus points are awarded for the variety of prisms used. Maybe a trapezoidal prism? Maybe a prism with an irregular cross section? All kinds of possibilities. Sure, there are elements of this that might be a bit time-consuming, maybe even a bit frivolous, but I can't imagine teaching students about prisms with letting them make some, and this context has been really productive for me over the years. See some examples below.

The cuboid challenge

Can you make three different 3D shapes that fit together to make a cuboid? They must be different shapes and you may use only one Prism. You have to actually make it. That is where the challenges come. Enjoy.

So I have written a lot about cones here without even going into the amazing world of conic sections. I think everyone should make a cone at least once in their lives and I recommend that teachers ask their students to do it. I have set out to exemplify a kind of task that hinges around practical experience of trying to make something that meets a certain description. I think I have demonstrated how this could be anything from a playful side note at the end of a day to the beginning of a significant bit of algebraic proof that ties all kinds of bits of mathematics together. Our department was once asked by the International Baccalaureate if they could send a film crew to watch us for a day, interview us and our students doing this kind of activity. It was brilliant fun, but I wish I had known before they came that the whole thing would be a complete fix. I had a class making cones. I have a vivid memory of the filmmaker telling everyone in the room to shut up and sit still while he just filmed one of the groups, asking them to repeat what they said etc. We all had a class filmed that day and my favourite bit of the video is when two students from Ollie's class (he is my colleague and classroom neighbour) were used in the video in the bit that was about Richard's class (my other colleague and neighbour). I suspect lessons were not actually that great that day, but they look excellent in the video! I don't pretend that this has always gone super well or is above questioning, but for me, it helps to achieve one of the key goals of helping students make important links by behaving mathematically. It's about cones, but also not about cones. Cones are as much a vehicle for being mathematical as they are the subject of this lesson. It's a permanent fixture and I even did a version of it on Zoom during the pandemic. Definitely a lesson to look forward to.

From the box to the classroom

Thoughts and themes

- 'One-question lessons' take some thought but can then take care of so much of the lesson management because the task is so easily explained and easily started.
- The 'one-question lesson' with possibility built in allows the teacher to spread themselves amongst groups and individual needs.
- Physically making shapes is a powerful way to explore their properties.
- Adding constraints to the shape can provoke different kinds of thought and strategy.
- Let students speculate and test their conjectures and be prepared to help individuals with carefully judged questions and inputs to help them make important links.
- Activities that have feedback built in are really efficient. They will know if they have made the cone correctly because it will meet the description.

Task to try

- Try making the cone as described.
- Try different variations on the cone or other 3D shapes.
- Try asking students to make two different shapes from one piece of card with a view to maximising area or volume. For example, two circles or two cubes.
- Try making a robot/person out of prisms.
- Try the cuboid challenge.

3 If the world was a village of 100 people

What's in the box?

Inspired by the wonderful book called *If the World Were a Village*, this is a chapter about perception, ratios, percentages and proportion and activities based on this book. These are activities that push our understanding while practising in the context of some profound statistics about our world. There is also a logic puzzle, and this gives us the chance to explore the role of logic in mathematics and why it's such an important feature of teaching, learning and doing mathematics.

How often have we heard people speak so easily of 'the basics' in the context of education, and particularly mathematics? It is such an easy phrase – *"you know, the nuts and bolts, the bread and butter"* and it all pulls on this key idea that you have to learn to walk before you can run. It is all full of so much obvious sense. At the risk of an early distraction here in chapter 3, I'll raise my favourite phrase that I feel should always go with it. The phrase about the importance of having things you want to run towards! Not an either/or, definitely an 'and'. But let's get back to these 'basics', and who wants to say just exactly what these are? No one, that's who. Everyone is happy to spout 'reading, writing and arithmetic'. We'll hear things like 'tables, adding, subtracting, multiplying etc'. With more subtlety, we will hear things like 'number sense', but there isn't a definitive list anywhere (or maybe there is and that's what I have been doing wrong all these years) for lots of reasons. Clearly I am happy with a general sense of curriculum hierarchy but keen to focus on some of the nuance within. Let me give you an example. One of my great friends, David, teaches biology across the hall from me. Part of our established banter is that he will pick me up on the way to the staffroom for a cup of tea and bend my ear about percentages. He'll say variations of *"So, tell me when you teach percentages again? We still get all these students that can't do them and if you could just teach them properly at an early age then that would be great"* (picture the cheeky smile crawling across his face). On days when I rise to the bait, I'll come

DOI: 10.4324/9781003266501-3

at him with a bunch of responses like *"What exactly do you mean by 'do per-centages' or 'teach percentages'?"* If I really want to shut him up (remember we are actually friends), I'll give him a problem like this.

> *If I have a full glass of red wine and a full glass of white wine and pour 10% of the red wine into the white wine, then 10% of what is now in the white wine glass back into the red wine glass, what percentage of each glass is now red and white wine?*

Mic drop. He goes very quiet and changes the topic. I am sure I have made my point quite clearly here. As I search for ways to help students understand the nature of learning mathematics, and because we recently had a live link-up with astronaut Thomas Pesquet (very cool), I recently found myself comparing studying mathematics to looking at the Earth in orbit from the International Space Station. The idea that you will orbit the same planet repeatedly but it wouldn't stop you looking for and seeing new things each time. Most of these analogies have limited value, but when a student says to me something like 'I have done quadratics in my last school' I am compelled to help them under-stand that 'doing quadratics' is not a thing and that it is a topic that keeps on giving! OK, so the orbiting analogy is a bit twee, but I like it for now. There is always something else to see and percentages are no different. I totally get the idea of basics, building blocks, walking before running etc, but only some aspects of a heading like 'percentages' might belong there. Have you answered the wine question yet?

This chapter will dwell on percentages, proportion and ratio a bit. Here is a thought. What purpose does the concept of percentage actually serve? Is it not just a human construct that we have become conditioned to need as a means of understanding proportion? Why say 60% when you can say six tenths or three fifths? These are genuine questions. Have you heard that a percentage is just a decimal multiplied by 100 to make it more palatable? The underlying question about how much of mathematics was 'discovered' as opposed to 'invented' is always a good provocation. It does seem possible to me that mathematics and the way it is used could easily have evolved without a focus on percentage as a concept. Not to say, of course, that it doesn't have value or is in any way alone in this respect, but it is a good example to share with students to provoke some of that thought. Is it true that expressing proportion as a fraction of 100 has some inherently more understandable quality? Questions like this have obvi-ously been hotly discussed and will lead into discussions about the emergence of the base 10 counting system as the prevailing choice. It is always a tricky balance to decide how much you want to encourage students to dwell on this, but not to at all is probably a missed opportunity. I have thoroughly enjoyed the series *Big Bang Theory* and it still makes me laugh on reviewing. I recently re-watched the one where Amy agrees to sit with Sheldon to watch *Raiders of the Lost Ark* as one of his favourite movies. It's all going well until she points out that Indiana Jones and his actions, in the end, have no bearing at all on the outcome of the movie. That if he had not been involved, the outcome would have been the same. You don't need to know either the *Big Bang Theory* or *Raiders of the Lost Ark* to get the parallel I am drawing here, but if you know either then you might want to check that out. Either way, it is a nice way into the conversation about percentages.

Anyway, all this leads me to bring up the wonderful book called *If the World Were a Village* by David J. Smith and Shelagh Armstrong. The premise of this book is to try and help us understand about the people, places, cultures, diversity and inequality of the world's population by, essentially, expressing proportions as fractions of 100. As percentages. The cover of the edition I have reads 'Imagine 100 people live in the (world) village, 9 speak English, 25 have televisions, 13 cannot read'. If you are not familiar with the book or the idea, which is available in numerous forms on the internet, then I am sure you understand. There is something quite captivating about trying to see the world's population as this one village of 100 people where only 9 of them speak English. For me as an anglophone, even living in France, this still makes me stop and think. Of course it is time-sensitive data and this is not a trivial issue when using this idea, but this can contribute to the richness of using the resource. The book takes us through various demographics and into areas about access to food and clean water, schooling and literacy, money and electricity and more before looking at how the village has changed and how it is likely to change in the future. Reading it is a thoroughly profound experience. No doubt it would be less of an experience without the proportional metaphor of the world village. Imagining that 24% of the world's population does not have electricity is somehow made easier by an illustration of the 100 people in the world village that has 24 of them in the dark. In that sense, even the percentage figure isn't quite the same as seeing it projected onto a population (100 people) that we can easily see.

So I love this book. When I see things like this then I am usually occupied with thoughts about how I can get them into my classroom. This is where things get really interesting for teachers. There have been many occasions when I have come across resources like this and enthusiastically brought them to my classroom to share and left disappointed at how flat they fell. Not that there is disinterest, but that the interest is fleeting because there is nothing, per se, to do with this interesting new information. Sure, it's great that lots of things cross students' paths: some of them will stick, others won't, but they should get shown things. The real challenge, as I began to say, is coming up with ways to help students to properly engage with them. So here goes. . . . How can we get students engaged with this idea of the world village?

Recreate the images in the book

It feels brave to start with this, but I am sticking to my guns. It's brave because I know how precious time is in school. I also know that many teachers out there are keen to make sure that little time is wasted. I am totally on board with this, but confess that I have come to think more broadly about time and about what it actually means to waste it. I don't expect agreement here, but I can't convince myself that 3 minutes won here and there at the beginnings and ends of my lessons really adds up to much. I never once complained if students missed my lessons for enriching experiences for other subjects and always expected colleagues to reciprocate. I take a broader view that 500 hours of secondary school maths lessons is a long old time. With this in mind, the time we got 100 students together to remake some of the world village illustrations for ourselves was time really well spent. No, I can't tell you specifically what mathematics was learned, if any, in the morning it took us to do it. No, I can't provide evidence that every child involved was thinking non-stop about the exercise. Yes, there was quite a lot of 'fun' involved and yes, you might have been able to catch some images of students seemingly wasting time. I can't provide you with evidence that the payback was worth it either. So it's up to you to decide. I am just telling you what we did. We spent the morning thinking creatively about how to recreate these images and then we fed off them for some time to come.

It does take some thinking and planning though. First of all, the number 100, whilst convenient for percentages, may not be for our groups. I had to plan so that I had the required 100 students and few helpers and all the associated time-tabling issues. Of course, redesigning the activity to suit the number of students you actually have is ripe for the mathematical taking, even if 'What if the world was a village of 79 people?' doesn't have quite the same effect. We'll come back to that later. There must be many ways to do this, even with after-school volunteers if that suits better. I worked together with the geography teacher at school and some students beforehand to think about how we might make the images and prepared some of the resources we needed in advance. Matt had some of his older students sketch a map of the world in chalk on the playground for us to use as our backdrop in a place where I could photograph it from the roof. Of course, with drone cameras, the overhead photo is now much more achievable. We did some other things that morning too, but, again, I'll come back to those in another chapter.

The net result of this was a terrific set of images to go with the world village statistics that had our own students in them that we were able to use for some

Figure 3.1 World village. What if the world was a village of 100 people? How many would have electricity? How many would have a college degree?

display and classroom activity that helped people engage with them less transiently! Check – objective achieved.

We will be interestingly divided into two groups here. Those that spotted the misspelling and those who did not. I briefly considered an interdisciplinary joke, but thought better of it. These are real photos of real activities! The mistake is immortalised. Sorry.

Some 'basic' ratio work (sorry – couldn't resist)

Thinking about readers working with different-aged children in different settings, I think it is worth saying that this notion of working with ratios can be presented in different ways with different twists to make it suit your classes. The details can be the same, but the choices you make and the way you present it allows for the broadness. One of the problems with seeing 'percentages' as in any way discrete from other topics, along with any 'doing' of percentages is that it is easy and not always so helpful to gloss over the inherent connections with other means of expressing proportion. As we said from the off, we can express proportion with fractions or decimals and we also use ratio to express proportion. It's a reasonable question about why we have so many means of expressing proportion and short answers are in short supply, but longer ones would surely dwell on the arguments about discovery and invention as well as how these different means have evolved to work better in some contexts than others. For example, to know that but 9 of the people in the village speak English is also to know that roughly 1 in 10 people do, or that for every 1 who does, there are 9 that do not. Just pay attention to the news and reflect on the different impact these different ways of saying the same thing can have on you – for better or worse.

All of that is without even considering the significance of all that estimating, when it's OK and when it's not. On one hand it seems acceptable in the context of a summary to say 'approximately 1 in 10', whilst a question that asked for a simplification of 9:91 would probably require you to say that it can't be simplified, or that it can be expressed in unitary form as 1:10.1 recurring. It is so easy to create undesirable confusion! With this in mind, it can be helpful to pick out some of the statistics that might avoid some of this. For example, there is this statistic about school. 'There are 36 school-aged villagers, but only 30 of them attend school'. There are lots of things we could do with this. We took some photographs of our map of the world and printed them on A3 sheets and laminated them (serial laminator alert). Counters then act as people.

This diagram represents the 36 school-aged villagers. The background is up to you of course. I like the laminated map because it is a further connection to (a) the specific context of the world village and (b) the personal experience

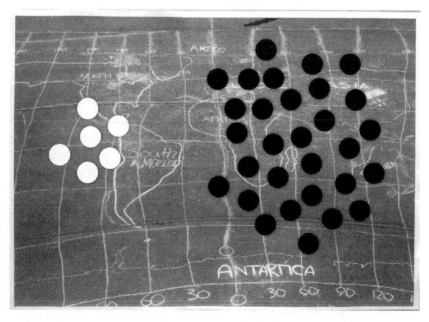

Figure 3.2 World village ratios. For every 30 school-aged villagers who attend school, there are 6 who do not.

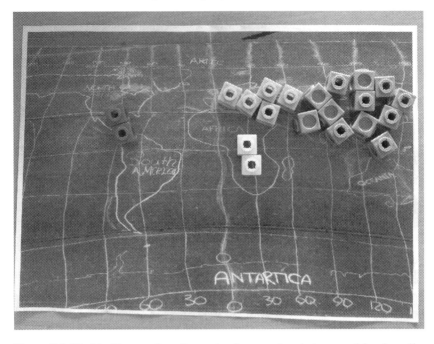

Figure 3.3 World village ratios. Example shows cubes being used to show the ratio of populations in four different geographical areas of the world in a given year.

students had of making these images. The counters are the students, 30 of one colour and 6 of another, so we are now showing the 36 school-aged people in the village. It is quite a nice experiment to present this to students as 'So we know that there are 36 school-aged people in the village but that only 30 of them go to school – can you use the counters to show this information?' and see what they do. This kind of question always carries the risk of the activity going in a direction that you had not anticipated. These are salient moments for teachers, right? Even two decades in I still get surprised that what my students see in their minds is not the same as mine. Imagine that! Still, they are worth asking so, if nothing else, you can find out what they are thinking. The chances are high that students will choose one counter per person, that some will decide that the 6 who don't go to school should be a different colour counter. Amazingly, some are likely to start organising them into groups of 6 where there is one yellow for every 5 greens, for example, especially if you prompt them to spread the students around the world. At that point, you may even get some that decide that all the yellow ones belong in one part of the world and then we have a good discussion on our hands.

Clearly, it would be equally possible to set it up a bit more and tell them to use 6 of one colour and 30 of another and then put them into 6 groups. So many variables here, so much depends on your class, timing etc etc, but I just wanted to offer the opportunity to let students show you that the organisation of this kind of information might actually be fairly intuitive and that it is often just the conventional language and notation that we introduce that is hard to learn or takes it away from the intuitive. I hope what you are now imagining is students simplifying ratios by means of coloured counters. I suspect that you might also be thinking this is not a revolutionary thought worthy of a chapter in a book, but I hope that you also realise that I am pointing out that even the simple ideas have subtleties worth exploring. What does the context of this book and the personal involvement of the students bring to the party? The idea of being the people themselves in the photographs, and then simulating them as counters before moving to a written notation, helps us to a well-established path of understanding. Then there is the nature of the questions, the way we ask them, the example numbers we choose. For example:

- What if, instead of telling students how many of the school-aged children go to school, why don't you tell them that, of the 36, for every 5 that do, there is 1 that doesn't. What will they do then?
- What if we use a statistic like, in a group of 30 people there are 21 adults and 9 children. How will that deconstruction go? How will that look in reverse?

Even as I write, I begin to think of new things we could do with these statistics. Each of the stats could be presented in a different way to draw the focus to a different aspect of ratio like cancelling/simplifying or splitting a quantity with a given ratio. Of course I accept that it takes some time to organise the information and resources to make this happen, but you only have to do it once, then you can use it again and again, and each year you are likely to find a new angle to pursue.

World village ratio puzzle

The 'World village' activity that I have enjoyed the most over the years is this puzzle that, through a series of clues, invites us to piece together all of the information about the world village. Students start with a blank grid and use the clues to fill in the blanks. I'll explain more in a minute, but first I want to tell you where the idea came from.

From the same source of unknown authors as the lost bone, I have carried around this 4 by 5 grid of circles that came with a series of clues about which colour counters should be put on each circle. For example, the clues might read like this:

- *Row 1 and row 2 are the same*
- *The ratio of blue to red counters in row 3 is 2:1*
- *There are twice as many green counters as blue counters in the whole grid*
- *And so on. . . .*

I have set this up in different ways over the years and made different versions of it. It's actually a lot of fun to make these puzzles, trying to make sure that there is enough information to solve the puzzle, but not so much that it makes it easy. Trying to make the clues varied and thought-provoking. Then I would often set up a group where, for example, each student had four of the clues. Students were allowed to read their clues out loud to the group as often as they liked, but they were not allowed to show them. This is an attempt to stop one person from the group taking over completely, which is one of the many potential pitfalls of such group work. I won't get too much into that; suffice to say that I have planned many group activities that have not gone well and some (I'll leave it to you to make a comparison between the words 'many' and 'some') that really have. There have been enough of the latter to convince me that working in groups is an essential element in a rich and varied experience, but enough of the former to convince me that it is never as easy as it I'd like it to be to set up and just one tool in the bag.

In any case, this activity is simple enough and does encourage a lot of problem-solving reasoning between students, lots of talking and listening to each other, lots of conjecture, speculation and checking and a lovely satisfying moment when a solution is found. There is a lovely moment of mathematics when students are asked to say whether they think they have the only solution and why/why not.

The last question is what prompted me to take this activity to my Theory of Knowledge class. In this class it turns up as a game of 'Human Sudoku'. Using a simple 4 by 4 grid in the form of 16 chairs, and 16 pieces of paper given to as many students. The bits of paper are four 1s, four 2s, four 3s and four 4s, and students are asked to sit down so that there is a 1, 2, 3 and a 4 in each row, each column and each 2 by 2 corner. With a class of 32 this is lovely as two 4 by 4 grids next to each other. The group dynamics are good fun as 32 people try to simultaneously solve the same puzzle. If I have a couple of students left over I often ask them to solve the puzzle on a piece of paper to demonstrate how much faster an individual usually is with something like this. As they finish and check, I'll ask them if they think they have found unique solutions. The ensuing conversations are fun as students try to articulate arguments for or against and we ask the question about whether transformations of the solutions should count as different. Often, a direct comparison of the two groups we have side by side is all we need to show that there is more than one solution and help us towards the idea that with a blank canvas there can be multiple but finite solutions. The discussion focusses nicely on the justifications we use. Then we will repeat the exercise but this time I'll sit some of the students down in fixed positions, as in the case of the puzzles we are familiar with. In this case, we will have a unique solution and students will be able to prove that it is unique by logical deduction from the starting points that shows each seat must be filled with a given number and so no other solutions are possible. All this is a model for the notion of going from axioms to theorems. A model for showing how, if we have undisputed starting points, we can deduce logically from them to the solution. If we don't, then the model is one of subjectivity where the multiple solutions are a product of the starting points we choose. Although mathematics is more than logical deduction, its abstraction is what allows us to have undisputed starting points that are much less common in other fields, like sciences and history. Of course, whilst this purity is rightly revered, the absence of context leads us to question its usefulness. This links back to the quote in chapter 1 about mathematics, certainty and reality.

I do recommend a game of Human Sudoku for lots of reasons, but mostly to help students think about the very nature of mathematics in a way that can apply to lots of their mathematics lessons as they happen.

So, back to the world village ratio puzzle. This is the same principle as the counter problems mentioned above and, of course, the same principle of logical

The World Village in 2010							
If the World was a Village of 100 people, what can we say about them?							
What language would they speak?	Russian	Hindi	Other languages	Spanish	English	Chinese	Arabic
Religion	Christianity	Muslims	Belive there are spirits in all natures	Buddhists	Hindus	Others/Athiests	
Access to food	Undernourished and Dying of Starvation	Hungry most or all of the time	Have enough to eat but not over weight	Have enough to eat and are Overweight	Undernourished		
Acess to clean water	Have clean water			Have not			
Acess to clean air	Have Clean air			Have not			
Have computers	Have computers			Have not			

Figure 3.4 World village ratio puzzle. The diagram shows part of the grid that needs to be filled in using the world village ratio clues.

deduction building from starting points to a solution as the Human Sudoku. In a teaching tragedy I managed to lose important elements of the counter puzzles I talked about above. Despite tearing various rooms and boxes apart to find them I finally conceded defeat. They were reincarnated as the world village puzzle. The table below shows a small piece of the grid.

Students will get clues such as . . .

- There are 6 Buddhists.
- The ratio of Christians to Buddhists is 11:2.
- Half of the people are hungry most or all of the time.
- The ratio of English speakers to Spanish speakers is 3:2.
- And so on. . . .

And, I have produced a list of the missing numbers that go in the gaps. This is key to being able to solve the puzzle. The whole puzzle is available at noblegoals. net/books.

And the rest is history . . . I mean maths. I can see that this puzzle might look a bit big and overwhelming for some groups. As it is, it is pretty difficult. I once used it at a conference session where a room full of 30+ teachers in small groups took well over an hour to solve it. The beauty of such a puzzle is that there is enough for everyone to get started and enough for some to be really stretched. It can be set up for different groups of students of different ages or differentiated by offering more clues or some of the answers. I will often say that students are allowed to ask me for three of the gaps. That way they have to think carefully about which of the answers will be most useful to them in terms of unlocking other answers. It could be made much easier by simply filling in some (carefully selected) answers before you share it with students. However you see it best fits your students, this activity has potential to engage students with lots of thinking about proportion, ratio and problem solving and is very much a highlight of my year!

Percentage perception

Beyond the world village, this kind of information is out there in all sorts of different guises. I once stumbled across a survey that asked a sample of people in different countries (and I know we should ask questions about that sample) about the percentage of people that live in their country that are Muslim. They also asked about the percentage they thought voted in the last election and the percentage who were unemployed and the percentage of immigrants. Their average guesses were then compared to the actual numbers. The questions and results were asked and presented in the same way as the world village: "Out of 100 people in your country, how many do you think. . ." and so on. Here we are comparing an actual 'country village' (what if your country was a village of 100 people) to a 'perceived country village'. The differences were fascinating and gave us lots of potential to explore difference and percentage difference and correlation. A survey in a newspaper that my students and I have been feeding off for a long time.

So we started out by talking about percentages and the basics. We raised questions about our preference for chunks of 100. We talked about a wonderful book and the problems of sharing it with students in a way that really invites them to engage with subject matter whilst providing an opportunity for mathematical behaviour and practising mathematical ideas – the holy grail of teaching resources! We even got to some of the fundamental epistemology of mathematics before engaging with a puzzle that can be set at various levels right up to 'fiendish', even for a group of maths teachers. Not bad for chapter 3, I think! That should keep David across the corridor quiet for a while at least, until he gets right back at me with some mind-blowing biology.

From the box to the classroom

Thoughts and themes

- Where do percentages fit in the discussion about proportion, and what do they offer that other means don't?
- The world village book offers the idea of seeing proportions of a village of 100 people. Why is this perspective of value, and how can we use these ideas as a meaningful context in which to explore ratio and proportion?
- A larger-scale, cross-curricular project can offer concrete experiences that give meaning to these statistics and produce resources that you can feed off.

Task to try

- *Try making some of the images with students for a school display.*
- *Use these images to explore different aspects of ratio.*
- *Solve the world village logic puzzle, which can be differentiated to use at different levels.*

4 Goodness gracious great piles of rice

What's in the box?

This is all about trying to give some concrete meaning to numbers that are quite hard to understand in the abstract or without a visual aid to magnitude. Based on the fabulous travelling exhibition from Stan's Cafe called *Of All the People in All the World*, where a person is represented by a grain of rice, we get into lovely layers of estimation, shapes, comparison and juxtaposition. The chapter goes on to reflect on general issues with 'infographics' and the heavy reliance on good mathematical design or mathematical investigation!

Figure 4.1 Jar of rice. How many grains of rice do you think are in this jar?

DOI: 10.4324/9781003266501-4

How many grains of rice do you think there are in this little jar? Go on, seriously, look at the picture. How many grains of rice do you think are in there? How are you going about making your estimate? I highly recommend giving yourself a few minutes to think about this and try to zero in on your best estimate. I promise, the answer will be revealed and, yes, I did count them all myself. I don't waste my weekends!

I am a hoarder (I know, stay with me), so my classroom cupboards are a treasure trove of mathematical goodies and memorabilia, otherwise known as a disastrous mess. Occasionally I am motivated to have a clear-out and employ the 'If I haven't been in that box in 6 months then I don't need it' rule or even the popular 'Does it bring you joy?' filter. Sleeves rolled up and ready for action, I dive in and then, something in the box catches my eye and I dig a little deeper and it's all over. I'll find an old piece of work, picture, prop or relic that does, in fact, bring me joy. It will remind me of an activity I haven't done for a while or an idea I once had, or a student I once taught and my head will spin off to something I want to recreate. It's just the way I am, for better or worse, and I love having boxes full of rubbish that I can occasionally sort through for this kind of experience. You'll be pleased to know that there are days when I am more successful and *do* manage to get rid of things that I really shouldn't be keeping. I was clearing out some cupboards just yesterday and came home with lots of good memories and ideas. It just feels like the longer you do this, the more aware you are of the huge number of possibilities there are for your classroom. This book is about the things I never forget to do, but there is a whole range of ideas and tasks that I have done once or twice and remember to fit in when I find some kind of reminder. There isn't time to do everything, so some things come and go when they could just as easily be permanent fixtures. So many ideas, so little time. My cupboards and boxes help me remember! I have thought, though, that one thing that must occur as a little odd to the cleaning and maintenance staff in my school is the frequency with which they find piles of rice in my room. It's fair enough, so I should probably explain.

The year was 2009 and I had travelled to Swansea for the ATM annual conference. I had agreed to be part of a session run by Anne Watson about mathematics and dance. There is more about that in a later chapter about 'Dancing Vectors', but for now, I like the delusion that you might be imagining me as some coordinated dancer type! My experiences of these conferences have always been wonderful for lots of reasons. Probably the most significant is to be surrounded by so many people who spend their days doing the same thing as me, having the same interests and then sharing expertise and experiences with them. Then the conference provides you with such a rich variety of contexts in which to do that. On this particular Wednesday afternoon, we were invited to visit an exhibition from the theatre company Stan's Cafe titled *Of All the People in All the*

World. If you have seen it, then you'll know. If you haven't, then what follows is a poor substitute for the real thing, but enough to help you see how this got into my classroom. The basic premise is quite simple. One grain of rice represents one person. The room is then filled with very carefully juxtaposed piles of rice that represent different groups of people. The biggest pile of rice in the room is labelled as 'The number of millionaires in the world'. Two or three members of the company wear brown coats and are continuously in the act of weighing out new piles of rice as the exhibition evolves in front of you. We, the audience, point and gasp and count and estimate and think and discuss as we look at piles of rice that tell us about our world. A pile of 6 million grains of rice is juxtaposed with a single grain of rice labelled as Adolf Hitler. Another shows us the number of male Nobel Prize winners shaped like the long part of an exclamation mark with the female Nobel Prize winners as the dot. Two more piles compare the number of daily births to daily deaths globally. This is just a little taster to help you get the idea.

It is a profound and fascinating afternoon that sparks so much reflection, even still as I think about it now. I'll spare you the full review and leave it to your imagination, and hopefully the opportunity to see it for yourselves. Let's move on to how we might be able to draw on this for some great mathematical activity for the classroom. As I said in the last chapter, this can end up being frustrating. Something that we experienced and enjoyed the deep mathematical nature of does not necessarily translate to our students in different circumstances. I'll confess though, that my first thought here was that this rice show was something I thought we could recreate at school and that is where it started. I think I am prepared to concede that sometimes my enthusiasm for such projects may have come at the expense of some other equally (?!?!) useful things I could have been doing. It's just the way it went for me and I think, in general, I would dive into projects without being sure of what would come out of them. The second time, of course, I was better able to add and design different foci that brought a bit more control. Often first times are a bit more intrepid. Having played with the idea a bit over the years, I think it is worth pointing out some of the ways in which this show is or is not potentially mathematical to get us started.

How much does a grain of rice weigh?

Having counted all the grains in that jar we opened the chapter with, I am happy that it doesn't make sense to count out individual grains of rice for this project. Well, at least for an amount beyond which the eye can't easily count them. For example, in one iteration of this project, students compared the number of people that could fit into different stadia. Each pile of rice was arranged in the oval form of a football stadium, containing thousands of grains of rice. In the gap in the middle, they diligently put 23 grains of rice. Two teams of 11 and a referee. So, counting the 23 was necessary; the crowds could be done by estimation.

Still, estimation is no simple thing here. There is no way we can get away with 'looks like' or 'I reckon', and students will reach this conclusion for themselves as they search for efficient ways to estimate. How can we estimate the weight of a grain of rice? One grain of rice won't register on even a sensitive set of scales we borrowed from the science department. Are any two grains of rice even the same? Does it matter what type of rice we use? This in itself provides an excellent opportunity for mathematical activity. Perhaps each student in the class can count out 100 grains of rice and weigh them to work out a mean average. Maybe you can pool the results of the whole class for something more accurate? Maybe you can then compare with the class next door? This kind of activity can go across the school age range, from those first encountering the idea of a mean average to those dealing with the fragile world of sampling, distributions and hypothesis tests. We could add in a focus on the significance of errors in approximation if it came up. Once we have established a meaningful exchange rate between the number of grains and weight, we can use this directly proportional relationship to measure out different piles. One of the barriers to reproducing this exercise in school is the limit to the amount of rice you can get hold of and so, it can be useful, in more ways than one, to get an idea of how much rice we will need for various displays before we start making them! So, already, we have a lot of mathematics going on here.

What shape is a pile of rice?

So the thing that struck me when I first saw the exhibition was the choice of shape for the piles. As I remember it, the piles were, for the most part, in the shape of cones. Lovely cones, remember them? That's what shape grain-like substances will settle into if the point of 'pouring' remains unchanged. Of course, a number of physical realities will stop them being perfect cones, but they will be close enough for estimation. These are naturally occurring cones, which is a nice moment. I wonder though, when we pour grains of rice and allow gravity and friction to decide the shape, will the height of the cone always be proportional to the size of its base? If the point of pouring moves at a constant speed in a straight line whilst pouring, then the result will be more like a triangular prism with a half a cone on each end. All this makes me think about the link between the number of grains of rice, the weight and then, the volume. I'll come back to this later.

So I hope, at this stage, that teachers across the age range can see plenty of potential here for mathematical activity, even if it is tinged with a little fear of spilled grains of rice all over the floor. It is true that there are slightly less inspi-rational, but equally important considerations about practicality to be made here. Lots of containers and trays and patience. We once ran this across our primary and secondary school, with classes from all the different year groups contributing to the display and working with the exercise in a way that was most relevant to them and their courses.

What shall we show?

What I have always underestimated about this task is how difficult it is to find and settle on the numbers and statistics we want to show in our exhibition. Try it; it's not easy. What piles of rice do you think it would be interesting to make and include in such an exhibition? What shall we juxtapose? Now add in the real-ity that there is a limit to the amount of rice you can have and display! Of course, as you think, you will inevitably want to know what a million grains of rice looks like as a cone-shaped pile and how many bags of rice you'd need to make it. Put this on your list of things to think about from time to time.

I remember, the first time I tried this, I got the rice out and said *"Come on then, what piles of rice shall we make?"* naively assuming that the great and feasible ideas would come flowing. There were plenty of ideas, but I had to shoot most of them down, which of course was disappointing. An important decision to make is an artistic one. I really appreciated that in the original exhibition, they stuck always to the 'one grain is one person' base. This is powerful for lots of rea-sons and terrific for helping us to reflect on the different perceptions afforded to whole groups of people as opposed to individuals. *"One death is a tragedy, 1000 is a statistic"* (origin disputed). Clearly though, if one grain of rice can represent 10 or 100 people, then this opens more doors for this activity, both in terms of mathematics and the numbers you can display. For me though, it does detract from the focus you get when you imagine that each grain of rice you see is a person. There are ways around. One of my favourite displays we ever made was about population density. There were 15 equally sized black square bits of paper representing 15 countries/places and on each were grains of rice that represented the number of people that live per square kilometre in that place. Australia juxtaposed with Macau was successfully provocative. As such, we found it more effective to go with 'rates' as an alternative to letting a grain of rice represent more than one person. Once you have made some decisions like this, it helps to prepare for the 'What do you want to show?' element.

Another time we made this display, I actually started a conversation amongst my colleagues from different subjects (different planets!). They set about think-ing about the kinds of things that they had been doing with students in their classes. This was a terrific way to spread this through the school and resulted

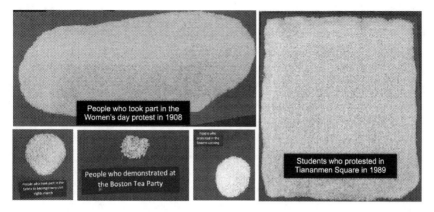

Figure 4.2 Protests. One grain of rice represents one person. These piles show the number of people estimated at various famous protests.

in some great ideas. Another favourite of mine was a series of piles of rice that showed the number of people that had been at different protests throughout history, including the March on Washington and Tiananmen Square.

In any case, my point is not to underestimate the challenge of finding statistics that you want to show that are feasible. I like to have suggestions ready to help steer students in fruitful directions. And remember, 1 million grains of rice is more bags of rice than you think! (well it was for me, anyway). At the time, Stan's Cafe toured with 12 tonnes of rice in the back of a lorry. Here are some of the things we did:

- People who were living in the Calais 'Jungle' at the time juxtaposed with people that crossed the English Channel daily, those forced to leave their homes, daily, due to persecution or conflict and the number of people who work for UN refugee help. This was also near the number of people who fit in the biggest stadium in Toulouse.
- As mentioned already, the comparison of different stadia.
- Number of people who work for Airbus in Toulouse, the number that can fit on an A380, the number for an A318 and the number of people who attended the Twenty One Pilots concert in Paris.
- Casualties from different battles and conflicts.
- As mentioned already, the attendance at various historical and current protest marches.
- Population densities for different countries and places.
- Historical populations of our school.
- Numbers of people in different professions in France.

A big display – OK, for sure, this was messy, but so worth it for my money. We have done this and put the piles of rice against the wall in our school reception. Yes, I was worried that it would get messy and yes it probably took a disproportionate amount of time to get ready, but we did it and for 2 weeks, students walked past the piles of rice every day and looked at them and talked about them. Teachers brought classes down to focus on some of the piles that were relevant to what they were doing. Parents and visitors perused as they waited in the reception, and it was an incredible focus. We even had a reception where we invited parents to come after school one day to see what we had done. I was pleasantly surprised that, barring a couple of accidents, everyone was very respectful and have always been glad that we did that. I have kept photographs of course and shared some of them here, and photographs are a good alternative to the display, not least because they are less messy, easier and allow you to reuse rice for different piles.

Spin-offs

One of the things we have come up against is that students get very ambitious with the volume of rice that they need to show their stats. I remember the enthusiasm that hit when a student said, *"Why don't we have a pile of rice for the populations of all the different countries represented in our class?"* "Yes", I said, *"that would be amazing, let me just go and buy all the rice within a 100 mile radius and we'll get started"*. The student was Indian and sat next to their Chinese friend. Not to be defeated, I sat with my colleagues and worked out that we could have fun with some spin-offs. Whilst it could detract from the original Stan's Cafe show, it seems right for a school. We decided that we could work on a principle of 1 mm^3 representing one person and then make shapes of different volumes to represent different groups of people. Here we got into one of my favourites.

Population pyramids (tetrahedrons) – We went back to the class that wanted to show all the populations and suggested that they needed to make regular tetrahedrons where 1 mm^3 represented one person. Now there is a task. What is the side length you need for India? That is another one I am leaving for you, but suffice to say the mathematics of that problem was perfect for that IGCSE class and varied and rich and engaging. A really wonderful project that ultimately resulted in the production of a general formula for converting the desired volume into the side length. It's just a terrific example of how experimenting with a simple idea can take you to places and opportunities you hadn't imagined.

Other classes worked with various cylinders and prisms to make some 3D infographics with this volume version of the rice show.

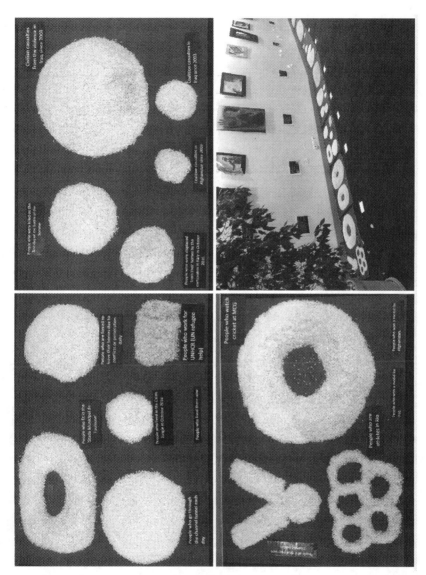

Figure 4.3 The rice show. These images show some examples of the display based on the activities suggested in this chapter.

This exercise crosses neatly into the world of infographics, and this too is really fertile ground for mathematical activity. Take the 'Billion Dollargram' as produced by David McCandless and Information is Beautiful. This is a rectangle divided into smaller rectangles, where the area of the rectangle represents a certain number of billions of dollars that are associated with the name of the square. Things like different countries' defence budgets appear alongside national debts and foreign aid contributions and any other numbers that may be in the public eye. It's not hard to imagine mathematical activity surrounding those rectangles and making them fit together. There is even good activity in checking the accuracy of the diagram! The internet is awash with infographics, and it will not come as a shock to many of you that there are some truly terrible and woefully inaccurate examples out there. The good news for teachers is that where these fail to communicate usefully, they do still have potential for investigation and activity. The theory is that such diagrams are designed to help us visualise information with a view to understanding it better. A noble aim indeed, but it doesn't always work out that way. Take for example, the use of a circle. Can you picture what two circles look like where one has twice the area of the other? And so the lid comes off another juicy can of mathematical worms.

I promised I would return to the jar of rice at the beginning. I am sure that you will all be familiar in one way or another with the idea of the 'wisdom of crowds'. There is lots to read about this, not least in James Surowiecki's book by the same title. In this context, the suggestion is that, if you ask enough people to estimate the grains of rice and average their guess, then you might get somewhere close to the actual number. Let's cut to the chase: I have never seen it work with the grains of rice! Sorry. I put together four different jars, one with foam packing peanuts, one with sweets, one with staples and this one with rice and spent several years collecting guesses at different events. Amazingly, the mean guesses got pretty close to the sweets and the packing peanuts, but not so much on the other two. This is a fun context to explore a bit of data processing and an even more fun context to discuss. Why might it work or not work? Under what circumstances? There are some lovely subtleties about data skew. For example, there is no limit to overestimating, but clearly no one is going to guess zero or negative numbers. Once again, a very easily created little project with lots of potential. Anyway, for now, there are 7596 grains of rice in the jar. How did you do?

The intention here was to share our experiences of playing with rice inspired by that amazing installation I first saw in Swansea. Even from writing about it again I am reliving, rethinking and excited for the next incarnation of this. I hope that teachers across the age range have seen potential for activity here and that you are thinking about trying one of them. Like the world village context, this rice-based adventure is a perfect opportunity to build some important horizontal links with other disciplines and see mathematics in real, relevant contexts about understanding the world around us. The activities tick a lot of boxes in the mathematical behaviour box, but the main attraction here is the way it feeds into the notion of mathematics as a powerful tool for understanding the world around us, a lot like the world village. Here there is a delicious crossover with the arts, their involvement as a medium for helping people engage with numbers and their associated ideas, just as they do for other important stories. This is all part of the human condition and the things we need and enjoy to help us engage. I thoroughly recommend such a school-wide project every now and then or, if that doesn't suit (and let's face it, there may be many reasons for that), put a scaled-down version on your yearly schedule and build displays over time. I also recommend the cycle of hoarding and storing and then clearing out your cupboards occasionally, although I think my cycles might benefit from some increased frequency. For those of you who made a considered estimate of the number of grains of rice, or even a random guess, or even those of you that are thinking about doing just as you read this. . . . There are 7596 grains of rice in the jar.

From the box to the classroom

Thoughts and themes

- Displays and infographics can be effective ways to help people engage with statistics and numbers.
- Making such displays can be a deeply mathematical task and feed into the view of mathematics as a powerful tool for understanding the world around us.
- All this provides excellent opportunities for cross curricular activity and understanding.

Task to try

- Try working out an estimate for the average weight of a grain of rice.
- Consider making, photographing and/or displaying piles of rice that represent different groups of people. This can be done across the age range and on a whole range of different scales.
- Try the activity where you have to deduce the side length of a regular tetrahedron whose volume in cubic millimetres represents the population of a country.
- There are multiple variations on the above.

5 How do I love thee, let me count the ways

What's in the box?

This chapter explores a few activities as means of exploring the principle of asking 'How many ways . . .' and how that freedom invites a degree of ownership over a task and releases the speculative mathematician within who is encouraged to think about what they could do as opposed to what they are supposed to do. We also point towards the playful, creative nature of mathematics as a pursuit. These are then the elements that can be used in the design and use of other tasks.

Much is made, quite rightly, of the role of memory in education and whilst I know we could easily dwell on this here, I'd like to skip to a possibly more concerning issue of teacher memory. I am aware that dwindling memory is a terrible affliction that awaits many of us in the future and so I am hesitant to make light of this, but it can be quite disturbing sometimes to realise how many things about my job I regularly forget. I am going to be kind to myself and put it down to the sheer volume of daily sensory input that I get. The number of classes and students that come in and out of my door on a daily basis can make it difficult to hold on to certain details. I sometimes have a cold sweat in the early part of a lesson as I introduce an activity – one I have been very much looking forward to – as it dawns on me that I may have actually done this with this class already. It is such a shattering thought; a gut-wrenching combination of disappointment that you can't do the activity and the realisation that you have no plan B and a class full of students. Although I have enough experience to navigate such a situation with students, it is still a little stressful. Anyway, because I am struggling to remember, I'll pause and ask a question to the class to see if they remember. Then it gets worse because it becomes apparent that you may well have offered the activity to them, but that it was not as memorable for them as you hope. Then you consider doing it again! You can see how this can spiral. As I wrote in the previous chapter about fishing through old boxes in my classroom reminds me of things, the number of things you have done in your classroom over a long period of time is enormous and it can be

DOI: 10.4324/9781003266501-5

fun to stumble across things you haven't used in years. At the same time, it can be alarming how much you forget. Even simple strategies that you used to use or things you know are good practice that you just got out of the habit of doing can be easily forgotten until a colleague talks about it or you have a sudden bolt out of the blue and you are suddenly all over it. Perhaps I have confessed too much here, perhaps it is only me, but I just have a sense that because there are so many more possible ideas and activities and strategies out there than there are lessons to teach I can only ever keep a certain amount of them in my mind at the same time.

This chapter is less about a particular activity and more about the ways in which the theme 'How many?' is such a wonderfully powerful approach for teaching and learning and can so often be overlooked or forgotten. Throughout my career I have gone through so many cycles of forgetting and rediscovering this theme and experiencing repeated 'Dory-like' fresh joy every time. (You know, the blue fish with the very short memory span who helps Nemo's dad find him.) As I have probably said already, I am taken with the idea that I have heard many people espouse that tasks themselves are less likely to bring richness than the way in which you use or present them and the exchanges you have and questions you ask along the way. There is of course lots of good writing about questioning, so this theme is just the tip of the iceberg, but I wanted to get it in early as it is so easily applicable to different students of different ages in different contexts.,

The basic principle I am getting at here is about asking students to find 'how many ways' something can be done. This simple question asked at the right moment in the right culture seems to release a powerful dose of motivation and engagement that leads to some very effective mathematical behaviour. The openness of the question, not surprisingly, opens a whole range of possible avenues and thought processes and is a key moment where students are invited to think about 'what they could do' as opposed to what they think they are 'supposed to do'. Thinking about examples that I wanted to offer here made me reflect that many, maybe even most readers might be thinking that this is an elementary notion that I probably didn't need to write about. Then I remembered two things. First, this is a book where I am writing about my favourite things to do in the classroom, so this belongs. Second, this key idea about the difference between 'could do' and 'supposed to do' whilst seemingly elementary is nonetheless significant in terms of what it might mean to do mathematics or behave or think mathematically.

As I try to articulate the significance of this, I am often reminded of the emotionally charged account that Andrew Wiles gives in Simon Singh's documentary *Fermat's Last Theorem*, when Andrew is trying to describe what it means to do mathematics. He likens it to first being in a dark room and shuffling around to try and establish where the furniture is. Once you know this you move with more confidence and eventually make a map of the room at which point you have effectively turned the light on. Then you find another door, try to open it and start all over again in a new room. OK, so all analogies have their limits, but I have often come back to this one and shared it with students in trying to help them understand the nature of doing mathematics. I even christened my classroom the dark room for a while, but as you can imagine, this name was not understood by enough people to prevent the associated confusion and inevitable, unfortunate misinterpretation that students in my room were often left in the dark. Hey ho. I still recount the analogy though and, when there is time, share some of the bigger story and let Mr Wiles tell it himself (oh, the joy of YouTube). The 'How many?' theme is a perfect way to let students experience a bit of this for themselves and help them to recognise it too.

We know that different tasks on different days will be made up of different ingredients and that over a time period we might want to keep a variety. Some will occur more than others but this one for me is like coconut milk to Thai cooking. So I'll keep writing!

Let me run through a few of them to help me share what it is that appeals.

Areas of shapes

This is a nice simple one to help us get the idea. How many rectangles can you draw with an area of 48 cm^2? Clearly much depends on what the students already know about area already and clearly the choice of number has a big impact on what follows. Perhaps the question comes with a picture of a 6 by 8 rectangle and a grid showing 48 squares, perhaps the class has already looked at area in a different context. The details here are up to you and your classes and I hope you can see that you as the teacher can set this up in different ways accordingly. Once that is done then you are away. There is something primitively empowering about the idea that it can be relatively easy to get started and that no two students are compelled to go in the same direction. Something enticing about knowing there might be any number of rectangles out there to find. Find one or two and then you are motivated to look for more. Of course, depending on your class, it may well not be long before students want to talk to you about having found them all, the relationship to the factors of 48 and the possibility of using numbers other than integers. In a breath, you have students exploring a proof that they have found them all, exploring the applicable constraints and asking questions about moving the task on.

Using integers might be an assumed constraint; what if we take it off and allow halves? What does that do to the number of possibilities? What about thirds? What happens with different starting numbers? When does the emphasis of such a task move to be about working with fractions of numbers?

Stop and think about what mathematics students might be using and practising in pursuing these questions. Think about the strategies they might use or that you could suggest and what it means to use them. Think about the conversations they might have and the reasoning they might use. I am just asking you to recognise the potential that can lie inside simple questions, depending on how you present them, what constraints you introduce or take away, and what freedom you give your students to ask and pursue their own questions.

Now imagine that you want to expand to 'quadrilaterals'. How many quadrilaterals can be found with an area of 48 cm^2? What new things might we encounter trying to do this? What if we bring in triangles? Different types of triangles? Why stop there? How many sectors of circles can you find? If the area has to be 48, can we generalise about the relationship between the radius and angle of the arc? We can get to surface area and volume of 3D shapes too and what about 3D shapes whose surface area and volume are 48 (cm^2 and cm^3, respectively)?

Clearly, this simple question can go for miles and miles (metaphor not related to area - sorry) and take in all sorts of mathematics along the way. I think it fits pretty well with Andrew Wiles's analogy.

Quarter the cross

All this leads me really nicely into the truly wonderful 'Quarter the cross' craze. I think craze is the right word. As my own children were engrossed in 'loom bands' maths teachers across the globe were engaged in 'Quartering the cross' and sharing their solutions on social media #quarterthecross. I first heard about

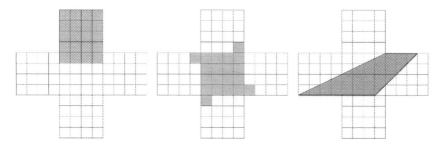

Figure 5.1 Quarter the cross. Here are three examples to help understand the goal of 'quarter the cross'. The starting shape is the same each time and the goal is to shade in a quarter of it.

'Quarter the cross' from David Butler who is a lecturer at the Maths Learning Centre at the University of Adelaide. David was riffing off a task that he traced back to a book called *Great Assessment Problems* (Dekker and Querelle, 2002) after some teachers on a workshop were talking about it online. David called it 'Quarter the cross' and I took inspiration from his work and have shared this task with teachers and students ever since.

The principle is simple. You start with a cross. Imagine a large outlined 'plus sign' and the goal is to consider how many ways there are to shade in a quarter of the cross. Although it seems that any shape could be the starting point for this, and of course it could, there is something about the 'fiveness' of the cross (at least as I can see it) that adds a lovely dimension to this thought process that, say, 'quarter the square' might not have. That said, I haven't tried. It seems quite likely to me that another 'quarter the shape' craze is quite likely and I am sure that many have dwelled on what features would make it an interesting shape to start with. This kind of thinking and exploring is very appealing with potential to be disruptively time-consuming. Anyway, back to quartering the cross. What gridlines, if any, you choose to put inside the cross definitely influences the nature of the task and the responses you get. Varying it then changes them, of course. It is also worth thinking about whether or not you want to add the requirement that the quarter is one entire piece and not made up of unconnected parts. You can always start or finish with the most open with no constraints, and this is recommended for the inventive thinking you are likely to see. It is a constant source of amazement to me how frequently I see somebody do something I have never seen before, either with students or teachers. This may also be a salient reminder of how constrained our own thinking as teachers can be! Maybe some are obvious, but then again, what is obvious to some is often not to others and vice versa, so it is great to watch it play out. It is also terrific to watch and engage with what happens when people find it harder to find solutions. Some students are competitive to start with but join others in collaboration when looking for original thought. Once a pathway is unlocked (the light is turned on, a new door is opened) there are often a few solutions using a similar technique.

After that it is all about what constraints you want to add to provoke or steer students towards certain thinking. Here are some ideas.

How many ways can quarter the cross with . . .

- Using one straight line only.
- Using two straight lines only.
- With triangles (with an isosceles triangle?).
- Rectangles (and then other quadrilaterals and other shapes). Let's say, for example, you have recently been working in some way with trapeziums

(trapezoids if you like, and I will avoid the discussion about 'at least one pair of parallel sides against 'only one pair'), then this might give the perfect opportunity to play with them and practice.

- Shapes that have reflective symmetry (maybe you want to be specific about how much).
- Shapes that have rotational symmetry (and again, maybe you want to be specific here)
- A shape with at least one curved edge.

Please try quartering the cross yourselves. It can be very engaging and gives you a good insight into some things your students might experience as they try

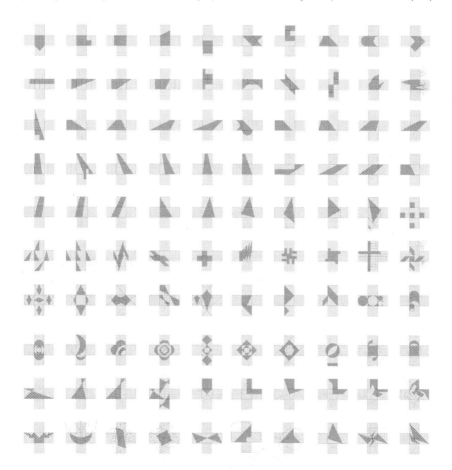

Figure 5.2 One hundred ways to quarter the cross. Here are 100 solutions involving a variety of mathematical ideas produced by David Butler.

Source: Image by David Butler.

it. Please also don't underestimate the task. There are some awesome solutions that involve lunes and integrated areas under curves. David was kind enough to let me use this diagram he made of 100 solutions that should really whet the appetite for getting stuck in.

In many ways this is a shining example of the 'How many?' theme because it encapsulates so much of the potential. It is easy to approach, it doesn't have to be done the same way by everyone, you can add and remove constraints as you wish and the task can go a long, long way. It's definitely a highlight and comes highly recommended, along with following David on Twitter to hear about the things he does and thinks about.

The 2022 game

I begin every calendar year with this game since it was first introduced to me. You start by taking the year you have just started. As I write, I am preparing for the 2022 game. Then you take all the digits that make up the date, so in this case 2, 0, 2 and 2 (lots of 2s). Then the task is to make as many of the numbers from 1 to 100 by using all the digits once and only once. For example,

> $2 + 0 + 2 + 2 = 6$, so I have ticked off the number 6.
> $2 + 0 + 2 - 2 = 2$, so I have ticked off the number 2.
> $2 \times 2 \times 2 + 0 = 8$, so I have ticked off the number 8.
> $\dfrac{(2 + 0)}{\frac{2}{2}} = 2$, so I found another way to tick off the number 2.

There are other possibilities. I can put any of the digits together to make a 2 or 3 digit number.

> $22 + 2 + 0 = 24$

Or I can use a decimal place wherever I like.

> $\dfrac{2}{.2} + 2 + 0 = 12$

I can use the digits as exponents.

> $(2 + 2)^2 + 0 = 26$

I can also use factorial (so, for example, 4 factorial, $4! = 4 \times 3 \times 2 \times 1 = 24$).

> $(2 + 2)! + 2 + 0 = 26$

Then there is the complete joy of the fact that $0! = 1$ and I'll get into that in a moment.

$(2 + 2)! + 2 + 0! = 27$

$$\frac{(2 + 2 + 0!)!}{2} = 60$$

We can even explore repeated factorials and double factorials. So, as you can see, what you might have started to think was going to be a limited exercise with all those 2s suddenly becomes something much more interesting. We turn quite a few lights on and go through quite a few more doors. This has all those desirable features mentioned already. Everyone can get started and plenty of feeling around for furniture can be done before anything gets too difficult. By the same token there is always more to look for than you think there is going to be. I love how students will be inventive in their thinking and come up with ways and means of getting numbers that I haven't thought of. In that sense, they often open doors for me too. Once you unlock a new idea it usually gives rise to a little cluster of solutions. I also really enjoy the dynamic with students who start out wanting to compete with each other *"I've got 23 how many have you got?"* giving way to the desire to collaborate and feed off each other's ideas.

Another important observation to make here is that often I will find students who want to work through the numbers from 1 to 100 in order and that this can be frustrating. There is something about being slaves to order that I find anarchically upsetting (we all have our occasional rebellious moments) and then I realise that I and my kind have probably played a significant part in that indoctrination and that there are good reasons for it too, but I do find it intriguing. Convincing students to just speculate with different operations and combinations is a big part of helping them to make that desirable move from 'What am I supposed to do?' to 'What could I do?' In that sense the activity, whilst being an obvious opportunity to practise arithmetic and operations is perfect for encouraging this important mathematical behaviour. The phrase 'you have to speculate to accumulate' is another of my favourites and seems appropriate here.

I said that I would come back to the factorial issue with 0! = 1. Clearly we get into some sophisticated ideas here. The use of the symbol is arbitrary so it can be easy to teach what it means. Explaining why 0! = 1 is less so. For better or worse, the way I have enjoyed doing this with students is by using the notion of arrangements and permutations which, in itself, is another opportunity for the 'How many?' theme. I'll ask a group of four students to stand as though in a queue and observe the order they are standing in. I'll change the position of two people so we can establish this is then a different order before asking 'How many different ways can these four students stand in a queue?' This can play out as a class activity, or students could be put into small groups to work on it. For uneven numbers a fifth person might be the director as it were, or you can provide different coloured counters for a simulation. A good deal of playing with four people in an actual queue though is pretty key. Then I'll stand back and watch and listen and learn a lot about my students. At some point, for some groups, I might suggest coming up with a systematic counting method (and as I am saying it, I'll smile wryly thinking about how I too am really a slave to order). I am sure you can imagine what happens next and think about the interventions you can make and questions you can ask. The outcome is a really nice model that helps us understand why the factorial is a way of counting combinations. A student on their own can stand in only one arrangement, two people can stand in two ways, (2 × 1). For a group of three, each can take a turn at the front while the other two do their thing (3 × 2 × 1 = 6) and for the group of four the same is true (4 × 3 × 2 × 1 = 24). So, we have imagined factorial as the number of ways that number of things can

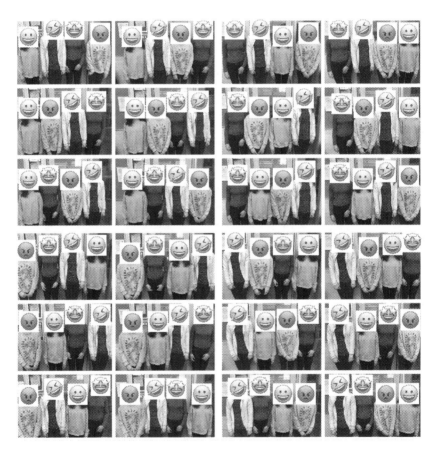

Figure 5.3 Four factorial. This image shows the 24 different ways that four people can stand in a queue as an activity to help students understand the notion of factorial.

be ordered and much as there is only one way to arrange one thing, there is only one way, but indeed one way of arranging no things. I am certain that there are better, sounder explanations and that it can be dangerous to oversimplify and that maybe, probably, I still have some things to learn about factorial, but I find it quite satisfying. I usually make an image of my group of four students like the one above as a visual reminder of what we did.

Now we are equipped with all the factorial options, we can go even further. Of course they tend to make big numbers, but then there is division to counter that. In the spirit of 'How many?' it is also important to also pay attention to the different ways in which a number can be made. We often find this out when we are collating a class set of results. I will sometimes introduce levels of competition to this that culminate in two or more classes competing against each other, which involves a given class collating their results. This is when we can discover the multiple ways in which a number has been made and we can enjoy comparing and discussing which might be the simplest, the most elegant or the most convoluted! Each of which has a certain merit worth sharing. Sometimes I have made a giant chart and put it in the school reception for some crowdsourcing as a school as we get into the hardest ones to find. This is a nice way to raise the profile of such a task.

I know a lot of students take it home and a lot of parents end up playing too. This is wonderful. The whole thing is a festival of 'How many?' and all the associated mathematical behaviour that comes with being asked to speculate and play. It has all the key features of accessibility and engagement as well as the stretch factor since we don't know in advance which ones have solutions and which ones don't. Again, this another nice model for mathematics as I think back to the moment it dawns on Uncle Petros (I mentioned him in chapter 1) that there is no certainty that there exists a proof for Goldbach's conjecture and his life's work.

Darts

I'll go with one more simple idea I like based around the game of darts and the significant mental arithmetic involved. A quick google will get you up to speed on the rules if you need them, but the concept is pretty easy. You have three darts to throw at a scoreboard and you score the points that correspond to the area of the dartboard you land in. You can score each of the numbers 1 to 20 as either singles, doubles or triples and the concentric circles in the very centre are worth 50 points and 25 correspondingly. So, provided you score with each dart you can get scores ranging from 3 (three single 1s) to the famed 180 (three triple 20s). How many ways are there to score 118 with 3 darts? Can you do it with only doubles or only triples? I'll leave that with you, but suffice to say there is a lot going on here and, once again, lots of potential. The dart board itself seems to have oodles of potential with all its circular geometry. I am now wondering, if each square millimetre of a dart board is equally likely to be hit, what might be the expected outcome of three darts? An investigation for another time.

In writing this chapter I have felt a good dose of imposter syndrome - *"Why is this guy writing about something so obvious?"* - but I have had a good time and have finished up by being certain that it is right to include it because of how often I have to remind myself of the potential that there is in the 'How many?' theme. I hope I might have now convinced some of you about that and reminded others. It is amazing how often this opportunity can arise. I am going to push the dark room analogy a bit more. I warned you. I think teaching is a bit like the dark room, only it's a massive house with loads of rooms, too many to know them all. I like some of the rooms more than others and even though I have been to lots of the rooms, there are others that I have never been in, some that I have been in but forgotten where the furniture is and others that it gives me great pleasure to rediscover whenever I am provoked to do so. I am enjoying that analogy but will limit myself to that. I take a lot of comfort in imagining that there are other teachers like me who feel that way. How many ways are there to teach and learn mathematics? Arghhhh!

From the box to the classroom

Thoughts and themes

- The principle of asking 'How many?' around a mathematical idea brings a mathematical freedom to a task.
- Students are not obliged to go in the same direction and are encouraged to think about what they could do as opposed to what they are supposed to do.
- Such tasks might offer a good view of what mathematics can be like. Playful and speculative.
- Adding and removing constraints along the way can bring richness and adjust the focus.

Task to try

- Shapes - how many with an area of 48. Change the number, change the shape. There are many variations here.
- Quarter the cross - Find different ways of shading one quarter of a cross in.

- The 2022 game – adjust to the year in which you are reading this!
- Explore factorials with the queue problems.
- Darts.
- Try to remember that a practice exercise can be enriched with a 'How many?' exercise.

6   Number searches

What's in the box?

This chapter revolves around puzzles and tasks involving subdivided shapes and, in particular the concept of a 'number search' arising from collaboration with primary colleagues. Such a simple activity that encompasses so many aspects of mathematical behaviour and is a delightful way to encourage and, more importantly, observe the different approaches there can be to similar problems. We will look at a simple example involving circles and demonstrate some of the many mathematical ideas that can arise, before showing how it can be used at different levels.

At the end of the last chapter I was brave enough to extend Andrew Wiles's dark room analogy for mathematics to teaching in general. I thought it was risky then, but now I am apparently still occupied by it. If my massive house of teaching, full of rooms for us to discover, indeed covers everything, then how different do the rooms that primary and secondary teachers visit look? How much time do they spend in the same room? How is it possible that despite it being the same profession, primary and secondary teachers know so little about what each other does and how strange is it that the systems, largely, seem to be set up to manage both differently, or perhaps more relevantly, separately? If we were redesigning school from scratch – and that really is a fun thought experiment – would we really validate these two (and others as well, of course) distinct sections with these clear boundaries between them? If we could free ourselves from the obvious pre-conditioning then I suspect not. That is not to say that I think it needs changing or doesn't work. It is just a reflection on how odd it seems that this all works so separately. Anyway, I'll get to the point. A huge bonus to working where I do is that we are a primary and a secondary school all on the same site. The two sections still operate almost independently, but clearly there are considerable advantages to the union and the geography. Liaison could always be more and better, but it is more frequent and useful than it would be otherwise. My own classroom opens out next to the kindergarten playground. We see each other regularly and teachers often do in-service training together. Lots of us

DOI: 10.4324/9781003266501-6

know each other pretty well and have regular opportunities to talk about what we do and bridge this strange divide I mentioned earlier. As a result I know quite a lot about what goes on in our primary school and vice versa. Clearly there is a significant difference in the job description and although we have lots of maths enthusiasts amongst our primary staff, I am still left to marvel about how their enthusiasm and expertise extends to so many other areas. I can match the enthusiasm, but not the expertise. This is all really great. Actually though, this is even occasionally annoying when I experience a strange possessive emotion about activities that I learn students are doing in primary that are MINE!!! I get to give them that amazing experience - thieves. When the class says *"I remember, we have done this before"*, it isn't even me just forgetting and I don't even get the satisfaction of noting that it was, at least, a memorable experience that I gave them, because someone else did. You can imagine cagey conversations between us where we are exchanging experiences and I suddenly forget key details about this activity so as not to give it away, literally. Forgive me, we are all human.

So we talk a lot about maths. It's great. Even better, I get a lot of great ideas from primary colleagues, ranging from playing with pattern blocks and Cuisenaire rods to different types of tasks (I'm not telling you the details in case you steal them haha). This chapter is about one of those that I believe to be universally known as 'number searches'. My colleague Simon Gregg put me on to these as well as on to the Twitter community that are exchanging them. Simon has been kind enough to let me share some of his work in this book. The idea is, once again, very simple. Students are given a diagram, typically a rectangle or a regular polygon that has been divided into different smaller shapes of different sizes and colours (or 'shades of grey' as it may be in the case of this book and I never imagined getting that phrase in). One of the shapes is left white and we are told that it represents a given number. For example 'The white square is 1'. Then the task is, 'If the white square is 1, what are all the other shapes?'

Hopefully you have taken the time to have a go with this. Also hopefully you can see that, like so many of the tasks offered in this book so far, they have potential that reaches out through lots of different levels of challenge. Much like #quarterthecross, Simon has been part of an active #numbersearch movement online and has an extensive collection. I am quite determined to be honest in this book and so am keen to point out that I am not a prolific number search user, but the spirit of the book is about the tasks I come back to year after year. This one sticks in my memory because I remember coming back from an epic school trip to Berlin and designing it on the plane as a means of staying awake. I had seen Simon tweet about

Figure 6.1 Number search. An example of a number search by Simon Gregg. If the white triangle is 1, what are all the others?

another number search and thought, there has to be a way for me to use this in my secondary classroom. This is one of the many nice things about having some contact with primary colleagues and being reminded of the variety of playful approaches they use and the ease with which a secondary curriculum can sometimes convince you there isn't time. (Perhaps primary colleagues experience this too.)

The following number search about parts of circles is high on the list. The principle is the same, in this case, the white square is 1. What do the other shapes represent? Again, please have a little go.

As you may have noticed, a lot is going on here. Let's start with π. This puzzle is a great context for seeing the wisdom of describing quantities in terms of π as opposed to wanting to calculate, and then round, the numerical values. I have already taken some responsibility for students' preferred behaviours, and I'll have to again here. The instinct that completeness is only felt when answers are 'calculated', must be at least in part a function of things we have asked from students in the past. The cycle that students go through here is interesting to watch. *"Mr Noble, my calculator isn't working. When I put 10π in my calculator it just shows me 10π and doesn't calculate it for me"*. Such a nice observation which is usually followed by a nice conversation. Ten minutes later students are beginning to feel the liberation that this brings and become serial 'Leave it terms of π' disciples. I love it when this too extends to calculations everywhere. *"Do I really need to put this in my calculator and give you the answer? I have shown you the calculation I would do, surely that's enough?"* and the cycle is complete! Years of complaining

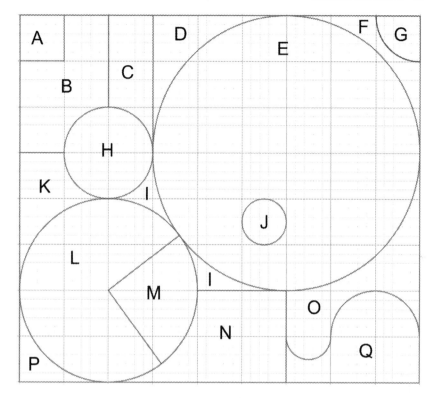

Figure 6.2 Circle number search. A number search designed to help students work with parts of circles and the associated algebra. If square A is 1, what are all the others?

that you didn't want to 'show your thinking' but now it's the only thing you want to show me.

It is once again a lovely feature that this task does not dictate a starting point. This brings a lovely level of accessibility to it and allows everyone to make some progress early. This builds into thinking strategically about which solutions might depend on others, or be easier if I have done others. The result is lots of different potential routes through the task which adds that great sense of agency that invites more of the 'What could I do?' thinking I wrote about in the last chapter.

Deductive logic

Although this may seem obvious, I do find I want to point out to students as often as it fits, when they are using deductive logic, as much as I would other approaches too. I like the idea that students become more conscious of which methodologies they are using to acquire knowledge and dwell on the strengths and weaknesses of them. In this case, we have a whole lot of 'IF THEN' going on and it's not the same for everyone. More than that, it has to be sound logic, so dwelling on the soundness of the logic we use in discussion with each other is every bit as fruitful.

Algebraic units

The effect of leaving answers in terms of pi often leads to some nice algebraic thinking. Although pi is not a variable, because it is being shown as a symbol, it invites us to treat it like an algebraic unit. *"Shape A is 3π and shape B is four times as big so it must be 12π"* and so on. Since students will have started in different places and taken different routes, these 'units' will be different and it is great to hear about how students are doing this. Another related moment is the thinking about how an area might be more easily worked out by taking something bigger and subtracting as opposed to adding up all the little parts. Those of you familiar with the basic principle of algebra tiles will be familiar with all this thinking. The notion of elegance is often used about mathematical solutions – Einstein's "poetry of logical ideas" comes to mind – and this task offers us a chance to reflect on it. Consider the least regular looking section of the diagram near the bottom right corner. There are a multitude of ways to work this one out, but which might you consider the most 'elegant' and why? How does elegance manifest in mathematics? This seems so much like a whole other book, but, for now, I think it is enough to suggest that wherever there exists the possibility for multiple solutions (and this seems pretty prevalent) we might take a moment to compare the different solutions in terms what we like about them and which might be more 'elegant'. Just as we did in the previous 'How many?' chapter and as we will again in the coming chapters. It is not just a mathematical appreciation cult, it is a fundamental part of knowing and recognising that there are multiple routes to solutions and that this is pretty useful as problems get more and more challenging.

Fractions

Oh, the great underestimated mathematical notation. Evidence from my experience suggests that adding and subtracting fractions is anything but basic. A vivid memory I have is of putting the finishing touches on marking some exam papers. There had been two parts (not equal but totalling 100) and I combined the scores as follows:

$$\frac{a}{44} + \frac{b}{56} = \frac{(a+b)}{100}$$

Hold your head up high if you have never done that! Context is everything and it is so easy to forget the ways in which confusion can be successfully sought! Needless to say, your classes had better be ready for some fraction work here and how great an opportunity it is to practise just that. Going back to the mention of elegance above, there is a role for elegance here as we work with the fractions too. The sheer joy too of course is that once you have all of the different shapes they should of course all sum to 72 (you may not have noticed it is an 8 by 9 rectangle). The answer is not a multiple of π. All but one of the shapes inside is, but the total is not. They should all elegantly cancel out as you sum the fractions. A whole group of irrationals summing to a rational. Ahhhhhh – so immensely satisfying and a beautiful point to think about knowledge!

When someone talks about richness, it can be ambiguous and, of course, subjective, but I see simple demonstrations in a task like this. We are practising areas of parts of circles, working in terms of pi, algebraic thinking, manipulating fractions, the pursuit of elegance ending up in basic geometric proof and inviting searching epistemological questions about rational numbers. All of this happens in an environment that encourages and rewards mathematical behaviour. I like this kind of rich. There is no doubt that it takes some management as a teacher, but students will help each other out a lot with their reasoning and, well, no one said it would be easy.

How can we take this further? In a multiverse, in fact maybe even in this world, there may be someone who has taken the number search idea and run much further with it. Thinking about making the number search was a terrific exercise too. I told you about making this one on a flight home from a school trip to Berlin. It was a lovely bit of recreational mathematics, dovetailing with thinking about my students and, well, my job. Even writing about it now makes me think about what extra features I could pack in or put in to a new one – without getting too greedy. Simon responded with one that had a 'lune' in it. How that might contribute to helping us understand how the area of a lune might be calculated? Another angle for developing the way we design and use such a task is about which area is the given one. This too could change the focus a bit. Time is limited, but one day I will. I like the idea that I have plenty of things to pursue as and when the moment arises. There is always more.

I hope then that you have played with these number searches and thought about what it can bring to classrooms. I hope that you have thought about making some! There is a lot of potential just waiting to be explored.

In related matters, I have been thinking about other tasks about shapes being subdivided. Here are some ideas.

Dividing squares into squares – Thinking back to the joy of 'How many?' For a given square, how many different ways are there to divide it into different squares? Which numbers of squares are possible and which ones are not? There is a famous solution to the problem of dividing a square into smaller squares where no two squares are the same. I have included a poster based on this solution made by my friend Pierre. How could this picture be used to stimulate some activity? What are the areas of all the smaller squares? How can I prove that it works?

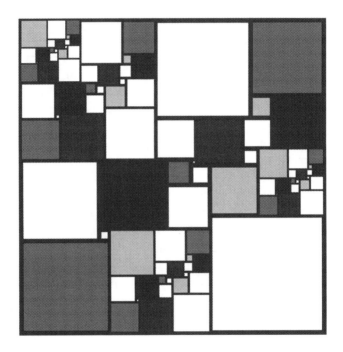

All square

Figure 6.3 A square of squares. A poster, designed by Pierre Claverie, of the well-known square divided into squares. How could this be used to stimulate mathematical activity?

Source: Image by Pierre Claverie.

Dividing circles – This is a puzzle I have traced back to John Mason and it's one that has actually become a benchmark in my own mathematical journey. I'll have to tell you the whole story. So I'm in Luxembourg for a maths competition (for students, not me). There is a lovely community of international schools that host these in different European cities for three different age groups every year. I've enjoyed going and hosting. One of the best events has become the teachers' evening on the first night. (I know, students getting in the way and all that). This evening involves 30–40 maths teachers getting together for dinner. Different host schools have done this differently, but there is usually a mathematical theme to the evening. This night in Luxembourg was my favourite. The round tables were covered in brown paper and the tables were decorated with puzzles and pencils. There was more to the evening and more to the form of this as well, but I just needed to set the scene. For large parts of the evening, teachers went up and down to the buffet, before returning to their puzzles. As more food and wine were consumed, there was slightly less puzzling as you can imagine, but not for me. I was consumed by this one puzzle. If you haven't heard of it, I urge you to try it and resist looking up a solution. Here it is. 'Can you divide a circle into congruent parts so that at least one of them does not touch the centre?' There you go. Try it. There are solutions! I am going to leave it with you. It was later when I described this puzzle to John and he told me more about the work he had done on it and the whole class of problems about subdividing shapes. Another mathematical rabbit hole. In any case, I was consumed by this problem and I kept hitting brick walls, but felt I was close enough to keep pushing. Eventually I came carefully to a solution that I thought might work. I constructed it more carefully and then justified its correctness to myself and for the briefest of moments, I felt like the cleverest person in the room. It is a unique kind of euphoria. I often think of it like those 3D magic eye pictures. You get little elements and then, when you have things just right, the whole 3D picture emerges before you and you can't believe you couldn't see it before. It's another reference to the dark room, isn't it? Anyway, I looked up to share my glory only to find everyone else had left the table and were at the bar! Still, that moment was mine and although it has come in different doses both before and since, that particular moment stands out for me. These are the emotions I want my students to experience in my classroom. Again, in different doses, but that emotion is so invigorating. Anyway, have a go at that one yourselves.

From the box to the classroom

Thoughts and themes

- The number search concept of 'If this area is 1, what are the others?' invites a good deal of productive mathematical behaviour.

- Although it is ostensibly a geometry task, it fast becomes an exercise in algebraic thinking and number skills.

Task to try

- Try the two number searches offered in this chapter.
- Look at the hashtag #numbersearch on Twitter to find more.
- Try making your own number search.
- Consider the square of squares poster as a stimulus.
- Try the circle division problem.
- Explore other subdivision of shapes problems.

7 Human loci

What's in the box?

One of my top five moments of the year when students become the points that have to 'obey the given rule' as we explore the wonders of loci and construction. Something so powerful about getting out of our seats and 'being the mathematics' before translating that to pen and paper activities and then on to some great challenges and the joys of construction that make up Islamic tile design.

It is difficult to put into words exactly how the first year of a teaching career goes. Of course, it will be different for everyone, but in my case it was a truly mind-blowing experience. I mean that in the sense of how many different things happened at the same time, how much I learned and how steep the learning curve was. Almost every day brought something new, and not always welcome by the way. Time has helped it all look a bit blurry, but some moments stick out. I worked in a wonderful school with terrific colleagues. It was not without its issues, but it was a good place to have that first year. Six of us started that year as newly qualified teachers and year 7 form tutors (11 year olds) and tradition dictated that year 7 would be taken on a residential trip to beautiful Bath at the end of the year and that one of us would get the honour of organising it. Guess who? I have already mentioned the youthful energy that I had at the beginning that may have dwindled somewhat since then, so obviously I said *"yes, please"* and dived into this new adventure alongside the others. I have lots of anecdotes about that trip, but I had better get to the point. Among the many things we did on that trip was a trip to the Roman baths. This is, of course, a given for a trip to Bath. Just as I have enjoyed in Rome, letting the mind wander to imagining some of these scenes 2000-plus years ago is pretty interesting. I am not convinced that 180 year 7s felt the same way. They dutifully took their black audiophone guides and held them to their ears as they followed the path and interspersed occasional looking and listening with laughing at each other, posing and having the general excitement of all just being out together. It is the age-old question of how to help children engage with such amazing stories and ideas and how much engagement can

DOI: 10.4324/9781003266501-7

be reasonably expected. It plays out in museums and classrooms alike and is a central preoccupation of educators. I know of many who are keen to correctly point out that engagement is not synonymous with learning, but, based on my understanding of the language, the latter can't happen without the former, so it is reasonable for it to be a preoccupation, just as long as it does not come at the expense of making it through to the latter. I think a lot and often about the circumstances in which I learn and what it is that engages me and I'd like to think that I am mostly engaged by the act of learning itself, but, whilst I may have made progress, I am aware that I do enjoy it when an effort is made to engage me. I like my history wrapped up in novels, I like my speakers to be great communicators, reading and responding to their audience and I like my museums to go the extra mile. I wanted to suggest to the baths that they get a refund on the audio guides and use the money to employ some actors to be Roman and fuel the imagination that I mentioned earlier. I wanted the students to be able to watch the Romans in action in that setting and be able to ask them questions. To be fair, I have no idea how viable this would be, but you can imagine my delight when, many years later, I visited Hampton Court Palace (a Grade I listed palace on the outskirts of London, famously a favourite residence of Henry VIII) where they had done exactly this. There was a welcome room where we watched a short video, with actors of course. The actors' portraits were on the wall and when we left the room they were there, in person, doing their thing. We were with French friends and Henry VIII walked past and spoke French to us! There was something so wonderfully immersive and engaging about it. We were given robes to wear and invited to pretend that we too belonged wandering the halls. In the Rijksmuseum in Amsterdam they made a real life freeze-frame of Rembrandt's 'Night Watch'. In the same city the NEMO Science Museum boasts an incredible 'chain reaction' amongst its many interactive exhibits. Science (and maths) museums have often got a better handle on this in my experience. I understand that we are all different and that ultimately we are after the same goal, but these things are so often windows into thinking. Perhaps you know the scene in the first Harry Potter movie where Harry, Hermione and Ron have to play a game of chess where they are the pieces? That is the kind of immersion I mean!

So that brings me eventually to the activity that I want to write about in this chapter. It is an example of something that can be broadly used in different contexts to make some learning experiences deeply immersive. The topic is loci and construction and the location is a big empty space, indoor or out (if you live in the south of France). You need a few plastic cones (or similar) and some string. The basic premise is, of course, that a locus of points is the set of points that obey a given rule, so each of the stages of this activity is based on a different such rule.

The locus of points that are a given distance from point A

Point A, in this case is a cone and the points are the students. I'll put the cone down and then stand still a certain indeterminate distance from it and then pick a student and ask them to stand somewhere that is the same distance from the cone as I am. Then another and another until I invite the whole class to do so. It is a fairly gentle introduction, but the first couple of points are important all the same. Sometimes the first person wants to come and stand next to me (a rare experience for a maths teacher) because it seems safer, but that might be mostly a function of not being comfortable estimating and replicating the distance I am. All you need is for a few students to have demonstrated that, but for practical constraints, there are an infinite number of places they can stand, so they just need to pick one. It is quickly apparent that this 'loci' is a circle, with the radius defined by me. We might stop for a minute to think about how accurate we have been. This scale is a nice access point for accuracy. Someone will notice the string I have brought with me and suggest that we use it to emulate a compass so we can check. Alternatively, it is quite fun if I am approximately a student's arm span away from the cone, then I can get a student to be an 'aeroplane' around the centre and hopefully narrowly miss everyone's noses as they do so.

I am deliberate about keeping the distance unknown because I, myself, want to be a variable. The advent of dynamic geometry software was enormous for teaching and learning mathematics, but it can be easy to miss the fundamental notion that everything you construct is dependent on the beginnings, the features you defined at the start. In this 'human dynamic geometry simulation' that is me. So I'll remind students that they all took their lead from me. Even if they took their lead from someone else, that person took their lead from me so, they all depend on me. Then I'll take a big step backwards and, not surprisingly, the circle gets bigger. I might do it again, and then gaps will open up which invites questions about the infinite nature of a locus of points. We are just a sample of points trying to show the whole locus, but we would need an infinite number of points to cover the whole thing. I might suggest joining hands to make this point. There are about 14 glass-walled classrooms that open up on the space I usually use for this activity as well as the heads office and I do enjoy imagining them wondering what we are up to as we join hands and run in and out like we are doing the hokey-cokey. I take photos when I can and I like the one we get when we use our feet to make the locus with a small radius.

I am sure that you get the main idea, and even though the first part is a relatively simple idea that I could have done more quickly, it does give us the opportunity to sow the seeds of the important ideas. The infinity of points and the dynamic nature of the construction and which features it depends upon. These are really important for what follows. The fact that the students themselves are the points on the locus is what immerses them in the mathematics and obliges them to think about what is happening. Although, yes, you can follow someone else, you still have decisions to make and you have to move, you have to take part.

The locus of points that are equidistant from points A and B

Now I have two cones, perhaps about 2 m apart, and I'll ask a student to stand somewhere that is the same distance from one cone as it is from the other. Most will go for the point right in the middle of the line between the two. Naturally. So the second point needs a bit more thought, but not much. You can hear minds whirring and muttering about where this is going. *"It's going to be a straight line - it is because ..."*. At some point, someone will be carefully trying to judge their position by gauging the distances by eye and we will naturally reach for the string and compass simulation to help them. It's a nice instinct to develop. As the whole class is invited to join I am always hopeful for one student to realise that this is a great opportunity for mathematical (and thus acceptable) mischief and go and stand absolutely miles away - because they can. On my best days I have been careful to place the cones in such a way that allows for this but using a convenient building for a limit. Again, it is a lovely instinct - *"this line will go on forever"*. There is lots of opportunity for discussion here, but I have to be careful not to push it too far. Perhaps we will talk about how we could have determined the line with the compass, or we will leave it for now. I have to notice the line between when I am getting super excited about everything that is going on and when they are. It is an easy one to miss and we don't have to do everything at once.

Trying to focus on the students immersed in mathematics, I am keen to get dynamic again, so I will step in and move one of the cones and then watch and listen as that one sinks in. Again, a simple thing that prompts a lovely moment of reasoning and momentum builds for the idea that they should only move half the distance I do. Then it gets really interesting as I get the last laugh on our mischievous character by moving the cone in a different direction! Haha. Depending on the classes and the numbers I sometimes have two groups, three cones and two lines. It is all to play for.

The locus of points that are equidistant from a line segment

This then introduces a new element because there is a line between points A and B, so the result is in parts. Again, the focus is on the discussion here. I like to emphasise that I want them to show the locus as best they can and this usually results in students being quite creative! At this point I have often created two or three groups and given them a list of tasks to try. Although, as ever, this means I relinquish some control, it does at the same time unlock a good bit of independent thinking and discussion. More people are prepared to put their ideas out there and more people are engaged with talking about what should happen. I get to hop between the groups and listen to the conversations, only chipping in with some questions that I think might help. The aeroplane can come out again for this one. Maybe I have specified a metre here and can use a metre ruler to test. Maybe students have to nominate a photographer to capture each of their solutions before they move on.

The locus of points that are equidistant from a triangle

This is made up of straight lines and arcs of circles. This takes some thinking about. What if the triangle is just an outline? Can part of the locus be inside? Will that have curved parts too? How can this be justified?

You can see that there are lots of questions you could ask based on these ideas and all of them can be catalysts for good discussion, puzzling, reasoning, justification and mathematical thinking and behaviour. All of them require the students to 'be the mathematics' and be immersed in the problem. Of course, though, we can go on. . . .

Challenge 1

There are two cones A and B. Can you all stand so that the sum of the distance you are from A and the distance you are from B is the same for all of you?

Challenge 2

There are two cones A and B. Can you stand so that you are twice as far away from point A as you are from point B?

So these two get really interesting. As I have written already, I am keen not to teach anyone to suck eggs, but my experience of doing this with teachers in workshops tells me that most have never done it. If you recognise them straight away, then fine, otherwise, do please have a go. (I am imagining you using a piece of paper and a pencil now, not rounding up 30 of your friends, but feel free.)

A couple of key things start to happen here. The level of problem has gone up a category and students' intuitive responses are often not the solution. This is a lovely journey, especially if you think that many of those intuitive responses have only just been developed. We begin to hit barriers. It gets a bit quieter, the

Figure 7.1 Human loci. These images show students engaged with the human
loci tasks written about in this chapter.

atmosphere is more pensive. This is definitely tricky territory for the teacher,
because it is the point you can easily lose students. Groupings, choices, interventions are all important. Doing this with teachers is great because you don't lose
many and you get lots of great discussion. With students I have to help more and
there are lots of ways to do this. *"Do you want this piece of string to help? What
about 'insert student name'? Are they standing in a place that meets the conditions? How can we check?"* Some playground chalk can help here so students
can collect points. It can be hard to know how to leave this. If a group solves it, I
might get them to explain to the others. Otherwise, time will run out and we will
need a change of medium.

   This is the next big moment for me. When it becomes more efficient to work
on your own with a piece of paper and a pencil. It's a classic transition from
concrete, through pictorial to abstract. What appeals to me here is that a lesson
that starts with an upbeat buzz because we are going outside, gets to a point
where everyone (almost) wants to go back inside and work on their own. Having
been the points, they can easily move to representing themselves as pencil dots.
These last two problems I think are much more approachable like this, but this
is fuelled by what we did first.

   I guess you get the idea by now. It was actually quite hard to write because
each time I do this, something different happens, which can be both the mark
of a good task and an extra challenge for the teacher. My favourite is when
students want to go 3D, trying to make a hemisphere around the first cone. It
is lovely thinking. I hope that you can quickly think of variations on these tasks.
There is opportunity to use objects in your playground, to vary the shapes and

the conditions, to play with the way you represent the outcomes or linger longer on the dependent, dynamic elements. I often come back to this when we are looking deeper at quadratics with the locus of points that are equidistant from a point and a line. I have also come back to it when teaching theory of knowledge looking at Euclid's postulates and their limits as a knowledge system. All this is to help you imagine children of all ages playing purposefully with these ideas.

Here are a few more spin-offs related to construction.

Giant triangles

Imagine a group of students is given the task of drawing a triangle with sides 1 m, 1.5 m and 2 m on the playground with chalk and I've also given them a long piece of string and a metre ruler. What do you think they would do? There is something of a thought catalyst to working on that scale with those tools. You can't guess and check very efficiently so a more elegant solution is necessary. I think, in this context, I don't need to teach children how to construct a triangle. How might any of this be different if I vary the lengths of the string given? Perhaps I give them one piece that is 4.5 m, or three pieces each corresponding to the side lengths, or just one that is 1.5 m long. Such little things can change the approach.

Imagine if two or more groups have been given the same task and I ask them if they have all drawn the same triangles. What then? Picture three students holding the long piece of string around the corners of their triangle and then lifting it and transforming it to a nearby triangle to see if it fits exactly on top. What if it does? What if it doesn't? Maybe they rotate a little and it fits on some but not others, then one of the human vertices takes their corner and limbos under the opposite side to create a reflection. I am sure you get the picture. So much fruitful activity here.

Maybe you have some giant cut-out angles now and some other tasks so that students explore the conditions for congruent triangles on this large scale. You might try other, purer (if I can get away with that) constructions without dimensions like 'equilateral' or 'isosceles'. There are countless other construction tasks you can carry out using this big scale. Try it and see what you think it brings to the table. As I have said, I think the scale invites or encourages good thinking and, like with the loci, at some point students make the natural transition to pen and paper willingly and, as a result of their playground graffiti, now do so with confidence.

Islamic tile design

I can't not mention here the potential joy involved in extending some of these constructions to the wonderful art of Islamic tile design. So much to say here. A colleague, Simon, and I did once run a small, somewhat undersubscribed, after-school Islamic tile design club, where we once did one in playground chalk. Inspired by the work of people like Eric Broug, Samira Mian and others, I always look forward to the lessons where we extend construction to Islamic tile design. It surely warrants much more than just this brief mention, but hopefully I have created a little spark for some of you. I recommend trying to construct an Islamic tile so you have that experience. If nothing else, you might find something you like to do. It has become a lovely therapeutic extracurricular activity for me. Beyond that you will get a glimpse of the experience a student might have in doing it and think about the value it can bring related to some of the wonderful geometry and the methods required to make the intersecting tiles.

Voronoi diagrams

More recently, I have come back to this human loci in the teaching of the perhaps lesser known Voronoi diagrams. For the uninitiated, a simple explanation might be to imagine a town with three mobile phone antennas and then finding a way to divide the town in a way that showed which mobile tower each house was closest to. Then imagine a fourth tower or a fifth and the complications you might come across as you did so. The resulting diagrams do depend on the construction of perpendicular bisectors. So, more recently, I have had 17 year olds constructing Voronoi diagrams in fake playground towns and playing on the scale to help them understand the significance of what they had been doing.

Parabolas

I am going to go on a parabolic tangent here. I won't be too long, but this is too good to miss. I am often given to saying that learning languages is the most significant thing I have ever done. It sounds good and is probably debatable, but there is something pretty profound in there. Perhaps this little example won't do that claim justice, but I got such a kick out of discovering that the French word for satellite dish is *parabole* and a similar one out of connecting the dots between the properties of a parabola that make it perfect for amplifications of a signal like a satellite dish or the sound mirrors that were built to give early warnings for incoming air raids. Going back to thinking about museums, I have always had in my head that mathematical minigolf would be a great exhibit. You could have all kinds of holes, but the one I am thinking about now is parabolic in shape with the hole at the focus of the parabola and an obstacle in front. The shrewd mathematical golfer will know how to bounce the ball off the edge to get into the hole, right? This will happen one day (I am sure it has already). Above, in describing the human loci, I mentioned putting down a point and a line and asking students to stand in places where they are the same distance away from the line as they are from the point. This involves another important bridge in understanding that the distance away from the line is the perpendicular distance and is the shortest. I am sure you will know that this locus of points will make a parabola. (And I forgive you if you didn't, I was a teacher before I learned any of the amazing properties of parabolas). This is a nice return to human loci with a nice reveal when the moment is right. I want to write about it here though because it gave rise to a problem that I really enjoyed trying to solve.

We have mentioned dynamic geometry and there will be more in this in later chapters, but the following problem involves using dynamic geometry. If you know what you are doing then go for it straight away, otherwise you might have to try and imagine it. One of many nice features is the 'trace' function. This means that you can add a 'trace' to a point that means it will leave a trace behind when it moves. In this context, it will show the locus of points. A simple example is the circle:

- Create a line segment, AB.
- Create a slider that is an angle.
- Put a trace on the right hand point, B, of the segment.
- Now rotate the segment about the left end, A, using the angle of the slider.

As you increase the angle by changing the value of the slider, the segment will rotate 360 degrees around A and point B will trace a circle, the locus of points that are equidistant from A and AB is the radius of the circle. You can start again, dragging point B further away and then make a bigger circle, just as we did with people before. So, here we go, now the challenge is to set up a construction using dynamic geometry so that when you move one dynamic element of it (the slider in the case above, but could be a point), another point in the construction traces a parabola. Please note, that, as many of you know, it is possible to input information as algebra, but it goes without saying that this is not the goal of this particular problem. There is no hidden parabola that your point will magically travel along. The point that you trace will trace the parabola because you change something else about your construction. Try it. It gave me a lot of pleasure. While you are there, try and do something similar for challenges 1 and 2 also listed above.

I started this chapter by talking about museums and putting out a comparison with how we might be expected to engage productively with museums and exhibits and how we might be expected to engage with ideas in a mathematics classroom. I wrote all the disclaimers in the beginning too. I think it is an interesting question. Here we landed on an immersive element that both offers and demands direct involvement from students in 'being the mathematics'. Like everything else, I'd say, try it. It offers something. On museums and maths, I am waiting for my window to go and visit MoMath in New York with great anticipation.

In the meantime I have had a lot of pleasure from the MMACA museum of mathematics in Barcelona and I know there are others. I once picked up a tweet from Dr James Grime of Numberphile fame, amongst numerous other things, where he was asking for ideas for a travelling museum that I think is now out there. This was a perfect opportunity for procrastination and I wrote pages of suggestions, including mathematical minigolf. I wonder if any of them made it. A museum is on my one day maybe but probably quite unlikely list of things I'd like to do. I'll keep you posted.

From the box to the classroom

Thoughts and themes

- Thinking about activities that invite students to 'be the mathematics' in an immersive way that provides a concrete experience for them.
- The idea that this concrete experience builds a bridge to a pencil and paper pictorial method and then more abstract conclusions.

Task to try

- Try all the human loci tasks with a class.
- Try introducing an element of 'dynamic geometry' where the students are the points.
- Spend some time yourselves with the two challenges and notice what happens.
- Try these as a dynamic geometry puzzle as suggested at the end of the chapter.
- Try the giant triangle constructions.
- Try large-scale chalk Voronoi diagrams.

8 Statistics telling stories

What's in the box?

On the same theme as the human loci, but now in the context of statistics, this one focusses on giving real depth of understanding to stats and diagrams that help us address the human connection referred to in the famous quote about 'One death is a tragedy and 1000 is a statistic'. More practical out of the seat activity that offers perspective on some important statistical ideas and how we use them to tell the story of the data.

Now, presumably, there are many great dangers with starting a new chapter by telling you about some of my favourite movies. You might not like them, you might know them, I might spoil them, you might wonder if I have lost my focus . . . and so on. The clue is in the title of the chapter though. Storytelling techniques are super interesting in the way they are designed to engage the reader or viewer. Like we have already said with 'What's in the box?', *"Why not just tell us the story and be done?"* Instead we employ metaphors, imagery and other techniques to conjure up pictures in our imagination and set the scene. We get to know the characters so that what happens to them means more to us when it happens. We are drawn into empathy and other emotions as a good storyteller slowly releases carefully timed bits of information to make us feel the story in real time. They give enough away to keep us interested whilst at the same time wanting more so we keep reading or listening or watching. I am going to assume, if we think about it, that we have all been sucked in by a great story told by a great story teller. Clearly it could be really dangerous to think about how this applies to a maths lesson, but many of the same features might apply. Even the teacher as narrator can work to a point, but lessons might be more like immersive theatre with the students playing the main roles. OK, I can see this all getting a bit wishy-washy, but I am enjoying the thought that the idea might play a part in what is coming in this chapter.

More specifically I have a couple films in mind as relevant examples. If you have seen either *Crash* or *Babel*, then you will know what I mean, otherwise you should be fine with the general description of a story that is told in bits. Messing

DOI: 10.4324/9781003266501-8

with time, locations and characters, the bits on their own seem unconnected and disparate. As the films progress you begin to put all the information together, and as they crescendo the story emerges with great clarity bringing so much more meaning to those seemingly disparate elements you had been collecting to that point. I love that! In our data-obsessed world I think this is the challenge. How do we put all those bits together so that they can tell their story and bring real meaning to them? You'll see I seem to have found yet another way to use the 'dark room' analogy.

So this is an activity aimed at bridging that gap between the statistics and the stories they can tell. Not surprisingly, it starts with a data set. Actually, it starts with four different data sets and the way you start depends on groups and numbers. The last time I did this, I used one data set, printed the numbers off big and gave each of the students in my class one of the numbers as they came in. I joyfully shout that they are no longer free people, but numbers now, forgetting (or more likely happy just to amuse myself) that they will miss the reference or even the subtle irony that the point of the lesson is almost the exact opposite. The task, at this point, is for students to work together to come up with different ways of 'telling the story' of this set of numbers. With a bigger class I'll split them into four groups and give each group one of the four data sets and set each group working alone with the cut-out numbers.

Common first responses include various means of 'classifying the numbers'. *"These numbers are whole, these are not"* or *"These are above 10 and these are below"* etc. I remember being surprised by the first one and it was a good moment to reflect about what students see when presented with a number. In the end it becomes a nice moment to talk about discrete and continuous data. The second classification often then develops into a kind of 'bar graph' where we begin to see the 'shape' of the distribution and students begin to get a stronger sense of what I meant when I said I want them to arrange the data so that it somehow tells its story. It's no longer a random seeming set of numbers.

Another common response is, not surprisingly, to arrange the numbers in numerical order. This seems reasonable, but doesn't seem to offer a lot until someone suggests that this arrangement would tell us more if they were put on a scale. Someone will notice that the number 20 has 19 on one side of it and 35 on the other and that this somehow doesn't seem right. Once the numbers are on a scale then, as with the bar graphs, we get more details of the story.

There is a good bit of freedom here for students to be creative. Sure, there is a little uncertainty to start with, but once they get into it, the idea of trying to tell the story of the data set takes centre stage and students have made

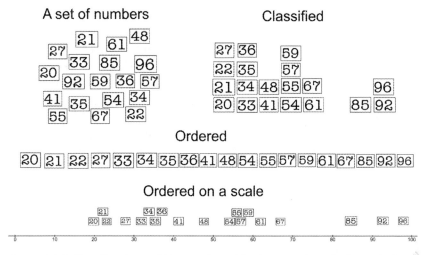

Figure 8.1 Telling the story of the numbers. The images show first, a set of random numbers, then the numbers put in order on a scale and in a bar chart.

some natural choices that have led them effectively to histograms and box plots. The process offers lots of opportunity for little discussions and connections with things they might remember about 'medians' being the one in the middle. Depending on what previous knowledge your students have or where you want to take this, you could steer this into a focus on box plots and the five-figure summary and so on.

Next up, having had four groups working on their different data sets, I will ask them if they can put all of the data sets onto the same scale. This too can be done in lots of ways, and as you may have noticed from the last chapter I have quite a thing for large scale. You can set up the scale with a row of desks in the classroom or a row of larger tables in an auditorium space or even with chalk on the playground again. The unexpected twist for students here is that the four data sets are all quite different and so they have all been working with quite different scales. One data set has a maximum of 12 while the other extreme is 100. So as the scale is decided, it has to be big enough to cater for everyone. This is where I often help by setting the beginning and end of the scale. Maybe it is 10 big tables in the auditorium, or maybe I'll have a tape measure ready. I'll give each group a line near the scale to help them organise and they set about putting the numbers on it. Here it helps if the numbers are big and written on A4 size or similar so that we can all see them from a distance. If outside and working with chalk, get them to write the numbers nice and big.

Now we can see how this way of telling the story of a data set offers us an excellent way to compare the data sets at the same time and we can start to discuss those differences. *"Look, this one ends before this one even starts"; "This one is stretched out really far even though there is a big bunch all together somewhere near the middle"*. The discussions are fundamentally about the shape of the distributions which is really a crucial element of understanding to get to.

I often feel a sense of scientist guilt as I experiment with students and teachers by waiting to see how long I can go before someone asks me anything about what the data actually is. I wrote earlier about aiming for activities that engage well enough that such questions are relegated to a lower priority and I think this is a good example. Having run variations of this activity many, many times, I can't think of a single occasion when either a student or a teacher has asked me what the data actually is. It is that bit of the story that no one has thought to ask but ends up being really important - I deliberately did not offer it. Of course this could be good and bad news. The good news is *"that it doesn't matter, it's a distraction, there is enough to work with and explore here even if the numbers don't mean anything"*. The bad news is *"that it's quite normal for us to be given completely meaningless things to do in maths class, why should today be any different?"* I can only hope that it is largely the former, even if it is mixed with a bit of the latter. Well, here is the punch though. The data is real. Each of the numbers represents the infant mortality rate of a country and the four data sets are systematic samples of countries from four different areas of the world. When this is revealed, and a bit of background on infant mortality is shared, students are usually stood up in a situation where they are almost immersed in the data, because of the scale. They can look around and point. *"Look, that must be Europe"* as they point to the narrow little data set all squashed up on the left. *"Look at that one - all the way out there"* as they point to the country with the infant mortality rate eight times higher than the biggest one in Europe. Such observations continue, questions arise and there is, it seems, a profound sense of meaning in the air. There is a serious story being told by these statistics and the way we have presented them and we are right in the middle of it. It is like those moments in the story where it all comes into such sharp focus. I have little doubt that my own perception of such moments is magnified a bit - OK, maybe a lot - but if I don't feel that way, then what hope do I have of helping students to feel that way? If you spend a lot of time with teenagers, the same teenagers, you do learn to read them reasonably well. It can be quite demoralising when the transient nature of the teenage brain doesn't seem to dwell for long enough on profound moments which accounts for why it is quite uplifting when the opposite happens. All we can do is try and provide the opportunities and this one has a high success rate even if it does leave us all somewhat disturbed.

I wonder if I have been able to do this activity justice by simply writing about it. I hope you have played a bit with the numbers as you go and tried to immerse yourself in the activity and imagine students immersed in this large-scale data presentation exercise. I hope that lots of you try it, or something similar. The immersive nature crosses over with the ideas in the previous chapter in a kind of 'being the maths' way. Especially if you get your students to kind of 'wear' the numbers and stand on the lines themselves. In the crazy age of data, I have seen some good memes (don't get me started on what that word means and how the answer to that question is very much generational) that try to get this message across. For example, a three-part image. The first is a giant pile of mixed-up multilink cubes and is labelled 'data'; the second shows the pile organised into smaller piles of same coloured cubes and is labelled 'information'; and the third has those piles arranged into some kind of chart and is labelled 'knowledge'. I know we could rage for hours over the simplicity of such a message and the meaning of those three words, especially the last one, but as a conversation starter, I think it is a good one and, in a sense, it is what we have done here with this activity.

Other human box plots

I hope that readers have imagined the different scope there is with this idea. As an icebreaker I have asked students and teachers to make a box plot of their heights. It is nice and visual, but kind of difficult. Clearly any variable will do, but I have avoided the temptation to go with 'your percentage score on your last maths test'. It can be as complicated or as simple as you think will work best with your classes. It doesn't have to be on a large scale; it can be manipulatives on a table working in small groups. It just hinges on students being hooked into the activity. You will know your classes best.

Cumulative frequency graphs

I have taken this further to get into cumulative frequency. Imagine having your class on a human box plot. I can think of an example where I had set up the scale from 1 to 100 with 10 large tables in the school hall. I was able to use this to help organise students into class intervals and make a histogram/bar chart (up to you if you want to get into the important difference) The hall has a balcony so it was easy to get a good picture from above (I do really *need* a drone though) Then, moving across the class intervals, I ask all the students to shift up the graph so that their line starts at the same height the previous one ends and then we have a cumulative frequency graph. I have described that quickly and there is, here, a good opportunity to discuss the midpoint/endpoint issue that secondary teachers know can cause some consternation. Like I said, keep it as simple or take it as far as you like. There is something about the simple transition from histogram to cumulative frequency that helps to dwell on the underlying concept.

On the same lines, any variation on this exercise that involves students having to focus on how the individual data points transform into the charts and diagrams can be an effective bridge. More than that, I have found it helps to bring real engagement with statistical ideas. These are always in context and always mean something tangible so it is important not to miss the opportunity to help students see that. Of course, I accept that there are lots of ways to do this, I have just told you about one I enjoy.

Going right back to a simple level – I was playing a card game at a friend's house (do you remember Ben for chapter 1? – I do have other friends) At various stages in the game you picked up cards that you couldn't play anymore. Each of the cards had a point value and their total was attributed to you as a player. I did really well and instinctively chose to represent my stash in a hybrid pictogram/bar graph, with each column being a different point value for the card. This of course told the story of my great success and facilitated the easy totalling of my points. In an unexpected twist in this particular story, the object was to have as few points as possible – oh well. Is it just maths teachers with that instinct to organise in that way? I don't think so. This was actually just after I did the activity above with the class and it reminded me again of the value of such concrete experiences.

Other charts and infographics

Among the many things I hope that this book does for people is that it sparks ideas. Perhaps you have already come up with some of your own ideas and twists on what I have suggested. Perhaps you already have something similar and perhaps you have completely rubbished my version and drawn up your own much better activity. That is all good. I have even found myself thinking on this theme (not the rubbishing, although I am prone to that occasionally too). The world of infographics is a fascinating development of the statistical diagram. All manner of rule-breaking goes on that highlights tension between different disciplines. Scientists do their box plots vertically and don't get more stated on some of the crazy diagrams you see in a geography classroom. The goal is always the same though – to offer a visual representation of a dataset or of information so that it tells us a story that we can't easily see from the data alone. The whole thing is fraught with danger and there are some horrendous efforts out there in the bad chart club. As such, I find it a useful focus for lessons. Pulling apart an infographic can be just as fruitful as designing one.

I get lots of inspiration for lessons from infographics. Of course, like with all information, the viewer has to be discerning. I already mentioned the 'Billion Dollargram' in chapter 3 and the great maths involved in checking its accuracy. In another I saw the 20 most populated cities in the world shown on a circle. In order. Each city was given an equal angle of the circle, but the corresponding sectors extended out to different places apparently corresponding to the populations of those cities. On close analysis, the population was proportional to the length of the radius and not the area. Clear or not clear? Useful or not useful? Could we do it differently? Could we do it better? Potential for maths tasks or not? I'll leave it with you.

So I suppose my point here is that 'the pictogram' that is so often seen as the 'basic entry point' in to statistical diagrams has kind of come full circle (no pun intended), and that although our curricula will be specific about charts and diagrams, there is plenty of scope for exploring infographics as a means of helping tell the story of the data set as well as a context for other bits of maths.

Data week

As a response to these issues crossing my path, I remember one year I organised a 'data week' in school as a project I did with my classes. With older students we designed an extensive survey for the whole student body and, in doing so, went through all of the associated issues. We are actually going to use this survey, so we had to think very carefully about the questions and all the issues that might come up (nothing like skin in the game). We even warned the whole student body in advance that we were going to ask them to track certain things during the coming week, like hours spent doing homework etc. We also set up some measuring stations during the week and asked tutor/homeroom teachers if they could spare some time to help make sure students had measured themselves and so on. Then we collected the data and with different classes we set about telling our story. It was quite an operation, but worth every minute for all the experience it brought as well as having the whole school buzzing about data for a couple of weeks. We did lots of things and some were more successful than others, but the result was a school decorated with the diagrams, charts and infographics that told the story of the student body. I'll give you some highlights.

On one wall in the reception we had a whole series of bar charts made of old books that we dug out of the library and various departments in the school (and then gave away to charity afterwards having dug them out). For each year group we had charts that showed the number of hours homework students had done in the last week and number of books students had read in the last 2 months. It was impossible to walk past these without staring at them and making comparisons. Each student in the school was a book in that display somewhere and everyone wanted to compare the year groups and pick out the surprising elements of the story that the charts were telling.

On another wall, we had an 'average student' from each year group. These were outlines of people filled with a photograph of every student in that year group. The height of the person was the mean average height of students in that year group and the outline had their arms spread out to the width of the average arm span. The average students for each year group were of course in order. It was a very satisfying exercise and a lovely thing to have on display. Students, once again, had this sense of involvement and were often caught comparing themselves to the average person on the wall. We approximated pie charts out of different coloured cubes where each cube was a person, we put dot plots and box plots on the wall to look at the shape of the distributions. We made scatter graphs where the size of the point was a factor too and the points were coloured with the flags of the place where the student came from, like the bubble graphs made famous by Hans Rosling and Gapminder.

I wanted to write about this project too so that I could offer examples of some relatively simple things that can be done here to complement that first example about the more worldly seeming infant mortality rates. I wanted to offer some statistics activity without getting lost in the related, tired but relevant cliches. There is of course much to be discussed about all of this and I find myself spending more and more time thinking about what we do with students and stats as 'data science' becomes ever more prominent. It is a minefield, but the fundamental notion remains the same. We are trying to tell stories with statistics and it can be a really rich exercise for all ages and on multiple levels.

From the box to the classroom

Thoughts and themes

- Organising data is quite an instinctive activity and most instincts lead towards creation of diagrams that are essentially those we need to teach.
- Offering students a concrete experience of 'being' or 'manipulating' actual data points invites a powerful level of engagement and understanding.
- Despite the epistemological issues associated with statistics, a central goal is to tell the stories with data and this should be part of a student's experience.

Task to try

- Try the 'telling stories' activity with four different sets of data about infant mortality as described.

- Try alternative approaches to human box plots.
- Try extending this to cumulative frequency curves.
- Explore other ways to make more concrete statistical diagrams involving people or manipulatives.
- Spend some time with infographics and possible associated tasks.
- Try having a 'data week' in your year group or school.

9 Match point

What's in the box?

While we are on statistical ideas, this activity asks us to think significantly about frequency distributions whilst extolling the virtues of the 'matching activity' as a way of inviting certain thought and reasoning processes in students.

This chapter is going to be about a simple matching pairs exercise. It is a classic concept that easily expands to a card sort and is broadly applicable. It definitely comes in the category of things I wanted to include but paused a lot to wonder if it was not just too obvious. On that, Derek Sivers was the successful CEO of CD Baby amongst a whole host of fascinating things he has done. His book, *Anything You Want*, about his experience with CD baby, is fascinating. Anyway, I only came across Mr Sivers because of a brilliant 2-minute video of his I found on YouTube that I use regularly when working with teachers and trying to encourage them to share. It is called 'Obvious to you, amazing to others' and centres around the basic premise that we all think our ideas are obvious but that other people's ideas are amazing. I have found this to be true amongst teachers. Even when teachers are talking about ideas that I think I am already familiar with, they will invariably offer me something new that I find amazing. The pretext here is that you are now expected to find something in this chapter new and amazing. OK? I like to start all my department meetings with a bit of maths (I don't always manage to – reality bites), but it is striking that however familiar any of us feel with the subject matter, when we dig deeper, we invariably get to new territory. So I am doing matching pairs. Here goes.

This particular activity came out of a conversation I was having with a parent who works in pharmaceuticals. I was actually on the way home from a teacher training event in Doha. (I couldn't resist that, I'm such a globetrotter. I will leave out that it's the only time I went and not dwell on the fact that I wasn't invited back.) It was a crazy, busy and fascinating weekend and I was sleep deprived, had a screaming headache and on the last leg of the journey from London to Toulouse. I get in my seat ready to zone out for an hour or so when, you guessed it, a parent from school slips into the seat next to me. Great. It actually

DOI: 10.4324/9781003266501-9

was, even if the timing was bad. I have enjoyed talking to this parent in the past and we got quickly on to pharmaceuticals. It's a spooky coincidence that someone in the row in front is reading the brilliantly titled *Bad Pharma* by Ben Goldacre. The spark came from a conversation about drug trials – something we all apparently pay a lot more attention to since 2020 – and how they are populated. It is a classic issue with students and surveys when they become fixated on needing to ask the same number of boys as girls for the survey to make sense. It is a tidy notion but indicative of not really understanding the concept of sampling, or at least not having thought about it for very long. Anyway, even with my screaming headache, I am being very clever about population demographics and stratified sampling when I am stopped in my tracks and made to realise that I too have not really thought enough about sampling techniques. She politely 'parentsplains' to me about why in trials you need the same number of different people in different age groups. Of course, there is less of a need for them to be the same and more of a need for there to be a minimum in each category for results to be significant which effectively amounts to the same. There you go. Classic teacher faux pas, picking up on a common misconception and then misconceiving with it.

So it made me wonder about what different distributions would look like. Try these.

- What shape is the population age distribution of the US? What about The Gambia?
- What does the frequency distribution of global literacy rates look like?
- What about annual income in different countries, the heights of a crop of sunflowers, the outcomes when two normal dice are rolled and the numbers added together?
- Think about the salaries of professional sportspeople. How different would that look for men and women?

The expression 'bell curve' is probably widely recognised and its basic principles perhaps understood, but it is really a mind blowing notion. On our curriculum we are required to 'do' the normal distribution and the binomial distribution, but what a syllabus will invariably leave off is that the very notion of a 'distribution' is a properly sophisticated idea that takes a good bit of thinking about. Which things might we reasonably expect to be 'normally distributed'? What other kinds of distribution are there? What causes a positive or negative skew? Is the normal distribution a naturally occurring phenomenon? I hope you have understood by now that I have no intention of answering such questions here, I just want to flag what I increasingly see as important under estimations of curriculum design. Perhaps, to avoid blaming the problem on a prescribed curriculum, I need to put it back on to me. It is often not until you have to 'do' the normal distribution that you start to think about how your choice of language and activity and approach for teaching in previous years can have a big impact of how ready students are for this 'doing' (Ok, I'll stop that now – I am sure you get my point).

Having talked about how sophisticated the concept is, it is broadly approachable by students of many ages. For example, I'll bet most classes could have a good conversation about how you might expect the distribution of birthdays in different months in the class/year group/school might look like. Of course, some of us might not want to have the conversation about how occasionally you can find a report from a northern European country where it is dark a lot and they really like Christmas, that has a little spike in births in September, but I am sure that we can all understand the basic principle. So I suggest that a matching activity like the one I am proposing could be used with students of all ages to be thinking about the concept of 'distribution' as long as the examples were carefully chosen.

In my distribution match, I have 12 examples, 9 possible distribution shapes and some debatable answers. A classic matching pairs exercise will work out neatly with actual discrete matching pairs. These are great and the process of elimination can be a real aid in the process. There is a huge difference between having to choose between potential answers and having to come up with an answer from nothing, as we see in multiple choice questions. It is a very powerful tool for inviting engagement with the task and reasoning between the students. My students get a bit upset with me when they work out (a) that it won't actually be all neat matching pairs and (b) that one or two of the answers might actually be debatable. . . . But the task is simple, try to match one of the examples with one of the frequency distributions.

In this example, please decide which of the pictured distribution shapes might be the best fit for the following populations.

1   A sample of 1000 adults had their IQs measured. This is the frequency distribution that resulted.
2   This distribution shows the heights of 500 fully grown sunflowers.
3   This diagram shows the distribution of people of different ages in The Gambia.
4   This diagram shows the frequency of babies born in different months starting from January.
5   This diagram shows the frequency distribution of a sample of baby weights.
6   This is a frequency distribution for the literacy rates of the world's countries.
7   This diagram shows the distribution of people of different ages in the US.
8   This distribution shows the frequencies of average household income.

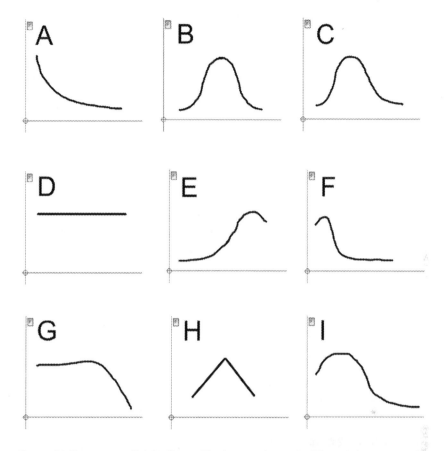

Figure 9.1 Frequency distributions. The image shows 9 different frequency distribution shapes, one of which needs to be matched with the populations described as a 'best fit'.

9   This is the frequency distribution for the wages of professional football (soccer) players.

10 This shows the frequency of different total scores when two of the same dice are thrown and the totals are added together.

11 This diagram shows the distribution of national standardised test scores.

12 This is the distribution of people of different ages selected to take part in a clinical trial for people between the ages of 20 and 30.

It's not hard to imagine that we could edit the list of examples and the list of distributions to change this activity to suit a class and so on. To continue, I'll go through some of the big talking points that come up.

What is a frequency distribution?

It rolls off the tongue so easily and sounds good and mathematical, but it's an easy to underestimate idea. Lots of early discussion is about this and, as a teacher, this is where I find I contribute most to help. This is most easily done in the context of an example. Looking at a normal distribution (bell curve), *"If this was baby weights it would mean that there are a few very low, about as many very high and most in the middle"* and so on.

Skew

It is a good mind-bending conversation to have about skew and when and why it occurs. Here is where I can often get out of my depth and am grateful to have some biologists in the class that can explain. There is something easy to understand about how, with measurement, there is an obvious minimum value but not a maximum, but the subtleties of skew go beyond that.

Literacy rates

This hits upon one of the big drivers from the Gapminder organisation and Hans Rosling that points to widespread misunderstanding about the world. Literacy rates are really high all over the planet. It is terrific to hear students comparing the shapes with what they think they know. It is really getting to the heart of understanding what the diagrams show.

Population Demographics

PopulationPyramid.net is really quite addictive. I recommend some time there. The pyramids are of course a more typical way of showing such data. They are two-sided with one side for each sex. How then, does that translate into a frequency distribution? This is then coupled with what we think we know about population demographics and how that might be different for the US and The Gambia. These are some salient moments of discussion.

Wealth and wages distribution

Many seem to be up to date with the idea that, globally, a very high percentage of wealth is with a very low percentage of people, so a shape comes to mind. How does this compare with the professional football players' wages? Is it the same shape? I based all of these diagrams on data I found, but have to accept that this will vary according to the many parameters that apply. It is for this reason that I am happy to let this trigger a useful debate rather than declare right or wrong.

Normal distribution

This is one of the more profound conversations to come up of course. The idea that this perfectly symmetrical shape might appear out of some natural, and some less natural, ideas is really very interesting and very definitely crosses over into our theory of knowledge lessons. A simple question about what things we might expect to be normally distributed can be very interesting very quickly. Then we can get on to the idea of applying it to other areas like, for example, exam grades. What are the implications of deciding exam grade boundaries using a bell curve? This gets pretty significant and piques interest. 'Two tourists running away from a lion, one tells the other that it's pointless, we'll never outrun the lion. The other replies that they don't need to, they just need to outrun them'.

Writing or talking about this always makes me think about the flaws there might be in this activity and then, in true teacher fashion, how to make the flaws work to our advantage. I am certain there can be a better version of this task, but suspect a reason that I have not set about making it, is that it already does what I want it to do. It is lovely when such a simple thing can give rise to a combination of such useful mathematical discussion and, at the same time, reflection about our world. I can see that getting really specific and making a complete set of matching pairs might have merit, but I think, as it is, it is more representative of the sort of thinking we are required to do when we think about the world around us. Just my view, please edit at will.

Even with Mr. Sivers's video in mind, I am sure that you will already know how effective the matching pairs or card sort activity is in provoking thought, reasoning and discussion in students. They are presented with so much to talk about straight away and the very simple nature of the goal makes it so accessible and lends it immediate focus. When designing these tasks, I think teachers get a rich experience too. There is so much good thinking in trying to isolate the connections you want to encourage students to make and then the value is multiplied when you see the connections they actually do make! As we have already said, this stuff takes time so we have to be realistic with ourselves.

I do also anticipate that this activity might be one that raises the most consternation amongst readers. Please remember that a principal goal of the book was to share my experiences of using activities that I look forward to. If you see flaws, then fix them when you design yours! I also anticipate that you have plenty of examples around you of this kind of activity and can easily think of different ways it can be employed with different students at different stages with different topics. Even a simple 'match the question to the answer' exercise brings a lot to the table because students have answers to work with and all the other reasons mentioned above. It doesn't have to be particularly sophisticated. Match the shape to its description or properties, match the number to its factors, match the boxplot to the data, match the function to its derivative. The last one has an extra edge if they are not labelled as functions and derivatives so any given card could be either!

I'll tell you quickly about another one I use every year. This one is all about quadratics and is a larger scale card sort and comes in three rounds.

Round one – 6 quadratic functions

For each of the 6 functions there is a card with a function plotted on a graph, an expression of the function, a factorised version of the function, the coordinates of the y-intercept and the coordinates of points where x is zero. So that is 30 little cards that need to be arranged into 6 groups of 5 and this one does work out neatly. This works super well at helping students to make important links between algebraic and graphical information. The coordinates can be seen from the image of the function and then the factorised form is juxtaposed really neatly with the coordinates of the zeros. There are functions with 0, 1 and 2 zeros to keep it interesting and groups of two or three students can piece this together pretty quickly.

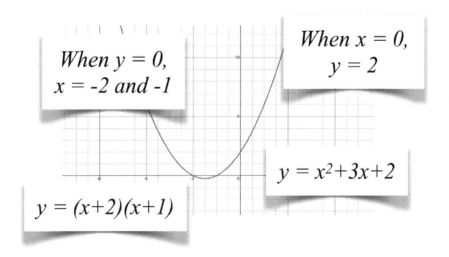

Figure 9.2 Quadratic links. This image shows a matched set of quadratic links cards.

Round two – 6 quadratic functions

Round two is the same but for the absence of graphs drawn on the axes. There are 6 cards with axes and students are expected to sketch on the graph (maybe it's just paper, maybe it's laminated and cleanable).

Round three – 6 quadratic functions

Round three only gives students the function and they have to add all the rest of the details.

I guess you see what's happened there and I am sure you can deal with the considerations about what you might expect students to know already before they start such a task. So often the crux of any kind of mathematical problem solving comes when students are able to observe things that they know and then put them together to logically deduce a new truth. Again, instead of 'What am I supposed to do?' and 'What can I do?', this activity offers good concrete experiences of this kind of behaviour that helps to get better at it and show its value. There is, as always, a risk that students can solve this kind of puzzle with simple 'pattern spotting' which might mean they weren't thinking as much about the given mathematical objects as we had intended. I won't pretend that I have a foolproof solution for this, but you can mitigate. For starters, the three levels of this activity demand more of a focus on the objects. In addition, that is what the teacher is there for. It is a beautiful notion to think that some carefully designed tasks just need to be distributed to students and everything will take care of itself. I don't think that happens. This is actually the bit about teaching I like the most though. The task brings the focus, engagement and activity, which leaves the teacher free to listen and then ask pertinent questions and offer helpful inputs when necessary. We will ask students to tell us what they mean when they say something and why they think what they have said might be true. We will help other students to be heard and generally help the students to make sense of the mathematics they are doing. I have sometimes asked groups of students to paste their cards to a sheet of paper and add annotations that explain the links and have sometimes done this as a formal whole class discussion. There are all kinds of outcomes here.

In summary, the humble card sort is to mathematics teaching what a hollandaise sauce is to French cuisine (I am much better at the card sort for what it's worth) in being a fundamental staple upon which so much can be built. I have offered two examples here that take it a bit further with an interest in exploring broader possibilities, but at whatever level with whatever topic, we have excellent tasks for promoting and exemplifying the mathematical behaviours that are so important. I, for one, find them amazing!

From the box to the classroom

Thoughts and themes

- The matching exercise offers a scaffold for students in providing possible answers and 'narrowing down' as an approach.
- In doing so, the activities prompt a good deal of reasoning between students working in groups.'
- They are great for helping students to make and/or reinforce links between different representations.
- Matching activities don't have to have neat and even outcomes.

Task to try

- Try the frequency distributions matching activity.
- Try adding/changing different populations and shapes to make this suit your class.
- Remember the value of existing matching activities you already have.
- Try the quadratic links matching activity.
- Try making your own again (it may have been a while) to remind yourself of this process and its value.

10 Prime pictures

> ## What's in the box?
>
> Our number system is such a source of fascination and prime numbers appear to be the DNA of it all. This is such an important thing to understand that it takes some thought about how to help students engage with it. With the help of some lovely visuals, this can do just that! The focus here is on multiple representations of mathematical ideas through visualisation and how we might make activities based around them.

People are fascinating, right? There is such a wide variety of interests and experiences out there and it is amazing to find out these things when you dig below the surface with people in discussion. It's actually quite sobering when you learn about some of the interests, talents and experiences of students you have taught for ages and never knew. We get lost in the primary focus of what we do and often never get, or take the chance to find out. Perhaps I shouldn't speak for everyone. I remember being really surprised when a friend of mine turned down a beer at dinner not because he turned down a beer but because he said he was 'on call'. *"You are an aircraft engineer and it's Saturday night, what are you on call for?"* I said. He said, *"Well if one of our aircraft is having a problem mid-flight tonight, then I am the person they will call for help"*. It's one of those things that was such an eye-opener to me, but that makes perfect sense once you know. Not much good waiting till Monday, right? Just talking to people about how they spend their days, their spare time, what they have done, where they have travelled can be very illuminating. I am sure you see where this is going. Let me tell you one of mine. Picture me on holiday, walking through a new city, soaking up the atmosphere and the history, camera at the ready. We are walking towards and admiring a famous landmark with lots of other tourists and my family notice that I have lagged behind. When they turn around to ask me what's up, there is a collective sigh followed by *"Don't worry, he is taking a picture of a drain cover again"*, and sure enough I am pointing my camera to the ground with my legs akimbo so they are not in shot, trying to find the best angle that eliminates the shadow, because this is a really good one. My poor family is used to this. You've heard of train and plane spotting, well, I am a drain spotter. I told you it's fascinating! I know I am not the only one. There is an online community on Twitter

DOI: 10.4324/9781003266501-10

that appreciates a good drain cover with unique or attractive geometrical properties. I promise, there is a world of amazing geometry on the ground beneath our feet, that someone, somewhere has often put a lot of thought into. I used to share them on an Instagram account until a friend famously told me 'she didn't get it', at which point I realised the photos were just for me and the little Twitter community.

I'd better go somewhere with this. I can't sell myself as a fanatic but there was indeed a form of unbridled joy when I found this one in London.

The reason may not be obvious, but I guess that it might provoke some thought in some readers. There was, for a long time, on the internet an interactivity that would allow you to make this kind of image that had a really important underpinning structure (I don't think it exists any more). But what might that structure be? Again, if you know, then you know, but if you don't you have some thinking to do. I might even tell you it represents the number 35 and you might now think that you have this sorted out, at which point I will ask you if you can then tell me what possibilities there are for a drain cover that represents the number 40 and then you'd be thinking! There is, of course, an underlying code for making such a representation and the first part of this

Figure 10.1 Prime drain. The image shows a drain cover that is a pictorial representation of the prime number decomposition of a number.

activity might be to give you the first 30 pictures that represent the numbers from 1 to 30 and see if you can (a) tell me which is which and (b) crack the code for how to make them. As you have a look at them, think about the following questions. If you know already, then try to imagine your students approaching these questions.

- Can they be classified in any way by things they have in common?
- What is the significance of the different shadings?
- What can you say about the groupings of circles?
- Can we recognise squares and cubes?

This could be like a matching pairs activity and certainly this brings all those advantages with it, but there are lots of ways you could present it to students. You could give them 30 different, nonconsecutive numbers. In another collection I have 30 different pictures, but some of them are different ways of showing the same number so the question might be *"How many different numbers are there here?"* The key though is in the questions that we ask to go with it. The goal is to decipher the code that is used to make the diagrams.

The topic of prime number decomposition just doesn't sound good, does it, but it really is. *"What did you do at school today?"* You'll know by now that the diagrams are ways of showing numbers decomposed into their prime factors. In my drain cover there are 5 groups of 7 because five 7s make 35. In another diagram there are 3 circles, each with 5 circles inside them that each have 3 dots in them. This is 45 because $3 \times 3 \times 5 = 45$. The different colours correspond to the factor at play. Yellow is 2, blue is 3, red is 5 and so on, with a different new colour for each new prime number. It is a delightful way of showing the kind of 'prime number DNA' of any given number. Of course, to many students, the notion of 'prime number DNA' will, at some stage be new and, of course, it is actually pretty cool and a really important exercise in coming to terms with the existence and nature of primes that are at once so fundamental in our number system and enigmatic. I know that none of this ever crossed my path until I was a teacher. Even then I may not have paid it enough attention when it did. When first encountered, the idea that any given integer must be a function of multiplying a number of prime numbers together demands inquisition. Few want to accept it without trying some more examples, and as you run through those examples it becomes obvious that it must be the case. Perhaps, like me, lots of students have not paid prime numbers enough attention; perhaps they have just been filed under 'anomalous', when they really should have centre stage. I find it all very exciting, especially when we get back to questions about whether mathematics was discovered or invented.

So the activity with the diagrams is designed as a task that first demands and offers the opportunity to practise behaving mathematically (What do you

Figures 10.2 and 10.3 Prime pictures. The image shows selected visualisations of numbers, based on their prime number decompositions.

wonder? What do you notice?) and then tries to draw students into this wonderful mysterious world of primes. Early in the piece students want to explore non-prime numbers of circles, but just think how many colours you would need! (OK, I know we are going to need an infinite number of colours either way, but I was thinking about sticking to two-digit numbers for now.) As students work on the task, they will make important observations about the colours and the number of circles. They are likely to identify the single circles as prime numbers which is a neat demonstration of their nature. Classes will vary and some do better than others. It is nice, when timing works, to let students share observations with the class so as to both let them enjoy the kudos and move the rest of the class along at the same time. Through lots of observation, conjecture making and testing and reasoning, the rules of the game emerge and there are some signs of illumination around the room. This is often accompanied by questions, good questions that search to test and extend any general conclusions that might be taking shape. All good stuff of course that is put to the test when students are asked to make some of their own diagrams. I have always quite enjoyed a bit of artistic freedom here. Even though the artistry might not obviously dwell on the maths, the visual record of the activity is worth it. Students do have to think about the different ways in which they can draw the numbers by using the factors in a different order. If you wanted to, you could get stuck into how you might actually construct these diagrams so that the circles are in the right place! Definitely not easy and starting to resemble the ancient Japanese mathematical art of Sangaku.

I have had a lot of fun with the task in various ways and it has helped me and students to explore the fascination of prime numbers and their role in our number system. Some of the artwork has been fun too. My favourite was the cake. Some students and I even took this activity to a local maths festival where prime cupcakes were prizes for anyone successfully decoding. What I like most about this task is the element of 'decoding' and how that plays on a natural instinct we have to want to solve a puzzle. We once had Dr James Grime (already mentioned) and his enigma machine in school and I have run code-breaking workshops for students as well, but still feel very much like I want to dive deeper into that. In this case, the code is written in mathematics of course and successful decoding is a lovely way into the otherwise dry-sounding prime number decomposition. *"Well, it was brilliant today at school Dad, we solved a good puzzle and opened the door on to the fascinating role of prime numbers in our number system and now I need to bake a prime cake for my teacher"*. I know, I am clearly delusional, but at least I hope you can understand why I was so excited to find that drain cover amongst all the other joys of London.

There are other prime number visualisation tools out there and perhaps you are aware of the work of Dan Finkel and his 'Prime club' game that is all based on the same idea. Working with this particular tool was a good example for me about 'cool things on the internet'. The idea that I often find cool things, let's focus on interactivities for now, and have so often been disappointed that my students don't get excited about them as I do. It is a good reminder that, at school at least, a task means so much more. A task has to take the cool thing and invite students in. It has to ask the kind of question or invite a level of engagement that brings all of its coolness out. This comes up a lot and is especially true when you consider that not everyone is a drain spotter!

The decoding idea is a bit akin to 'reverse engineering', which is something I will write about a few times in the coming chapters, especially those involving technology. To extend this chapter I want to dwell a bit longer on the kinds of activities that bridge a gap between a mathematical idea that can be written and also drawn. This is an idea I have thought about a lot and which resulted in making a set of images for classroom walls with a friend of mine who is a graphic artist. We will talk about mathematical ideas and he will make a picture of it. It's great fun.

Power pictures

One example I have worked on with students is to look at visual representations of indices. For example, what numbers do you think are represented by this picture?

There is something lovely and concrete about seeing how powers work in this way. Take 3^4 for example. Start with 3 objects, say squares, and then out of each square you should draw three circles (That will be $3^2 = 9$ circles), out of each circle, you can draw 3 triangles and out of each triangle there should be 3 stars. There will, of course, be 81 stars, 27 triangles, 9 circles and 3 squares and the diagram will be showing the first four powers of 3. Clearly, the artist might want to get a bit more imaginative with the shapes and the way they are drawn to give it their own artistic influence, but the principle is a nice one and, I think, lends a good deal of power to the power. I find this myself, but as teachers it can be easy to forget that we have been pushing ideas around our heads for much longer than our students so this kind of thing can be of value. Let's not forget how excited we can all get about fractals as well. Don't knock it until you have tried it. For digital artists there is the potential to go to higher powers here as well without spending hours drawing thousands of squares. I remember a student once crafting a beautiful 3D model of 3^4 too. I know this crosses time boundaries and I would never ask for it, but selfishly I quite like it

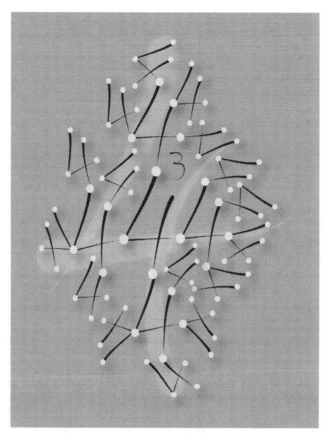

Yellow Constellation

Figure 10.4 Power picture. The image shows a visual representation of a number expressed in index form.

Source: Image by Pierre Claverie.

when students voluntarily get lost in a bit of maths related activity given I know how often that happens in other subjects. We can even come back to this when we get to summing geometric sequences and how many 'things' there are all together. As inspiration to get your classes thinking and talking, try googling 'hand fractal' and wincing at some of the 'power pictures' that people have created.

Fraction pictures

On another note, I remember a colleague once showing me some 'Mondrian-inspired' work their students had done that went like this. Each student was given a fraction to work with (in built differentiation) and a large rectangular canvas (OK, piece of paper). Students should split the rectangular canvas into two more rectangles where one of the dimensions is split according to the fraction they were given. This is then repeated at will. Not all rectangles need to be split, but some can be split as often as you like, or is practical. The resulting collage of rectangles is then painted (coloured) in red, yellow and blue and each new Mondrian is a visual tribute to the fraction they started with. In the process students have done a good deal of measuring and working out fractions of quantities. In an elaborate twist, the classroom can be set up as a carousel where students do a division on the rectangle they start with and then rotate to a different one with a different fraction, and so all the artworks become 'collaborative tributes to a fraction'. The art of fractions!

I know that there are those who raise good questions about display, but I am a fan. I suppose my ideal would be whiteboard walls to my classroom and plenty of display space above or in the corridors. Either way, I love to look at these things and have convinced myself at last that they have value in the area of 'episodic memory'. That sounds good to me, otherwise, I just think they look good on display. More importantly, students have had a valuable experience in the notion of multiple representations which is a central pillar of mathematical thinking that allows us to recognise and use mathematical ideas in different forms. That, dear family, is why I stopped to take that picture of that drain!

From the box to the classroom

Thoughts and themes

- Multiple representations are an important bridge in mathematics that allows us to recognise and use mathematics in different forms.
- Visualising concepts is a good way to exemplify the above.
- Such visualisations can be used for 'decoding' or 'creating', both of which invite engagement with the underpinning idea.

Task to try

- Try the prime pictures activities as 'decoding' activities.
- Try making some prime pictures and noticing what happens.
- Try making some power pictures and asking questions about them.
- Try some fraction pictures as described or variations on the theme.

11 Population growth

What's in the box?

Mathematical modelling is more prevalent than ever in the current climate and this activity is about getting students to think about its very nature and how it relates to other things that they know. In this example we look at some population growth data and explore the technique of 'taking some information away' as means of designing a task.

I have come to the conclusion (a bit late probably) that there are simply too many interesting things to do, read, watch, see and play with. The information age has simultaneously provided, and made us aware of, so many more of these whilst making it patently obvious that we will only ever have time to scratch the surface. A double edged sword indeed. At its worst it's a terrible dose of FOMO (fear of missing out) specific to things I want to bring in to my classroom somehow (FOMOOTIWTBITMCRSH – doesn't quite work as well). I'd like to think that I have become better at treating the internet like a constant stream of information that, at various points in the day, I will stop and watch. If I happened to see it come by then great, if it goes past without me noticing then I am sure it will come around again. I probably haven't become good at that, but it is, at least, the goal.

I am sure too that it is a well-established principle of advertising and publicity that if you want people to take notice of things then you have to make sure, amongst other things, that they cross people's paths regularly. That's as far as I am willing to go into such areas of which I have less than little expertise. It is relevant when I think back to first hearing about the Gapminder foundation. I remember a couple of colleagues talking about it with high praise and putting it on my mental list (and that is worse than the little bit of paper that you will probably misplace) of things that I must check out when I get the chance. It was probably a year later, after several more such encounters of people referencing it, and distant mental puzzling over what the connection might be between the name and the London Underground, before I finally sat down and had a proper look. Of course, when I did, I was full of *"why didn't I do this years ago?"*. Things just have to go past you. That is why I will be metaphorically wafting this book under your nose a lot. It is a sensational resource though. The Roslings and the

DOI: 10.4324/9781003266501-11

foundation have done stellar work to bring data into the public domain and present it in ways that help us to understand and encourage us to ask questions. I think I have mentioned it already.

So, one day, as the last class of the day says farewell, I am winding down by watching the internet stream past me and I catch sight of a new post from the Gapminder foundation about a new graphic they have produced on population growth across the planet. The post says that they are really interested in feedback from teachers about how they might use it in class and get students to interact with it. On my left is a big stack of marking and on my right my chaotic teacher planner and these are two of many signs that I should just let it pass. Unfortunately though, this has 'shiny new project' written all over it. I convince myself that the distraction is justified, that an element of teachers' work is creative design and artistry (We are all entitled to a bit of self-delusion) and that artists don't work to order. We have to strike when the moment presents itself. It is amazing what we can say to ourselves when we need to. So I spent the next couple of hours bashing out some ideas about this. The resource was a really nice presentation of how the population has grown over the last 200 years with the world divided into four main geographical areas. The main word though there is 'presentation' and I know I could have presented this to my students and it would have interested them just fine for its duration. It's just that it would not have been very long or very deep and students would not have engaged properly with either the factual information being presented or the various bits of mathematics that were going on. This is regularly the challenge of 'task design meets interesting thing on the internet'. It is, again, our work to create the task that can do this. So here goes.

I went to find my colleague Matt in the geography department and get his input and we put together an idea for a big project that would give birth to lots of little ones that we would be able to use for some time afterwards. At the time of writing I think that would have been about 10 years ago – so the effort was worth it. We have just begun to talk about it again. We drew up some plans and sent them back to the people at Gapminder and were really excited when they wrote back to say that they really wanted to see this in action so would send someone down to the school to see what we were up to. This means, of course, we'll have to do it.

We decided we wanted to remake the graphic but with students on a map and a time-lapse video of population growing. We did. It was great fun. Matt had some of his older students draw a scale map on the school playground – it was pretty big, about 15 m by 7 m and we coordinated some classes so that we could have 100 students with us for the exercise. (I mentioned this when I talked about the world village exercise – we did all this on the same day.) Then we had worked out that each student would have to represent about 93 million people.

We started in 1800 with enough students on the map to show the populations at that time and then, at regular intervals, we added more students to different areas of the globe with someone in the corner showing the passing of the years. Do you get the picture? We set up time-lapse cameras and video from the roof and recorded it so that the end result was a video of the population growth in those four regions, much like the graphic that Gapminder sent out to start with. Listening, as I do regularly, to the social media teacher machine I can hear great choruses of things like *"Classic waste of time" "What learning has happened there?" "What is this obsession with engagement and fun all about?"* It really is like that sometimes. You have to be brave to put your ideas on social media. I don't yet know if putting them in a book is better or worse. I'll be honest, I wouldn't attempt to argue that this particular exercise ticked anything in particular off our list of learning objectives. I don't think anyone had a profound learning moment and yes, it was a lot of fun. There are so many good reasons to do this sort of thing occasionally and the best one of them is the way you can feed off the experience and what you produced afterwards – and we'll get into that. First though, I just want to mention something important. Schools are often adorned with their 'mission statements' and various other manifestations of their lofty goals and hopes for the school community. There is good reason for healthy scepticism about how much of this is manifest in other day to day realities, but most of these lofty goals are admirable and very present in our daily thinking. My point is that there is so much more in the goals of a school than the objectives on my curriculum and so the 'broader goals' of education need to be on our mind too. This experience was such a lovely community event that we enjoyed, recorded, celebrated and talked about for a long time afterwards and this is real value before we even get into the thought provocation that came after.

Modelling population growth

So this activity is the main subject of this chapter (haha finally). It is high on my list of lessons I look forward to and stems very much from what I have just described there. One of the great joys of Gapminder is that behind every pretty graphic there is data and it is easy to get your hands on. The data behind the graphic gives you the population for every region for every 20-year period from 1800 to 2040 (with that latter being a prediction). As a graph junky in the age of Desmos (or your favourite alternative of course), it's very tempting to just stick that in a grapher and look at the outcome, but I don't want to get there just yet. What I have done here is take a careful selection of the data out of the table and present it as an incomplete table where the goal is to complete it. What numbers do you think go in the gaps?

Can you place the four geographical areas? They are the Americas, Asia, Europe and Africa.

You have to decide what numbers you think go in the gaps. You also have to decide which column you think goes with which geographical area. For example, in the third column, what goes between 0.05 and 1? And how will you make that decision? This is where it gets interesting and we can reflect on what might be a natural instinct to split the difference and pick a number halfway between the two. The lovely moment is when someone points out that this is not consistent with the way the other numbers change in the column. This points to at least some benefit of lots of looking at sequences over the years! *"It doesn't appear to be growing in that way"* is the desirable observation that someone in a small group will always make. Next of course, you have people trying to establish just how the sequence appears to be growing by analysing the other numbers. We may recognise this as an instinct for mathematical modelling and provides another example of how we can draw on natural instincts. Just quickly, it is probably worth questioning the use of the word 'natural' as I have already pointed out that this instinct or behaviour may well have its roots in previous experiences students have had in a mathematics classroom. Later we will get to a point where we put the numbers we have into a graph. Once we have this kind of visual it does become much more 'instinctive' to put a number on the natural path between the existing points.

There is a lovely logical level to this puzzle too. The fifth column is 'the world' and, as such, should be the total of the four columns. This introduces an extra check for students. It might be seen as a constraint or a clue I suppose, but either way it has to be considered and does its job as a prompt for

Year	Years after 1800					World
1800	0		0.07	0.03		0.95
1820	20		0.07	0.03		1.04
1840	40	0.76	0.08	0.05	0.27	1.16
1860	60		0.09		0.31	1.23
1880	80	0.79	0.11	0.1		
1900	100	0.89			0.42	
1920	120	1.04	0.15	0.21	0.47	1.86
1940	140	1.23	0.19	0.27	0.55	2.25
1960	160	1.67		0.42		3.03
1980	180	2.58			0.75	4.43
2000	200			0.83		
2020	220	4.48		1.03	0.84	
2040	240			1.16		

Figure 11.1 Population growth table. The image shows the table that needs to be completed for this task. What numbers should go in the gaps?

thinking that helps give students an approach to take. In a group, one student is likely to be looking out for this and might take on this role. My experience with this task is that students will happily run with this. There is enough information and approach to make it a feasible seeming puzzle. This is another moment where me as the teacher gets to listen and ask and help students to move along.

The next stage for me, or viable alternative starting point, or differentiation technique, is to give students the actual numbers that go in the gaps – but obviously not in the right order! This makes the puzzle a bit more like matching cards from earlier. We now just have to match the questions with the answers. It does change the nature of the task a little and certainly makes it more approachable. I like to let students have a go without first and keep the numbers up my sleeve. This lets me help some groups that might be in need sooner and let others make as much progress as they can. When they are given the numbers the instinct is to want to see which ones are closest to the ones they already have. The discussion goes on and the puzzling continues. This task often gives rise to the rare *"I really enjoyed that today Mr Noble"* comment. I like to believe that the rarer thing is the saying out loud. Invariably, students will get the numbers in the right place eventually and at some point I am likely to have encouraged at least some to plot the points they have on Desmos and use this technique to help them put the numbers in and check the answers they already have. This is another potentially helpful stage to the task.

By the time students have put the numbers in the gaps they have spent some enjoyable time solving a puzzle, they have demonstrated and used genuine modelling techniques that we can draw on later and they have had to draw on some general knowledge about the world to decide which column is which. If you haven't done so already, do have a go. Teachers on my workshops have gotten every bit as much out of this activity from my experience. It is really just a more elaborate version of a simple 'fill in the gaps' in this sequence question. The context perhaps changes it significantly largely because the data is real and therefore not an exact sequence. This is the reality of real data and really does help us get to the heart of what it means to use mathematical modelling. The addition of the fifth 'total' column introduces a nice level of logic to the puzzle and the size of the table all combine to make this an altogether deeper experience.

This key principle can be used in a variety of different contexts, but the tasks can be easily created. Start with a completed table of information and then take some of it away. In chapter 3, I mentioned the results of a survey that asked people *"what percentage of, or how many people out of a 100 as people may prefer, of the people in your country do you think voted in your last general election?"* amongst other similar questions. I wanted to use this as an opportunity to explore the difference between absolute and percentage difference and when we might usefully consider either of those. I made a table with the country, the average guess, the correct answer, the absolute difference and the percentage difference, then I took out some of the numbers and asked the students to try and put them back. I should say that this is not a random exercise, some thought has to be given to this to make sure there is enough information left in the table to deduce the missing gaps.

It is an odd reflection that, just as simply as asking *"What's in the box?"*, a huge amount of valuable engagement and mathematical behaviour was generated by taking this really interesting thing I saw on the internet and taking some of the information away. I think it is also an important reflection that often, engaging students with some of the awesome stuff on the internet, often involves taking it away from the internet and seeking engagement on a much simpler level. The internet is so full of 'answers' where a classroom needs so many more 'questions' to provoke productive activity.

From the box to the classroom

Thoughts and themes

- Incredible internet findings often need manipulation into tasks before we can expect students to engage productively with them.
- Taking information (answers) away and asking students to fill it back in is one way of doing the above.
- Mathematical modelling begins as a healthy instinct. The algebraic representation of these models might be the greater challenge.

Task to try

- Try the population growth task as described above.
- Try making your own task using the principle of taking information away.

12 Starting from scratch

What's in the box?

This is the first of three chapters with a focus on technology. Seymour Papert's *Mindstorms*, first published in 1980 is a seminal bit of thinking about the impact of teaching and learning of technological developments. Not so different from Papert's original ideas, this is about how we might merely scratch the surface of 'Scratch' to unleash some mindstorms in my classroom.

I enjoy the conversations where people from different generations reflect on the nature and magnitude of the changes in society that they have seen in their lifetimes to date. You know, you have probably had them all. People of my generation have some pretty big claims to major paradigm shifts. I mean, computers, the internet, the smartphone, we have seen all these pervade our existence to such a stunning degree of dependence and normality that it is quite extraordinary to think back to our youths that did not involve them at all. My poor children must be bored silly hearing the *"I remember the first time someone told me about e-mail and the internet"*. Of course, my parents will talk of cars, TVs, antibiotics, men on the moon and nuclear reaction, as well as all the tech so I guess, for now, they win.

I would assert though, that I have witnessed a technological revolution in teaching in my career. We saw and used, once I think, a BBC computer at school. I was lucky enough to have a Commodore 64 at home with the programs loaded up by cassette and a joystick. During my degree I did a course called 'Technical Communication' aimed at getting us to use word processors and I remember handing my first assignment in handwritten on the grounds that it communicated much more clearly than anything I managed on a word processor. We had brief exposure to computers during teacher training, and at my first school there were one or two decent computer suites where I first got excited about technology and mathematics teaching. I can remember vividly the first time I saw an 'interactive whiteboard' and began the subsequent campaign to get them in my school. When they arrived this was actually the first time I had a computer in my classroom, which was huge. I have since been lucky to have taught where we have lots of access to technology. In the beginning I was like a child in a

DOI: 10.4324/9781003266501-12

sweet shop, but it is interesting how wide access to technology has helped me become more discerning about what and when I want it. There are, of course, lots of arguments raging about all this technology and its impact. I know there are plenty who don't like interactive whiteboards and I often remind myself of an occasion when I was talking with Anne Watson, who has been a mentor of mine at various stages, about these 'interactive' things and she would simply point at her ordinary whiteboard and say "*Look, I have an interactive whiteboard too*". The point is salient and it is easy to get carried away with assuming that more tech is just better by default when obviously it is not. In a greedy reaction to all of this though, I much prefer to solve debates about 'either or' with 'both please'. I don't always get what I want, but I feel like everything has potential that you can't access unless you have it! Let the debate rage on, it's a good one, but for me, classroom technology has had a profound effect on ways in which students can see mathematics and behave mathematically and has proven fertile ground for our 'lessons to look forward to'.

I didn't read *Mindstorms* by Seymour Papert until I had been teaching for about 10 years. I had been shown the program Logo during teacher training and experimented in those computer labs I mentioned earlier, but had not reflected quite so much on the paradigm shift that this kind of technology had offered teaching and learning. The activity I am going to write about here is just one of many potential takes on these 'mindstorms' that Papert wrote about, but I am including it because it is, for me, such a clear vehicle for working with and thinking about the ideas. Every year, this kind of activity provides me with further thought and inspiration. This is especially valuable as I become increasingly aware of online movements/teachers/researchers who are not so sure about Papert's ideas. (That was diplomatically put.) Differing views and arguments are what provokes progress and so I always read and listen and then I come back to 'mindstorms' and try to look at it with fresh eyes. I do observe things that I can do more of or do differently as a teacher to better facilitate the mindstorms, but I am still convinced that the mindstorms are there and I see mathematical behaviour flowing from my students in the things they do and say, the questions they ask, the problems they set themselves and the way they set about answering them.

So let's get down to it. In the original Logo there is a turtle on the screen who will respond to coded instructions that you enter. You can type 'move forward 10' and the turtle will move forward 10 steps. You can ask it to 'turn right 90 degrees' and it will oblige. So the classic problem involves, for example, 'Can you write the instructions that will draw me a square?' In the first case, students might write the following

Move forward 10
Turn right 90

Move forward 10
Turn right 90
Move forward 10
Turn right 90
Move forward 10

And then we introduce the 'repeat' instruction which allows is to write that more efficiently as

Repeat 4 times
Move forward 10
Turn right 90

I feel certain that this has crossed the path of practising teachers, but if it hasn't and if you are new to all this, then this is the basic idea and it can develop pretty quickly into some lovely problems. What I will do next is just splurge a few such problems and then elaborate on what I think the key features are.

To start with, it is important to say that, these days, all this is happening with the program Scratch from MIT. This is the Logo turtle on steroids and some. Using the Scratch program the way I am proposing is a bit like driving a Formula 1 car to school. Let's not dwell on that for too long. At its basic level, it does all the things that Logo used to, albeit with a friendlier interface if you can look past the tools you don't need.

Polygons

So let's say that you have drawn the square using a repeat function. The next questions you might ask are . . .

- Can you write the instructions/code to draw a regular pentagon?
- What about other regular polygons?

Something about this simple problem and context is what provokes the mind-storms. You need to get this little animal to draw a regular pentagon, so how can you do it? How far does it have to turn each time? How can I figure that out from what I know about angles so far? And what we observe is that the context has set students a 'puzzle' that they want to solve. It is one where they can arrive at a conjecture and then try it out with instant results – if the turtle doesn't draw a regular pentagon, then we still have work to do. Trial and improvement is encouraged here and the iterative 'debugging' of the program is a lovely rea-soning process that is a pleasure to watch as it mixes with analysis of what is happening. For example, a student might deduce a turning angle of 72 degrees (360 divided by 5) as a conjecture and learn quickly from it.

Variables and a growing polygon

The algebra started, of course, as we introduced the repeat brackets, but it kicks into gear here when we ask students to express the turning angle as a function of the number of sides. Of course, for mindstorms to happen this has to be a necessary step in solving another problem, otherwise we take away the incentive. So here is a problem that can do that. Can you write a program that draws the shapes in Figure 12.1 in one go?

This might be a lot in one go, but for the purposes of this book I wanted to crank it up pretty quickly before anyone assumed this was all going to be easy. In my classroom I have an interim exercise that helps students learn about the 'variable' idea. They are asked to write a program that asks you to 'enter the number of sides' and that the program then does the necessary calculations to work out the turning angle. This of course is effectively asking them to generalise about exterior angles of regular polygons which is something I think it is reasonable to expect students to deduce themselves. *"If I need to turn 5 equal turns that make a total of 360 then I need to turn 72 degrees"*, which generalises to *"for an n sided regular polygon, the turning angle is 360/n"*. The thrill of making this conclusion is the same thrill as solving a puzzle. The word 'discovery' is much maligned and probably inappropriate as it implies a kind of wandering around until you find something then pick it up. This is much more mathematical in nature. You have a problem that needs solving, you have knowledge of the scenario at the ready and you put bits of this knowledge together to deduce new knowledge. Now that is doing mathematics.

Then they have all the tools they need. They know how to use a variable, they know how to use a repeat function and they know how to draw a polygon. So now it is a genuine puzzle. To solve it, you have to set up the program so that . . .

- There is a variable for the number of sides that starts with a value of 3.
- There is a polygon program in there that draws the polygon with the number of sides as set above and does the angle accordingly.
- That the number of sides is then increased by 1 and the program then repeated up until a polygon with 10 sides is drawn.

The order of all this is important too. What follows is a frenzy of activity as students make conjectures about how they think it can be done and set about testing those conjectures and learning from what happens.

Amongst the tech developments we now have available is 'network software' that allows me to see, on my computer, any or all of the screens of my students. I can sit there and watch them work. I generally prefer to walk around

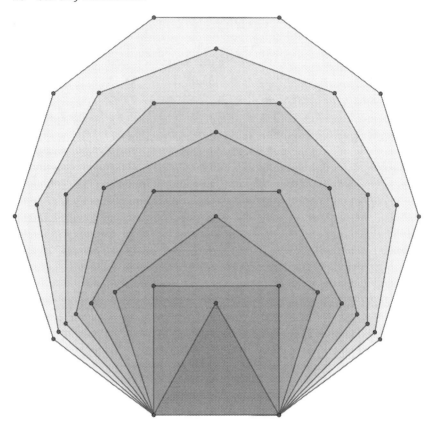

Figure 12.1 Growing polygons. The image shows concentric regular polygons. Can you write a program that will get the turtle to draw this combination of polygons?

the room and watch though. The network software has, perhaps understandably, become popular for surveillance which was probably the motivation behind its design. The pleasant side effect though is that I can, very easily and whenever I want, share the screen of any of my students (with their permission of course) with the rest of the class so we can look at their program and use it to move us on. This is particularly fabulous when I want to show two solutions side by side and have a conversation about 'elegance'. This is a word often associated with solutions and explanations in mathematics and this is an opportune moment for demonstrating what we mean. Clearly, I could copy and paste the polygon program 8 times and enter a different value of *n* each time, but the program that repeats and deals with the variables is so much

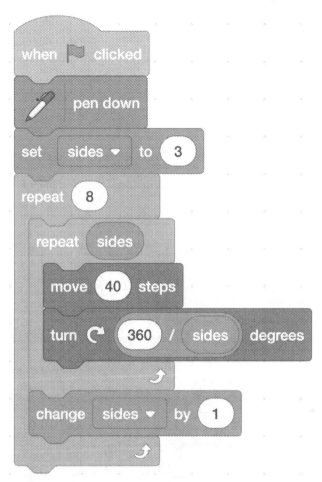

Figure 12.2 Growing polygons program. The image shows code that would draw the concentric polygons puzzle.

shorter and more 'elegant'. All the while, students are busy repeating, generalising, conjecture making and reasoning with each other and from the results of each try. It is another lovely example of a simple-sounding task, this time augmented seriously by a powerful medium, that creates the circumstances that encourage and reward mathematical behaviour. It is generally just one of those wonderful moments when it all comes together and this one doesn't let me down very often. There is more though and I do recommend having a go at these.

Shifting polygons

Can you write an elegant program that draws the following? Can you make it be defined by certain variables that you can change so you draw variations? Which do you like best?

Here we enter another new world, although the fundamental principles are the same in terms of what students need to know how to do in order to solve the problem. We can draw the first polygon, but what happens before we draw the next one? How many more do we draw and how do we get the program to stop drawing at the right time? How does the number of sides on the polygon and the number of polygons in the pattern affect the aesthetic of the finished

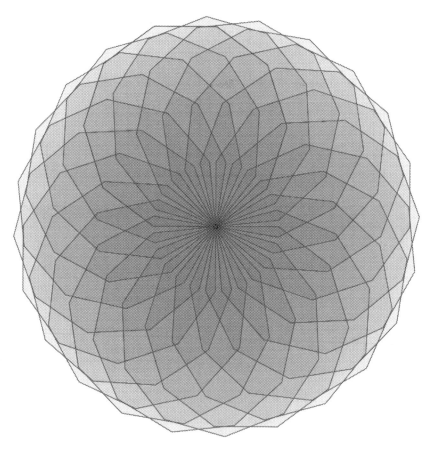

Figure 12.3 Shifting polygons. The image shows the shifting polygons program. Can you write a program that will get the turtle to draw this combination of polygons?

drawing? These are all the questions provoked by the challenge which students will ask and pursue.

I confess that I am seduced by the 'colour tool' on Scratch that allows us to change the colour of the pen along the way. I also like to change the background and have a bit of fun with the aesthetic. This is a confession because it clearly has less to do with the mathematics, but I do think it adds to the incentive to produce the finished product and so here we have a plausible argument I think.

Shifting and growing polygons

With this one we kind of combine features of the previous two challenges. Have a go!

I really hope you have opened up Scratch and tried to do this, or at least made a note that you want to. Countless students have done this in my

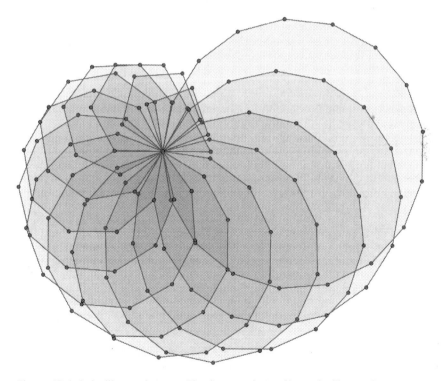

Figure 12.4 Spiralling polygons. The image shows the spiralling polygons program. Can you write a program that will get the turtle to draw this combination of polygons?

classroom, but I have also loved watching many teachers in workshops do this too. I think I said early on that it is a principle of mine (for better or worse) that on my teacher workshops, they spend a good chunk of time behaving mathematically. The buzz in the room when maths teachers get to do maths is joyful and a striking reminder of how important it is for us to have the same experiences as our students as often as we can. The yelps of pleasure and triumph when the problem has been successfully reverse engineered are the same from teachers as they are from students. What follows is often a lovely creative moment where people try out different bits of programming to go on making satisfying patterns using the same principles. I have always been a bit of a control freak in my classroom ("Ha!" says the rest of my family), and so am not always that comfortable with this freeplay, but I bring myself to allow it because of some of the wonderful things it produces from some students. In fairness, some of the things produced that I perceive as less 'wonderful' are probably so to the artists. It does help me to learn more about students though. Clearly, as the teacher here, I am over the moon with the sustained focus on angles and regular polygons and elegant algebraic programming. While I set the tasks, this is the prevailing activity. When those problems are solved, the freeplay tends to separate the group in two. Group 1 (the disciples), those that have been caught by the beauty of geometrical poetry, and Group 2 (the disrupters) those who do not crave the geometric regularity and take the first opportunity to go all Jackson Pollock on me. Still, I allow it for a while. My day has been made on occasions by students who show me, next lesson, what they went away and worked on.

There are of course lots of good ways to get into this kind of activity and I often start with a discussion where *I* am the turtle and I ask students to give *me* the instructions needed to draw different things. This could be me actually drawing on the floor (or playground outside) or me drawing on a board – there are lots of ways to simulate the turtle. I can be a particularly obtuse turtle when I want to be in an attempt to get students to use the right vocabulary and be precise with their instructions. Increasingly fewer students get the references I make to *I, Robot*. I don't expect many of my students to have read the Asimov classic, but it used to be true that many had seen the Will Smith feature film. Anyway, aside from the whole robot laws discussion, there is a moment where Smith finds a hologram of the late doctor that is left to help him solve the mystery of his death. The hologram only answers the questions asked of it when Smith asks it the right question. I quite like this little clip for helping to focus on accuracy and precision of language.

Thinking about varied approaches to this, here are three more ways to present the problems or work up to the activities.

1   I like the idea of showing students some code, before they have access to Scratch, and asking them to deduce what they think the code will draw or not as the case may be. This can involve some examples of code that works and some of code that contains errors (bugs) that students need to identify and correct (debug).

2   This might be extended or replaced with a matching pairs exercise (we talked about them) where students are given 10 bits of code and 10 images and asked to match the code with the image they think it will draw.

3   To help with Scratch, a decent technique of helping students to get into the activity is to give them some or all of the bits of code they need, but ask them to put them together to make the right program.

I just wanted to offer some good ideas for varying an approach to tasks like this that can oil the wheels or shift the focus. This is my favourite thing about a good task, and my approach to one might vary year on year after thinking about the possibilities.

Having spent some time on this kind of activity, I might, for example, give students this diagram, which is a chain of regular polygons and ask them to work out as many of the angles there as they can. Although it can be approached in a number of possible ways, I think many will use the context of the turtle to help frame the problem. *"What instructions do I have to give the turtle to make these drawings?"* and then the reasoning flows. Have a go and notice the reasoning you are using at each stage.

Then we might look at some various 'proofs' for interior and exterior angles of polygons that draw on this reasoning. See the images in Figure 12.6 as starting points for proving generalities about interior and exterior angles of polygons.

I think then that we have taken a lovely journey from a task that starts with using Scratch and coding to reverse engineer some mathematical structures as a means of provoking reasoning, to applying this reasoning to a static situation and then generalising to a written algebraic proof. It's a nice journey.

In summary, I hope to have provided provocation for the exploration of Seymour Papert's *Mindstorms*. I hope that this has prompted you to think about how the task, and variations of it, might work in your classroom. To help, here is a summary of those key elements.

Coding and precision

The task is based around the notion of providing precise instructions and there is something productively cold about how unforgiving such coding can be. The turtle will only do what you tell it to do. This gets us thinking about the much written symbiosis between coding and mathematics, between language, precision and logical structure.

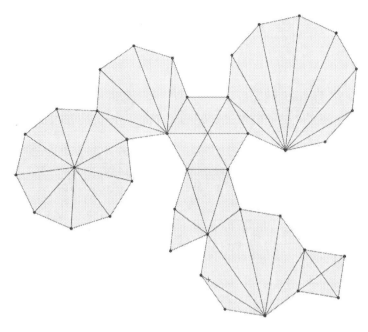

Figure 12.5 Regular polygon chain. The image shows a chain of regular polygons, divided in different ways. The challenge for students is to deduce as many of the angles in the diagram as they can.

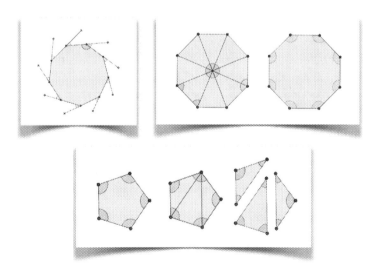

Figure 12.6 Polygon proofs. The images show three different starting points from which we could prove formulae for interior and exterior angles of polygons.

Reverse engineering

I will dwell on this more in the later chapter 'Dancing quadratics', but this is a clear example of a task based on the idea of reverse engineering. Students have to examine the finished construction to look for the key features of it in order to determine how to reproduce it. This builds on the fundamental 'notice and wonder' function where we ask ourselves what we notice and wonder about a given mathematical scenario in order to try and understand it or elaborate on it. *"I notice that the turtle turns an amount before drawing the next polygon", "I wonder what happens if I play with the amount of turn"*. The context of a reverse engineering problem is accessible, inviting and can lend instant focus.

The sandpit and the medium

Exploring mathematics through different media is a productive way of seeing it from multiple perspectives and, as such, developing a rounder view of it. Here the medium offers us a powerful sandpit. As we try to reverse engineer the object we have the ability to speculate quickly and test the associated conjectures. If we are right, the turtle will do what we want. If we are not, we will have to pay attention to what the turtle did and adjust our instructions accordingly. This instant feedback is highly efficient for teachers and students alike.

Behaving mathematically

This, again, is a perfect example of a task that provokes debate about what it means to teach and learn. I am fairly confident that you can read highly qualified expert research that says asking students to solve these problems on their own is not efficient. I am equally sure that you can read highly qualified expert research that it really is. I do feel that, as teachers, we must read and engage with research as much as we can and that it must play a primary role in training. I also think that critical analysis of research methods, what variables are considered and what is not and the limits of certain conclusions has to be discussed as well. This is not in any way to point to a conclusion that we can always argue what we want with research, but rather to reflect that little research is likely to offer us incontrovertible evidence for every child in every school in every scenario. Teachers have to try things for themselves and notice, as objectively as possible, what happens in their classrooms in the short term and the long. We have to regularly go back to aims and objectives of teaching and global goals and we have to talk about it. I (OK, Mr Papert) offer this kind of task as an excellent sandpit for such exploration.

Sorry – didn't necessarily expect to open that can of worms just there. It is just on my mind as I write as I am sure it is on the minds of some readers too.

Everyone else as well now! I just think the worst thing any educator can do is not acknowledge different points of view and evidence and I think this activity and the principles of *Mindstorms* are great topics to discuss. For my money, students are doing an awful lot of mathematics in these tasks.

At this end of the chapter it is interesting to reflect on what I said at the beginning about seeing a technology-driven paradigm shift in maths education during my career. Whilst technology continues to move at breakneck speed it is sweetly ironic that in my book I am writing to you about the principles of Papert's book first published in 1980. Perhaps this is something that permeates through education in general. Sometimes there will be great leaps, facilitated by one thing or another, but through all of that some fundamental principles remain.

From the box to the classroom

Thoughts and themes

- Technology is more than a medium for tasks and offers us new opportunities and new tasks for facilitating mathematical thinking.
- In this case, coding and programming are a prime example.
- The original ideas in Seymour Papert's Mindstorms are as alive and well as they ever have been.
- There are options for how to present such tasks that might be used to help, differentiate or change the focus.

Task to try

- Try the Scratch tasks lists above.
- Think about writing your own program that you might ask students to recreate
- Think about and try the different options for presenting the task.

13   Indestructible

What's in the box?

This is the second chapter to focus on technology. This task brings out some of the wonder of dynamic geometry. What is the actual DNA of a shape? What are the limits and possibilities? Can a trapezium also be a rectangle and does everyone agree? Precise definitions are crucial in mathematics, but to what extent are they arbitrary? All these questions and more are addressed in this activity about creating dynamic mathematical objects and everything that it tells us about mathematics.

So I have to get something off my chest here as we set the scene for this next chapter. I like to think I have an open and international perspective on most things. I am also keen that this book sells internationally, but I still get irrationally upset at issues relating to what I call a trapezium. Apologies in advance to North American readers and probably others. I can deal with 'math' even though my intrinsic Britishness means I have trouble saying it. If I have to, I am prone to adding a slight accent in a vain attempt to justify the absence of the 's'. Again, I apologise. I can even deal with 'trapezoid' despite the low-level grating and suppressed desire to rail against it. It is completely irrational and seems like a uniquely British issue and I make no attempt to justify it. Where I really get stumped though is on the idea that in different parts of the world there are different definitions of a trapezium (I have confessed to my irrationality, surely you'll allow me to call it this). The two definitions differ as follows . . .

1   A trapezium is a quadrilateral with 'at least' one pair of parallel sides.
2   A trapezoid is a quadrilateral with 'exactly' one pair of parallel sides.

The second definition excludes, for example and amongst others, all rectangles from being trapezoids.

All flippancy aside, I actually find this a fascinating point for reflection on the development of mathematics and the lovely discussion on the extent to which it is 'invented' and 'discovered'. Whilst this is clearly a debate of an epistemological nature, it does have a pivotal role in the way we teach and talk about mathematics. I will, probably in vain again, attempt to boil this down to

DOI: 10.4324/9781003266501-13

an oversimplified distinction between what mathematics is invented convention and arbitrary against what mathematics is innate and can be logically deduced from other ideas and must be that way. There are some easy examples like notation and terminology that are very much arbitrary conventions. We mentioned in chapter 3 that possibly percentages are to maths as Indiana Jones is to *Raiders of the Lost Ark*. I have read some interesting discussion about BIDMAS and I should add PEMDAS, as this chapter almost certainly dictates that I must. This is the idea of 'order of operations' that might, on the face of it, seem like an arbitrary decision but that actually has roots in what makes sense and logical deduction. Like any good debate, there are depths to reach. In any case, I think it helps to raise this idea with students when you can or, better yet, let them raise it. There is much that I might reasonably expect them to deduce logically or that I might show them or help them how to deduce. There is also much that I just have to tell them or that they have to be told one way or another, and I seem like as good a source as any.

In the case of the trapezium/trapezoid (See how confused I am right now?), clearly it is possible for two, at least in part, arbitrary definitions to exist.

We have to pull this right back to the classic question about whether or not a square is a rectangle. Many early experiences with shapes will lead to a natural distinction between the two that marks them as mutually exclusive, when deeper analysis clearly shows squares as a subset of rectangles. This is a key point for education in general about when it makes sense to oversimplify things, almost to the point of being actually wrong. The means might be justified in order to facilitate some important steps that can evolve in future. I certainly don't want to get stuck here for too long, but I do think it's important to think about it as teachers regularly. For me, I think the topic of shapes, and in particular quadrilaterals, gets much more interesting when we start considering all the subsets. I love discussions about and attempts to summarise them in Venn diagrams and then reflecting on how much of their definitions are arbitrary or not.

All of this pushes us to think about how we want students to engage with these ideas and there are obviously lots of ways. For the purposes of this chapter I am going to stay on the technology side and dive into some dynamic geometry. Before though, I want to tell you briefly about an activity one of my colleagues, who teaches younger children, does. Each year they get a bumper new crop of Wild West-style 'Wanted' posters. A student, for example, might have been asked to create a wanted poster for a trapezium. There will be a detailed description of the shape, followed by a long list of 'akas', where the public might be warned that the trapezium could be masquerading as a rectangle, a parallelogram or a square. It always makes me want to make a set. It's lovely. We mustn't underestimate how much a fun, relatable context like that can put the focus on the key ideas. I love that most of the students I get have done that already when they get to my class.

So, on we go to dynamic geometry. It is a provocative name – well, at least it is for 'math' (slight American accent) teachers. If I asked you to draw me a rectangle on a piece of paper, I am guessing that most of you would draw me a sketch, and be happy to accept its definition as a sketch. If I asked you to construct me a rectangle, I am sure that you would all remember how to construct perpendicular, and thus, parallel lines from chapter 7 and just do it. That's how things work in my classroom. Everyone just remembers everything we do. Honest. So now I will ask you to construct one using dynamic geometry. What will happen now? The idea is that you draw me a rectangle in a dynamic geometry program that I can move. I can pull the corners and sides and it will move and change. I can make it bigger and smaller, longer, thinner. I can even make it into a square. The catch is that, whatever pulling and pushing I am doing, the shape is always a rectangle.

Now, just to move on quickly for those that want to get cracking. Can you now do it for all the other quadrilaterals? In Figure 13.2, each is one of 7 quadrilaterals and has its set of properties. Whilst you can still move it, you can't stop it being the quadrilateral it is. A metaphor for humans?

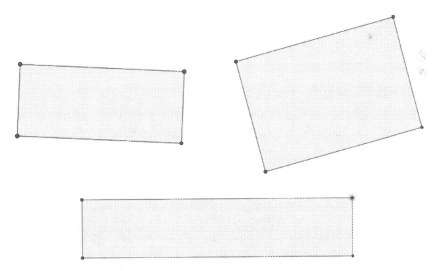

Figure 13.1 Dynamic rectangle. The image shows the same dynamically constructed rectangle dragged into different positions by pulling and pushing any of the dynamic elements.

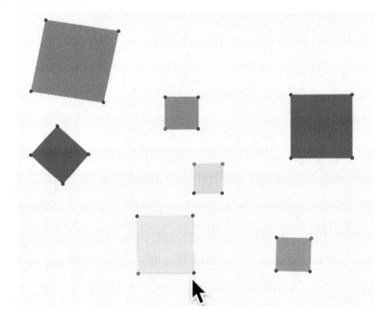

Figure 13.2 Dynamic quadrilaterals. The image shows the dynamically constructed quadrilaterals. Each one has its set of properties so, whilst you can still move it, you can't stop it being the quadrilateral it is.

For those that want to reflect a bit longer first, it is important to think about a few things.

Software training

Running and walking – It is as true with teachers as it is with students that you can't be expected to use software to do mathematics until we know how to use the software. As such, we have to acknowledge that some of our lesson time must be given to teaching students how to draw points, lines, segments and polygons. I am sure that most teachers and schools didn't need me to tell them this, but it is quite helpful to have this built into various points of your program so that students are regularly learning new skills with the software so that they build know-how as they go. Alternatively, you could devote whole lessons whose main objective is learning the software. Either way, it is a great help that students are often flexible enough to figure things out on their own and kind enough to help each other out.

The other reason I wanted to mention it is because it might be a good analogy for the age old notion that we have to learn to walk before we can run that came up in an earlier chapter. It makes so much sense, but I will raise the counter again about 'needing something to run towards'. My argument here would be that you need to know how to do a few things on the software before you can have a go at the task. You don't need to know the software inside and out before you do anything interesting with it. Teaching and learning mathematics might be the same. With a few mathematical ideas, we might be able to do some running – and probably should!

Definitions

Clearly the fundamental definitions of the quadrilaterals come into play. My guess is that students know them, but are less good at articulating them. These might be arbitrary to some extent, but if you provided 100 different quadrilaterals and asked students to classify them, it seems to me that these categories would make themselves right? Be mindful of the interplay between the task and the definitions. It might be tempting and useful to provide definitions – as a reminder – but it might be more useful to assume students know and let the articulation materialise as a product of the task.

What is allowed and what is not?

The rapid evolution of dynamic geometry software can be hard to keep up with. As soon as they have a 'trapezium tool' (ooh, that will create a stink), then the task is over. That said, it is increasingly possible for teachers to control the tools that students have. You might allow the 'perpendicular' or 'parallel' line tool, you might require these to be constructed too. It all depends on the nature of the class and what you want from the task on any given day. You might consider offering partly completed constructions and asking students to finish them. As ever, oodles of options and possibilities to work with.

Build up

'Sometimes, always, never' – you will, of course, be considering where this fits, what students have done before, and what particular things you want them to build on. That's why I like knowing that they have all done the wanted posters or variations on that task. I have an applet that I have already made with the 7 quadrilaterals in it. The applet is set up so that all the shapes look like a square until you move them. Then there is a moment where we focus on a particular shape and play a bit of 'sometimes, always, never'. For example, take shape A and change its size and position in as many ways as you can. While you are doing that, your goal is to take the statements below and decide, for each one, if you think they are sometimes, always or never true. Example statement might include,

- This shape has one pair of parallel sides.
- This shape has four equal sides.
- This shape has one pair of equal sides.
- One pair of equal angles.
- Four right angles.

Etc etc – What you put on your list is what makes the focus.

This does set the scene nicely for the part where students have to construct their own. It can be done individually or as a whole class where a student might volunteer to show how they think a shape can be changed so that there is a case where there are four equal sides.

Once you have the above decided and set up, you are good to go. How would you construct this rectangle? The others? I really do recommend having a go here. It is really interesting to focus on the different ways it can be done and there are some surprising challenges hidden away in there.

What happens?

As ever, I encourage you to pay attention to what happens to you when you try and then try to notice and solicit responses from your students when they are trying it. Like any good puzzle, there is an easy way in and so students will start drawing/constructing happily and then test their answers out on each other. Someone will argue that they have done it and another student will be invited to test it. Virtual pushing and pulling will ensue and discussions about order will be on going. The medium allows students to speculate quickly and then test conjectures and then improve on their solutions. They collect evidence and reason with the results. Then it allows for different solutions that can be compared and shared, just like the Scratch activity. There are some nice points to think about each of the individual quadrilaterals, some of which I'll mention here.

Rectangles and squares

The rectangle is a relatively easy starting point. Two pairs of parallel perpendicular sides. This can be quite satisfying early on and help to get students involved in the task. The square on the other hand, less so. . . . And this is a surprise to many. How do I keep the sides the same length? They have to be dynamic, so they can be made longer and shorter, but they have to stay the same length as each other. I hope you have tried (and by the way, I am sure it goes without saying that the regular polygon tool is not available – see note on technology below). You might think about two perpendicular lines and a circle.

The parallelogram and the rhombus

This has a similar feel to the last one, but not a similar solution. The parallelogram is pretty easy, but the rhombus needs a bit more thought. Students might need to think about midpoints and reflection.

The kite and the arrowhead

I am sure we can offer up different names for the arrow head. Would you be happier if I called it a concave kite? Do we agree then that the concave kite or arrowhead is a subset of the kite? Again, the diagonals come into play here.

In the last chapter I talked about the network software that can quickly allow me to share the screen of a student and this, once again, is excellent here for sharing work, publicly testing their efforts, examining solutions (students can hide and unhide their construction lines) and then comparing different solutions which is all good material for reflection.

Much like the Scratch activity in the previous chapter, here the medium is providing a perfect sandpit for making and testing conjectures. Equally, there is an element of reverse engineering about it as well, along with the notion of elegance – which is the most elegant way to do it? Where it differs is the focus on the dynamic nature of mathematical ideas. We looked briefly at this in chapter 7 too, when we were playing with 'human dynamic geometry' and every student's position was dependent on mine and other examples. In this activity, the constructed dynamic rectangle is, in a sense, every rectangle. Students get to explore the notion that each construction has a degree of freedom that is entirely defined by the elements that were used to construct it and the order in which they were used. It is a profound mathematical idea that goes beyond geometry into set theory and the anatomy of a variable. In many ways it is a much more natural way to see mathematics that a set of static images might be and really helps get our heads around the idea of generalisation. "Many things here can vary, but the following will always be true".

Writing about it has made me think back to a blog post I read from Dan Meyer who, at the time of writing, was heavily involved with Desmos. He was asking the question about whether or not computers were a natural medium for mathematics. The question has made me think a lot over the years. I think that I have decided that computers can be a natural medium for teaching and learning mathematics. Sorry if you were hoping for a ruling. This seems like a realistic response. The post dates from 2012 and there has been much progress since then, but there are still good arguments for how much teaching and learning mathematics is done with pen and paper (even if that is stylus and touch screen more and more). Still though, this activity is a good argument for why the computer is a natural medium. When programming/constructing with dynamic geometry, there is no 'rectangle tool' (yet), in order to construct one you have to know that a rectangle is made by two pairs of parallel sides intersecting at right angles. When you program it correctly it will always be a rectangle regardless of which points are moved. At the same time it represents the dynamism and generality of the construction in a way that is much harder to grasp with a static image. The process of drawing a rectangle on a piece of paper is not at all the same. In a sense, the environment is uniquely mathematical in that it expects and reacts only to the language of mathematics.

I like this. There is a danger in imagining that mathematics lives only in a parallel universe with different rules because it can appear otherworldly and alienate people as a result. On the other hand, it is true to some extent and I do often find it 'otherworldly' in a positive sense. It would be wrong to assume that this is only true of mathematics. Different areas of knowledge might be seen as lenses through which we look for, produce and acquire knowledge, each with its own framework for doing so. So I think this is OK and working in this dynamic geometry paradigm is all part of 'behaving mathematically'. The question about whether or not mathematics is a natural medium for mathematics is bigger than this point, but I think this task provides an argument for why it is.

Now going back to where I started this chapter, we might ask good questions about the main goals of this activity. I am aware of and frequently guilty of often wanting to do too many things at once and this is a real consideration for teachers, of course. The problem with a good task is that it often intersects lots of different bits of maths. The teacher has to play this carefully. This task might be about properties of quadrilaterals, it might be about constructions, it will involve midpoints, diagonals and transformations and it really might be about set theory. In the last item there we have a concept of huge significance for mathematics, logic and knowledge in general. In my theory of knowledge class I am keen to build on such an activity to look at Venn diagrams for exploring the notions of sound logic and logical fallacy which, I would assert, depends heavily on good understanding of sets, subsets and intersections etc. As I spend probably too long reading another Twitter thread about education or politics, the significance of these issues is often exposed. Do you see how we started with properties of quadrilaterals and ended up with world peace? Haha, poor students, trying to make sense of me.

Perhaps as you are reading you have thought about other foci these tasks could have. I don't imagine that we can have it all at the same time, but I also think it is a missed opportunity to treat them in isolation. Probably, different parts of this task can be done at different times for different students at different levels.

- The sometimes always never element where students get to push and pull shapes around a pre-prepared applet might be an excellent exercise to help younger students broaden their definitions of quadrilaterals, either individually or as a whole class.
- An older class might find themselves trying to construct a Venn diagram of the quadrilaterals. For a real stretch, they might actually try to do this with dynamic geometry and make it interactive.
- Somewhere in between, a class might have been using the context of quadrilaterals to practice and explore the nature of construction.

Perhaps this is a good moment to remind you to go back to chapter 7 and try the dynamic geometry challenges I set there, now that we have spent a bit more time on that idea.

A note on dynamic geometry

In what might be a combination of frustrating and liberating, I have tried not to be specific about what technology I use here. The term, 'dynamic geometry' is obviously generic and people have to go for what suits them best. I can see though, that for the uninitiated, it might seem like a steep learning curve. I began using the pioneering French Cabri Geometre software and have since been seduced by the all-conquering 'GeoGebra', which I think can be a bit much to get into at the beginning. That said, I think there are a few starting points worth considering to help.

- Opening GeoGebra in a browser is easy. Finding a few YouTube tutorials to get started with drawing lines, segments, points and shapes, is also pretty easy.
- If you follow this with a bit of playing around yourself, you will find that you are doing basic stuff pretty quickly. The basic stuff is all you need for this activity.
- There is a decent chance that in your school, be it primary or secondary, you have someone that knows their way around. Invest in them and get them to run a 1-hour tutorial/workshop in a meeting for you. This investment will pay you back many times over.
- For next level stuff you have options too. Perhaps your local expert can do this too. Failing that, find someone you can pay to come to your school and run a half day workshop. Failing that, it is hard to look past YouTube.
- In GeoGebra (and others I am sure), you can create applets that you can share with students where you give them a much reduced user interface

that helps both make it more user friendly and to make sure the focus of the task is where you want it.

- This, by the way, is just the tip of the iceberg.

I might consider myself an intermediate user of this stuff (because I got to decide just then). I have met plenty of brilliant people who can go to much greater depth and have learned a lot from them. My take though is often to keep the technology as simple as possible and focus on mathematics. In my workshops for teachers, I often come across teachers who have spent little or no time with this. They have known about it, but never taken the plunge. I like to think (and again, it's my book so I can say what I like) that in workshops I have shown how simple bits of technology can be quickly learned and powerfully employed in a small space of time.

More challenges – one of the best side effects of running workshops for teachers is that it provokes me to go looking for puzzles and challenges that often go a bit past what we might like students to do. When asking a room full of teachers to engage with mathematical ideas, I mostly go with tasks that we would offer students for lots of obvious reasons, but any good teacher knows they have to be ready with some extension, right? So this is a good moment to remind you to go back to chapter 7 and try the dynamic geometry challenges I set there now that we have spent a bit more time on that idea.

And now back to my trappy shape thing. When we argue that all squares are rectangles, we might start by defining the rectangle as a shape that has two pairs of parallel, perpendicular sides. For a square we might add the word 'equal'. The absence of the word equal in the first definition is what allows for the two sides to be different lengths. If we construct our 'indestructible' rectangle and allow it to be pushed and pulled in to all manner of different sizes, there will be a moment when we are dragging a point, changing the length of two sides, where that length is instantaneously the same length as the other pair of sides. At this point it meets the definition of a square. As such, there are, amongst the rectangles, some squares. Happy?

> As we make our indestructible parallelograms, we will have such moments when the shape is a rhombus.
> As we make our indestructible kites, we will have such moments when the shape is a rhombus.
> As we make our indestructible trapezium, we will have such moments where the shape is a rectangle, a parallelogram, a rhombus and a square.
> To limit a trapezium to 'exactly' one pair of parallel sides means that all of these instantaneous moments are excluded.

How then, would you make this indestructible trapezoid where there was never an instant when it had two pairs of parallel sides? For me this is inconsistent with the definitions of the other quadrilaterals. It is like saying that the rectangle instantaneously stops being a rectangle as soon as it is a square.

The goal here is not to decide who is right about all this (that's obvious - haha only joking) but to go back to that point about arbitrary mathematical ideas. Can we just define these things anyway we like? Is it OK as long as we are just consistent? Or is there something more inherently logical about these sets and subsets of shapes? I am leaving that with you.

From the box to the classroom

Thoughts and themes

- Mathematics is dynamic by nature - dynamic geometry software is a great tool to help us understand that and work with it.
- Indestructible quadrilaterals is a great task for understanding about the possibilities and constraints related to the properties of shapes.
- There is a balance to be struck between learning how to use software and then using it to be mathematical.
- There are ways to keep the technology accessible so that the focus is on mathematics.

Task to try

- Try the Wanted posters for quadrilaterals.
- Try working with dynamic quadrilaterals and 'sometimes, always, never'.
- Try constructing your own 'indestructible quadrilaterals'.
- Try making a Venn diagram of the quadrilaterals.
- Try constructing it in dynamic geometry.
- Try the extensions - parabola and ellipse - from chapter 7.

14 Dancing quadratics

What's in the box?

Here we talk about a class of problems I have called 'animated questions' where, based on an animated clip of a dynamic mathematical object, students are asked to reverse-engineer the animation based on what they observe and then effectively program it for themselves. We will focus particularly on an example involving quadratic functions but again demonstrate how it can be pitched along a big range of levels.

It seems quite incredible to me that I have written a book about mathematics where not one but two of the chapters have the word 'dancing' in the title. This might be vaguely justifiable if I could, in any way, claim dancing-related expertise. I can't. The best I can do is some desperately contrived and cheesy metaphor about how I see mathematics. *"Where others see abstraction and randomness, I see order, patterns, routines and rhythm"*. Hmmmm. How did I do? It's not good and, I suspect, even if you were lured in by the tantalising title (who am I kidding?), you are going to be disappointed by the absence of actual dancing. Sorry.

There is a link though. I was lucky enough to visit California as a young impressionable child. I got locked in a cell in Alcatraz, was caught in a flash flood at Universal Studios and crossed the Rio Grande for the afternoon. An amazing trip, but of all my memories of Disneyland, one that has endured beyond family folklore is the 'Dancing Waters' show at the Disneyland hotel. Multi-coloured water jets spitting, symmetrical parabolas of all shapes and sizes across each other in time to the music. I love that stuff; it's right up there with drain covers. The parabola in all of its glory. You can see it in parks all over the world now and I never miss the opportunity to photograph them. My children have learned to groan *"yeah, they're parabolas Dad, we know"* before I get the chance. Secretly though, I think they have acquired a similar level of appreciation. More recently, I saw the display in the fountains of Montjuïc in Barcelona, which is a city that pays more than its fair share of homage to the wonderful parabola thanks to Gaudi's influence. Activity in this chapter might lead you to the creation of something similar to the dancing waters!

DOI: 10.4324/9781003266501-14

This is the third in this little miniseries of technology-based activities and centres around the graphing applications that represent another significant tool for working with and exploring mathematics. I am going to set the scene a little though, to help readers see where this fits. The back road around our school, which leads to the staff car park is called 'Avenue Rene Descartes'. This is a detail that is easily missed. I know that I drove along that road for many years without noticing. This has led me to a nice metaphor for mathematical ideas. As I may have mentioned, I am given to railing against the idea that anyone has 'done quadratics' or indeed any other topic and I assume that maths teachers everywhere are the same. All that ever happens is that you take another walk up and down 'quadratic street' and try to look at some things you have never seen before. Maybe this is even cheesier than the one I opened with, but I have come to like it. That is how mathematics has been for me. Every time I revisit a topic for myself or in preparation for teaching or mostly during teaching, I always notice something I haven't seen before and this is often pointed out by a student. So the 'Avenue Rene Descartes' metaphor works for me. I also love to fill in some gaps for students about Rene, Cartesian grids and the French word for 'map', and am pretty sure that they pay more attention to the name of that street at least. This all makes a great contribution to our exploration of the evolution of mathematical ideas and how many of them are arbitrary as compared to logical progressions. The multiple representations of coordinates grids, equations, points and lines are a constant source of thought and activity.

The same colleague with the wanted posters often makes a human coordinates grid out of a bunch of chairs where each chair marks a set of coordinates. Students might be asked to sit down where the 'y' coordinate is the same as the 'x' coordinate, or where the 'y' is 2 more than the 'x' or where it is 2 times the 'x' and so on. You get the idea. It embraces so much of what I talked about in earlier chapters about having some mathematical skin in the game because you are the object and you have to be in the right place. These are great exercises for developing thought about the link between an equation that reads '$y = 3x + 2$' and how this has multiple solutions, each of which can be represented on a cartesian grid as a set of coordinates and how those coordinates make a pattern that is related the equation and its gradient and so on. This is such a rich web of interlinked ideas. It can be a bit overwhelming, and I think it is an area where I am least satisfied with how I have taught it over the years. There is a wonderful TEDx talk from Roger Antonsen where he extols the virtues of looking at all things, and particularly mathematics, from multiple perspectives. In each case he suggests that each alternative representation of a mathematical object might be seen as a metaphor that helps bring a new level of meaning to the idea. This is an excellent thought that is worth dwelling on.

So it follows that sequencing of focus on this web of interlinked ideas needs careful consideration and understanding. This next activity dives in a bit further down the line, but we will spend some time later exploring how the principles might appear elsewhere. The problem we are looking at is an idea I stumbled across while playing around with the notion of a dynamic constant. Much like in the last chapter, we are going to be defining some algebraic functions in terms of a variable whose value can change. For example, earlier we mentioned the function where the x coordinate is the same as the y coordinate. This is the function '$y = x$', where clearly, each x value has a corresponding 'y' value. If I rewrite that as $y = ax$, then 'a' becomes my dynamic constant. When $a = 1$ the function is $y = x$, when $a = 2$ it is $y = 2x$ and so on. Now imagine that I enter such a function, $y = ax$ into a graphing app and I am able to vary the value of a. In the beginning, assuming that $a = 1$ by default, we see the line $y = x$. Then, as I vary the value of a, the line moves, it dances! (I warned you.) Imagine I showed you the dancing line and asked you to work backwards to figure out what equation, using one dynamic constant, a, would result in this spectacle when I vary the value of a? Of course, you would tell me that the answer is $y = ax$. Well done! My goal here is to set up a genre of problems.

It is somewhat of a double-edged sword that I am trying to explain a dynamic mathematical object to you through a static medium and, at the same time, demonstrate to you the value of the computer as a medium. Some imagination is required for what follows.

In Figure 14.1, you can see a quadratic function whose vertex is on the line $y = x$. The quadratic function is defined in terms of one dynamic constant, a. When I change the value of a, the quadratic moves (boogies? shuffles? grooves?) along the line $y = x$. Like John Travolta sliding into the bridge of *Saturday Night Fever*, the vertex of the quadratic slides along this line. What is the function? Please try. At the time of writing, I find this kind of thing fantastically easy using the Desmos online calculator. When you enter a function in terms of y and x, and include the letter a, it will ask you if you want this to be a dynamic constant (although Desmos will describe this as a 'slider', which is much more in tune with my dancing metaphor). You can then just change its value. As ever, there are multiple options.

This will appeal to those of you who have already walked up and down quadratic street a few times, and certainly, your students will need to be quite familiar. I have tried to keep activities accessible to lots of levels, but, at the same time, I wanted to make sure we see these principles of task design applied across the hierarchical maths levels. The attention is drawn here to the structure of a quadratic function, the different ways in which it can be represented

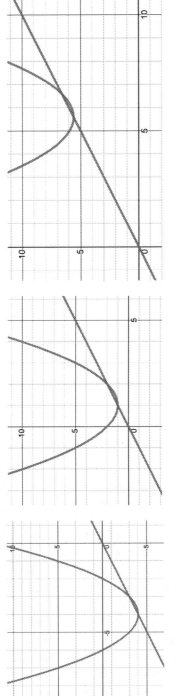

Figure 14.1 Dancing quadratic. The image shows a quadratic function defined in terms of a single dynamic variable in different positions based on the changing value of the dynamic variable. The vertex of the quadratic moves along the line .

and the influence that this dynamic constant has on the position and shape of the parabola it produces. After wrestling with and succeeding with this one, what about this:

- If you can make it dance along the line $y = x$, can you make it dance along the line $y = -x$?
- Can you make it dance along any given straight line?
- Can you make two quadratics dance at the same time, both defined in terms of the same, single dynamic constant. One dances along $y = x$ and the other $y = -x$ for example?
- Can you make the quadratic dance along $y = x^2$?

I think you can see where we are going. There are many, many potential questions here and you can choose them according to where you want the focus. For example, you might choose that your dynamic constant changes the shape of the quadratic instead of just moving its vertex. Solving them involves some delicious algebra. Once you have done a few, the ultimate challenge is to make your 'Disneyland dancing quadratics show', where you have a number of quadratics that are all defined in terms of one dynamic constant, when you change the value they all move in a beautiful, coordinated, symmetrical routine that captivates the masses just like the fountains do! You have to try it to get a feel for what kind of thinking is required, and it would be better if I could show you some moving (in both senses of the word) examples.

Animated questions

I have enjoyed milking this dancing thing a bit. It is not necessary for many, but it does bring something to the party for a lot of students. We are all different, so you feel free to leave it out. I played with this for ages in the beginning. I was convinced that I was going to get my first viral YouTube video with dancing quadratics. Call me delusional, but I still argue that views are on the (very) early part of an exponential curve. The publishing of this book is bound to help. It got me thinking about a whole genre of problems that technology has opened up. I went to a few conferences with a session called 'Animated Questions' where the theme was to show little animated videos of dynamic mathematical objects. All the objects are dependent on one dynamic constant and the video clips show the object moving when it is varied. The task is to reverse engineer the animation with a view to reproducing it. As mentioned in an earlier chapter, this kind of task is ready and waiting for those that have been asked to 'notice' and 'wonder' a lot. Being asked to pay attention to details and explore reasons for why certain things might happen or look the way they do is surely at the core of getting to grips with underlying structure and so this bit of mathematical behaviour is right up there on the desirable list.

The tasks are lovely and simple really, but I have had a lot of classroom joy out of these over the years. Much is rightly made of different 'models' for educational technology that I know you can all read about elsewhere if you haven't already. With animated questions, I think we are in an area where technology is more than just an alternative medium and we are using it to design and set tasks that would be very difficult (impossible?) to emulate without the technology.

I wanted to include the dancing quadratics to convince you I do things other than geometry. Not surprisingly though, geometry does lend itself nicely to the idea of animated questions. I'll give an example I love that I think is well suited to younger students and definitely bridges into number. Perhaps because a book is not a natural medium for animation (unless you are drawing on the page edges and then flicking them through your fingers quickly) I will do this differently and tell you upfront about the engineering.

Repeated rotation

Use a dynamic geometry application. Draw a shape, any shape somewhere towards the bottom left of your screen (for spacing reasons). Add a point in the middle of the screen. Create a rotated image of the shape by rotating it clockwise around the point using an angle of 'a' degrees. You'll need to set up a slider for 'a', and you should let it be an angle between 0 and 360 degrees. Now you have two copies of the shape, unless you have 'a' set to zero, in which case they are on top of each other. It might help to set the value of 'a' to 10 degrees or similar so you can see both the original and the image. Now rotate the image of the shape in the same direction around the same point using the same angle 'a'. (Note, you must use a, and not its particular value. This is our dynamic constant and so we want everything to depend on it.) Now you have three shapes. Now take the latest image (the third shape) and rotate it the same direction around the same point using angle a. Repeat this, always rotating the most recent image, in the same direction using angle a, until you have 12 shapes in total. The original and the 11 images. You got it? I am enjoying the thought of most readers doing this in their heads and trying to hold those images in place. Here comes the real challenge. What happens when I slowly increase the value of a, the dynamic variable? What happens when the value of a increases slowly from 0 all the way through to 360? What do you notice? What do you wonder? I'll leave this one with you.

So, all in all, we have had a lot of movement and patterns and if that doesn't qualify as dancing, then I'll hang up my dancing shoes. In three chapters focussed on technology I have set out to show the kinds of tasks that might only be done using technology. These are tasks that might not be possible, at least not in the same way, without the software and this is probably the most exciting thing that these changes have brought. It is clearly a whole other series of books and it was difficult to pick just three. The chosen three using Scratch, dynamic geometry and graphing offer a cross section of software and mathematical topics, although all three offer important crossovers between geometry and algebra. The whole notion of a dynamic variable is about as algebraic as it gets, right? I get pretty excited about all the things we can do with a spreadsheet as well and all of that is before we look at the other advantages of the medium. I will now add to my growing list of disclaimers that this is just a small window on the influence of technology to mathematics teaching because they have a cast-iron place in my lessons to look forward to. Apologies to those who were hoping for some actual dancing. Keep reading for dancing vectors, there is real choreography in that one.

From the box to the classroom

Thoughts and themes

- The dynamic variable is a powerful tool for visualising generality and the effects of changing values.
- Reverse engineering is an excellent way to draw on the practice of 'notice and wonder'. Observing what happens and puzzling to replicate it draws out lots of productive mathematical behaviour.
- Animated questions might be a type of problem/task that can only really be done with technology. More than just a medium.

Task to try

- Try the dancing quadratics and the various stages including the questions listed above.
- Try the repeated rotation problem described above.
- Experiment with dynamic variables and think about generating your own 'animated questions'.

15   Hot Wheels

What's in the box?

Any excuse to raid my son's Hot Wheels car racing supplies and travel around the world with them to make distance time graphs explore them up at multiple levels including an introduction to calculus! This activity, and suggested variations, are nice examples of how students make the journey from concrete, to pictorial to abstraction and keep track of it (pun fully intended!).

It feels terribly clichéd for me to start this chapter with a childhood memory, but I guess it's a bit late to start apologising for such things. Deep down I have convinced myself that the roots of ideas are an important part of them. I think the journey from first idea to activity is a really enjoyable, reflective part of the job. Maybe it's just me. I'm going to tell you this anyway. So picture me as a proud 9-year-old Cub Scout all decorated with toggle and badges and gearing up for the biggest night on the Cub Scout calendar. The annual car race. I am sure this was just a local thing, but it was a small community and we knew everyone and it was the talk of the town in the weeks leading up to the event. We were given a certain amount of raw materials (really not much), some rules and a brief to build a wooden car that would go head to head with other wooden cars in a gravity fuelled drag racing competition. That's two cars, two tracks, one clock. There would be some preliminary qualifiers and then the heat cranked up for the knockout rounds. I can see my car. Its black with red flaming, and apparently very effective, go faster stripes and it has left all comers in its wake to earn a place in the final. You can hear a pin drop as anticipation grips the room. Final preparations are done and the two cars are placed in the blocks that will be removed in a matter of seconds to start the race. It's like watching in slow motion as my car – yes my car – is ahead out of the blocks and just keeps increasing its lead down the hill towards a majestic victory. The crowd goes wild! Oh yes, what a night. The thrill of letting a pair of cars go at the top of a track to see which one wins is a classic childhood memory. Who am I kidding, I still like it and it still has a place in my life, once a year, when I raid my sons 'Hot Wheels' stash and take it to school for some distance-time work.

DOI: 10.4324/9781003266501-15

In fact this particular lesson has taken a lot of different forms over the years, so I'll describe some of the possibilities.

Hot Wheels tracks

It is actually pretty difficult to do a speed time analysis of a Hot Wheels car racing down a track. I am sure you can imagine the tracks attached to the top of a desk or filing cabinet and then a roller coaster–style track offering a lightning quick descent. The whole thing is over before you have said go and pressed start on the stopwatch. The challenge then was to make this journey into something longer. This involved the upsetting realisation that the friction coefficient on most Hot Wheels cars was too high. If the slope is too steep it all goes too quickly; if the slope is too shallow, the car doesn't go anywhere. So the car is replaced with a golf ball and the starting point changed to a small pile of books about 3 inches off the ground. With about 4 m of track, the journey of the golf ball lasts about 10 seconds. This is workable. This one usually happens in a corridor, or on a series of tables put together.

- We lay out 4 m of track in a straight line, representing the y-axis and distance travelled.
- We add a scale with a tape measure.
- The x-axis is then added going from 0 to 10, where this is time in seconds.
- One person has a stopwatch and when they say go, another releases the golf ball.
- Ten students with counters are primed and at the ready along the length of the track – graph side.
- The timer counts out loud in seconds.
- When they say 1, the first person puts their counter down where the ball is on the track.
- When they say 2, the second person puts the counter down next to the track where the ball is.
- And so on until the ball stops moving.
- Then each of the counters is transferred horizontally along the x-axis until it corresponds with the correct x-coordinate.

Hey presto – distance time graph. OK, not quite so quick. Some lovely things happen here. In the first instance students line up diligently, equally spaced along the track. That doesn't work. Here we get our first sense of the type of model we will get and begin to use non-linear language. We have to line up a couple of times before people are roughly in the right position. All this is clearly vulnerable to some accuracy issues, but where a student is wildly

Figure 15.1 Hot Wheels. Making a real live distance time graph with Hot Wheels tracks and a golf ball.

late or early or just plain wrong putting their counter down, it stands out like a sore thumb. It is also great to watch this conversation ensue and listen to the justifications offered for what the ball would have to have done to make that point correct. It is nice to hear students discuss the differences between what they would expect to happen, what did happen and why etc. Anyway, after a few tries, we get something that we think is a pretty accurate distance time graph of the golf ball. Of course, it is now very easy to get photos of the resulting graphs for later use. I like videos too, as reminders of what we did to produce the graph. I'll get into what we might do with that later. You can of course assign photographers.

As an alternative, or to make sure more students are involved, you could run two of these side by side. Or you could even consider some smaller versions of this and have 5 or 6 groups in your class each making their own graph.

Larger scale

I have often used a larger-scale alternative that I really like because it incorporates more of the 'being the mathematics' elements that have come up so regularly through this book. Now I am outside on the playground. The axes are drawn in chalk and measured with a trundle wheel. The golf ball is replaced with a football and a student is charged with the job of gently kicking the football along the y-axis. You can imagine that there are many who take pride in their ability to control a football to order. The students with the counters have been given a piece of chalk and stand in the correct place along the x-axis as if ready to start a sprint. The timer does as they did before and when they say '"go" and start counting, the students are supposed to move with the ball until their number is called and they stop and mark their spot on the graph. This too is quite funny the first time, but once again, with a few attempts, we do end up with some pretty accurate distance time graphs. We have a bit of playground directly below a second story window which is perfect for some aerial shots and footage of all this for later. I have often thought that a drone would be excellent, but know, in the first instance it would take me a while to figure out and there is enough going on. One day I'm sure.

Anyway, I am sure that you can imagine that there are numerous variations on this kind of possibility and there is no substitute for just having a go to help you see what things you need to think about to make it work. The question we should now be asking is why we might do this and what we might do with the results. So here goes.

It is fun. I have made no apology about this. I have found that I need this as much as students do. Something that adds variety to the global experience, something practical that gets students out of their seats and sometimes out of the classroom and something that makes us laugh a little is always welcome. Of course there is a point to it as well, but I have found that making the effort to do this kind of thing occasionally pays us all back in lots of ways. The more you do it, the more students know what is expected of them when you do and the less management issues it throws at you.

It is a concrete experience. It is skin in the game. Much has been researched and written about the journey from concrete, to pictorial to abstract in teaching and learning mathematics and I have raised it once or twice already in the book. Concrete, of course, does not always mean getting out of seats and classrooms, but I just mean to offer this as an example of a concrete experience. A drawn distance time graph might seem obvious to many, but all of us can benefit from actual experiments, even if they simply confirm what we thought we knew. Even me trying to work out what kind of set up I need to make a journey that lasts about 10 seconds was a fruitful exercise.

It is provocative – As mentioned briefly already, engaging with such an experiment provokes all kinds of thoughts and conjectures about what is happening, what should be happening, what is wrong and why. Students will make links between their understanding of physics and the mathematics of expressing it.

There will be good discussions around accuracy and error. There is measurement and procedure to be discussed and a really healthy dose of collaboration. Yes, I accept that there is much scope for students to opt out and hang around the fringes here without doing all of this. We can mitigate it to some extent. Carefully choosing the roles different students get can help. Ultimately though, I accept that this situation is all a bit harder to control. I have often reflected that even a more straightforward classroom environment does not offer you as much control as it appears to. Just think back over some of the meetings you have been in while daydreaming about the Maldives, or even just the weekend. We are all human.

It provides a rich resource on which to build – In the next section, I will talk through various possibilities for what you might do next with this, either still in the practical area or moving to pictorial and abstract. The point is that the activity has provided a context and resources for further analysis. You have a physical, large-scale graph to work with in situ. You have photos of these to work with in a pictorial way, you have videos you can watch to remind yourselves what you did. You have a memory of a concrete experience that can bring meaning and power to the next steps.

So we have had some fun and some variety, we have provoked thought and conversation and we have had a concrete experience that provides us with context and resources for further exploration. I'd say this is a good haul. We could argue all day about whether or not this adds value to alternatives. It seems entirely possible to me that at some point in the future we may have access to research that comes close to proving that this little exercise does not add any kind of value. That is the nature of knowledge and how we evolve. I can't offer you any more proof than my own experiences, although I should add that these are all informed by countless brilliant people who have done research and do know about research, so I am not a complete cowboy. If that day comes, I'll happily interrogate the claim and accept it if it stands up, but I'll probably also quit. I think that in reality, all classroom experiences that have been thought about, have the potential to add value and the potential not to and that it is more about the teacher, the students, the day, the margins and, if I am honest, the way the wind is blowing, that pushes the debatable value metre in one direction or another.

What next? Lots of options, of course, so let's have a look at a few.

Different experiments

If you are exploring distance time graphs then you might want to try and generate some different graphs for different situations. What happens when the ball goes faster or slower? What does the graph look like then? Is it possible to get something that accelerates? What about a remote-controlled car? With something like this you could get students to be inventive about journeys, varying their speed, stopping and so on. With this kind of model, you could easily have a bigger x-axis with more people on it for a much longer journey. If you want to get into displacement then you could allow backwards movement. Without a remote-controlled car, you could even just replace the ball with a person walking or on a scooter or skateboard. They could easily vary their speed etc. You could even have some example speed time graphs printed big and challenge the student who is walking along the y-axis to walk a journey that would result in the distance time graph you started with. This would provoke a whole other level of thought. I can see this being a regular thing – a weekly distance time graph experiment with a new challenge each week and a new student to 'walk the line' as it were (very happy to squeeze in Johnny Cash reference; I can hear the soundtrack). If routine, this could all be done very quickly. I am just throwing ideas out here to help people think about different ways with different age students. I have colleagues who like to recreate this exercise with a motion sensor from the science department. This is great too. It only involves one student at a time, but is much quicker and, of course, much more accurate. I can see this as a nice addition.

Focus on gradient and intro to calculus

Where speed varies, this is of course represented by varying gradients, so it is easy to make this a focus. I tend to use this activity with older students who are just beginning their study of calculus, so we can approximate gradients right there in context. With the big large-scale chalk graph, I will pair students up and ask them to approximate gradients at different points on the graph with different intervals. It gets pretty messy with chalk, but it's a great place to start. They might manage an interval of 1 second, then a half a second, but it is a good shift when we move back inside and start working with pictures instead. If the photo is put on an axis, then we can zoom and measure more accurately. The goal here is to demonstrate the process of taking approximations over a smaller and smaller interval, working towards an instantaneous measurement of speed. We might combine this idea with the varied experiments listed above. For example, let's imagine our remote-controlled car travelling at a constant speed and thus making a nice straight line, then repeating a slower speed and making a line with smaller gradient. I think it is really important to dwell on this link between 'distance over time' and 'rise over run' which eventually relates to 'Change in y with respect to x' and 'dy/dx'. On occasion, when the wind has been blowing with me, I have even progressed to plotting the gradient on the same graph as a speed time graph and a derivative. The key thing to notice as a teacher is the optimum point at which you should switch from working on the large scale and move to the smaller paper-based scale. This is tough because you have lots of students, but you still have to make the call and it will be different depending on all the different variables. If you get it right then the students too, feel a sense of relief that their task has become more manageable because of the change of scale.

The two previous sections show, I think, the potential range of difficulty we can employ here with this experiment. There are many ways to pitch in between the two and, as ever, I hope it has made you think of some variations too that you might try. It seems appropriate then that this activity might lead to some other graphs of a similar nature that the students didn't make and progress towards a more abstract understanding of the ideas. You don't have to stick to distance time even. The notion of the human graph may be applicable in lots of different ways and be a recurring theme. It does all take a bit of planning, but once you have done it, that reduces. I have adopted a pattern of using a whole lesson to run experiments and record them, which buys me time to prepare any evidence I want to use from that for the next lesson. No one said it would be easy, but this definitely ticks the 'looking forward to that' box.

I want to throw in a couple extra more general points. If I can talk about my childhood memories, then I can talk about my children, right? It is quite illuminating to have my children in my school and in my classes, I may have mentioned this. I will focus quickly on a conversation we have had about science and experiments. *"Why do we have to do experiments in science? If they already know what is going to happen, then why don't they just tell us? It would be so much more efficient"*. I'm just going to leave that there for a moment.

What would your answer be? Where does that question come from? I remembered about all this while I was writing this chapter and thought it probably deserved an outing. For me, it was mostly salient because my impression has always been that students generally enjoy science practical lessons. It's the part where they get to put on coats and goggles and be scientists. I know that is a limited definition, but I was just putting myself in the shoes of a student. So it was quite a revelation to learn that there are those students who don't and an important reminder that lots of assumptions we make about students, even if correct for the majority, are likely to be wrong for at least some. I think we could spend a good bit of time pushing this thing about experiments around and I think I can make some pretty good arguments about the value of experiments as I am sure we all could. What I do focus on though is the combined notions that (a) knowledge is the ultimate goal and we should take the most efficient path towards it, and (b) that the relationship between knowledge and experience has a pretty big impact on the efficiency mentioned in part (a). I suspect that some students have recognised that success as defined by a typical school can be achieved by simply knowing the outcome of an experiment and that actually carrying it out will not impact that level of success. This too is a stark reminder that there is a game to play here and that many of our students are driven by grades – for very good reasons and less convinced by the need for other experiences and education that does not visibly contribute to this. I don't blame them and whilst I'd love to have a big pile on the school system, I am not sure it is too helpful to do so. My business has mostly been to try and do the best with what we have. I do also think that, broadly, students are on board with the idea that education is much broader than exams, but when these are the only symptoms that are measured we can see that priorities change.

The next question is to be clear in our own minds why we think that experimental experiences (I love that the French word for 'experiment' is *experience*, by the way) do have value so that we can help convince any of our students who might doubt this too. Here we get to the very heart of methodologies like 'the scientific method' where we understand that, in the sciences, much of what we know, we only know because of observational experiments. The fundamental difference between inductive and deductive reasoning is that with inductive reasoning there is always room for little doubt, and so we are constantly searching for replication and improvement. Much of what sets mathematics apart from other subjects is how much of it is done in the abstract and, as such, is demonstrably provable through logical deduction. This level of certainty is comforting to mathematicians but unsettling to others because of its abstract nature. Wherever possible I like to occupy the intersection of this Venn diagram so that students might understand that experiments and observations are methodologies that facilitate the production of knowledge, and that learning how to go from one to the other is a big part of what we want them to learn at school so as they might be better equipped to do something more original in the future where no one can tell you the outcome. Again, I suspect my attempts to illuminate this depth will convince some and not others. More importantly, I have convinced myself.

I hope then that you are ready to have some fun with some or all of the ideas that are born in the simple concept of racing cars. I should tell you now though, because I suspect that statute of limitations has passed on Cub Scout car race appeals from the early '80s, that we had a secret experiment going on with our winning car. My mother, amateur, experimental scientist extraordinaire, was convinced that the addition of several layers of 'Pledge', the furniture polish, were going to give our car the edge. As I write I am thinking of the science that might explain that in context, but for now, we only have experimental evidence. We won it 3 years in a row. Then we left the country.

From the box to the classroom

Thoughts and themes

- A distance time graph might have more concrete meaning to students if they have made it themselves.
- Experimenting with making real distance time graphs brings out so many key ideas. This happens while the experiment is running and through observation and discussion of the outcomes.
- All this lends a lot of useful experience and context to working with these graphs on paper.
- Experimentation is a key element in knowledge production.

Task to try

- Try any of the suggested variations of the Hot Wheels distance time graphs mentioned above. There are many!

16 Maxbox

What's in the box?

It's such a classic problem about optimisation that can get us to so many wonderful bits of mathematics from simple volume right up to calculus. This problem could be used from primary school right through in different ways and even revisited as a result. We will look at ways in which students can engage with the problem and where the opportunities are to optimise as teachers. It also allows us to look at conceptual, mathematical bridges that link areas of mathematics. It's a well-known problem but still worth thinking about the ways in which it can be used and lead students on a long mathematical journey that brings so many of the things we have done here together.

Once, with a class who were studying set theory, we drew a giant Venn diagram on the school playground with three intersection sets. The title was 'What did you have for breakfast this morning?' One set was the set of people who had toast, there was another for fruit and another for cereal. Perhaps you can tell where we live. OK, so it's not the most hard-hitting of surveys, but the year before the class had chosen 'pro-abortion', 'pro-death penalty' and 'pro-euthanasia', so this was some welcome lightness. I felt much better about inviting the whole student population to participate in the 'Big Breakfast Venn'. Each student and teacher in the school was invited to put themselves on the diagram by drawing a little stick person version of themselves in the diagram. This involved everyone from age 5 and older, so you might imagine the younger students came out with their teachers and perhaps explored it a bit first and stood in the right section before drawing themselves. At break times, my class stood guard with some chalk that they gave to students when they wanted to add themselves. Now I want you to picture the two art teachers on their hands and knees drawing some quick self-portraits! It was a lovely simple thing that we all got a lot out in the kinds of ways that have already been discussed in this book. I am only mentioning this here, somewhat tenuously, so that I can bring up Venn diagrams. Subsequent attempts have involved four and five sets and some exploration of how you can create a five-set diagram where every possible interaction exists. To be honest,

DOI: 10.4324/9781003266501-16

although this was fun for us, nothing has worked as well since the Big Breakfast Venn. Venn diagrams are everywhere, especially in the world of internet memes. I have a book called *Venn That Tune* where some titles are represented as Venn diagrams. Only trouble is none of my students know the songs, but we have had some fun making our own. More recently Venn diagrams have come up as a means of exploring the soundness of logical arguments and we mentioned in chapter 13 the task of making a Venn diagram for the quadrilaterals.

I have increasingly come to see Venn diagrams as a perfect tool for recognising complexity in the world (perfect for me anyway). A student was once writing an essay about the relationship between descriptions and explanations and wrote the essay through a series of Venn diagrams. Perhaps descriptions are a subset of explanations, perhaps they are the other way around or perhaps there is simply an intersection between the two. The purpose was to explore their respective roles and differences in acquiring knowledge. Another year there was a question about change and progress and in both cases, the Venn diagram was very effective as a means for exploring the complexity. Perhaps you agree, perhaps you don't; I am just offering you a view.

As we write and organise our curricula as teachers and educators, this all comes very much to the fore. A syllabus is, normally, a list of specific and discretely expressed learning objectives. A curriculum or scheme of work will organise those objectives into a coherent plan that covers them all but groups them all in a way that facilitates an understanding of links and builds logically whilst considering opportunities for revisiting ideas. The trouble is that there are so many ways to do it. I have often enjoyed telling teachers on IB workshops *"I have designed the perfect order and scheme of work to deliver the course in* [pause for anticipation] *at least five different times"*. It is such a beast of a job because the Venn diagram of mathematical ideas is so rich and complex and varied that there are so many ways to do it. It is a good question about whether one team of teachers can do that and then just share it or whether or not teachers need to do it for themselves. As ever, I'd like to think there is a neat and satisfying compromise. True to form, I have just uncanned another worm farm to leave them wandering all over the place for your thinking pleasure. For a control freak, it can be unsettling not to know exactly what the best way to do things is, but at once liberating to know that, given the number of possible paths, yours, if you have given it a degree of thought, is probably one that makes sense. This has been a good excuse to combine a little love for Venn diagrams with a little philosophical provocation so as to raise the issue of all the potential cross pollination that exists in mathematics curriculum and how actually 'indiscrete' (I am thinking about this word) items on a maths syllabus are.

It is also designed to lure you into reading about an activity that everyone already knows, but that does bring out many of these points and always makes me think about how creative we could be with schemes of work beyond the traditional headings of algebra and geometry and so on.

Many will recognise the title of this chapter and nod accordingly because this has been a staple of mathematics teachers for many years, so I do feel a bit of extra pressure including this one. Stay with me though, because I find this to be the activity that keeps on giving and feel that there is always something to learn from it. Even when I hear someone describing an activity I think I know they usually hear something new. I am repeating myself now, remembering the video from Derek Sivers I wrote about earlier. The classic 'Maxbox' activity is perhaps maligned for many of us who experienced it as a popular GCSE coursework piece in England. I really don't want to start the coursework debate, although it's clearly good. I just want to get into the task.

Making the biggest

It is pretty easy to describe. Give students a piece of A4 paper (for example), help them to recognise (remember in many cases) that if an equal size square is cut from each of the corners, then the resulting shape is the net for an open top box. The question is simply 'What size square should you cut to make the box with the biggest volume? 'Let's say from the off here that, although many of us will recognise this as the opportunity to get into calculus and optimisation, there are lots of stops on the way to appreciate and I think the task as described can be given to students young and old to try. It really just involves a little understanding of a net, a pair of scissors and the ability to measure and calculate volume. By the same token, 100 variations on a simple version of this task exist where there is never any intention to get beyond measuring side lengths and volume. For example, given a piece of paper, make the cuboid (maybe closed this time) with the biggest volume. Remembering that the size of the paper can vary, what about 'make two cubes from this piece of paper with the biggest combined volume'. A task like this could vary to include all kinds of different shapes. Some of these are mentioned in chapter 2. In all such cases it would be super fertile territory for repeated practice of measuring and calculating volume, of working out nets as they try to fit stuff on the paper given. All the while there is an awful lot of conjecture and subsequent testing of the ways in which volume could be maximised. There is oodles of good activity in this paragraph.

Back to the Maxbox problem, which is easy to explain and start. There is a great moment when students start thinking about strategy and offering justifications. You have those that want to waste the least amount of material and then make big-based but shallow empty boxes. Then there are those that see value in depth (how can we disagree?) alongside those that predict that it makes no difference and the quieter ones who shrewdly anticipate something in the middle and have a good guess. What is notable here is that I can't recall a single student ever just getting out their calculator and crunching numbers. I wouldn't stop them if they did, of course, but it is an interesting observation. It's probably, first, an indication that there is appeal in the variety of cutting out and making boxes. Secondly, and more importantly I think, it draws on a fascinating human thing of wanting to guess, wanting to let our intuition go for it and putting faith in our ability to answer such questions in this way. This is a huge point. We do that a lot and we do it often where we shouldn't. I think maths class is a great place for us to learn about our intuition and that our intuition is better trusted in areas where we have experience.

In the beginning of his book *The Math Instinct*, which is obviously all about just this point, Keith Devlin talks of the dogs who can do calculus, which is a thing you can read about in various places. The short summary thought experiment goes as follows.

> You are on the beach with your dog, standing where the sand meets the water. You throw the ball directly along the beach and the dog runs in a straight line (ish) along the beach to retrieve the ball and back. Next you throw the ball directly out to sea at right angles to the beach (because you are a maths teacher) and the dog swims there and back in a straight line to retrieve the ball. Good dog. Next, you throw the ball out to sea somewhere between the straight line of the beach and the right angle - you throw it in a diagonal path. What does the dog do?

There is apparently evidence that some dogs will set out along the beach and then, knowing that they run faster than they swim, intuitively work out the optimal point at which they should leave the beach to swim the rest. Dogs that do calculus! I have summarised quickly and do recommend the rest of that particular read. I think that it is easy to imagine why that happens and that humans might have a similar intuitive ability because their intuition is informed by having done a lot of walking, running and swimming. It's not far from making good judgments (hopefully) about when it is safe to cross the road. No one is estimating the distance and the speed of the approaching car and making associated calculations. We are informed by our experiences. In the context of the Maxbox, it seems like students have not had enough similar experiences to make a good judgement here.

Box-making ensues and we end up with a variety of boxes, and students are asked to calculate the volume of the box and write it on. There are a few practical points to pay attention to here. First, be careful with A4 paper. It is not 30 cm by 20 cm, which would be really helpful so you have some important choices to make. You could prepare some bits of paper that are exactly 20 by 30 (a bit of guillotine time). Alternatively you can tell students to assume it is 20 by 30 and calculate the volume based on that assumption. This can work quite well because the alternative, measuring their actual shapes, invites a certain degree of inaccuracy. Teaching is full of these little margins that can make or break an exercise. You are likely to get some students quicker than others here and so when this happens I usually ask those students to make a second box and I give them a square size that we don't seem to have yet. This helps to make sure that we got lots of different boxes from lots of different square sizes.

Assuming all this has all gone well then you should now have a whole bunch of open-top boxes. For reasons I can't really justify, I like to use different coloured bits of paper so this collection of boxes has some aesthetic appeal. We are who we are. Then I ask students to put them in order, being quite deliberately non-specific about what measurement they should use to do this. Students will, therefore, typically come up with two ways of doing this. First, we see

Figure 16.1 Maxboxes in order. The boxes are displayed in order of first square size and then volume. Then they are displayed on a graph that shows square size on the x-axis and volume on the y-axis.

them put in order of square size because this too offers a pleasing aesthetic for the ordered mind. They become taller and narrower as in the picture below. Then the other way is to order them by volume - which was after all the goal of the exercise. This grates a little though because there doesn't seem to be a natural looking order to this. Funny how we have become so conditioned to look for such order.

This is where the thinking begins and people begin to ask questions about what is happening here. Then I will ask if there is a way I can show both orders at the same time. I can see how this might sound a bit contrived and these things don't always work out the way you planned, but there is a nice moment where students come up with something like *"put them on a graph"* that I think it's worth leaving the potential for. It is nice to recognise that the 'putting of things on a graph' is actually a natural step in trying to understand information that presents itself as opposed to 'that thing we do in maths a lot'. I suppose the two intersect, but I hope you get the point I am making about students thinking for themselves.

The result is a beautiful graph and I usually leave a display board for this free in my classroom in a very 'here is one I prepared earlier just in case' kind of way. In the spirit of the loci, box plots and distance time graphs, instead of points on the graph though we pin the actual boxes. This again is a concrete link. This point represents the volume of the box that had a square size of 2 cut out of each corner.

As teachers I think it is easy to underestimate the significance of this transfer to a mathematical model of the situation. It's really difficult to avoid the constant compartmentalising of mathematical topics that make them all look discrete when the reality is a beautiful and complex Venn diagram full of fascinating intersections. When opportunities arise to demonstrate this, it is important to point it out and lend it the significance it deserves. We now have this graph that shows data from an experiment and which begins to show us the relationship between the size of the square 'x' we cut out and the volume of the open-top box that results. It also answers many of the questions we asked, without quite settling on the value of x that gives us the maximum. At this point we have some options about what we might do next.

Interpolate

We can discuss the shape that data appears to show and use this to interpolate. Probably because of a previous focus on quadratics and symmetry, there is a will for it to be symmetrical, but evidence to suggest it is not. Probably students have seen less cubic algebraic models.

Fill in some gaps

We can make some more boxes to try and fill in some of the gaps. As we have discussed previously, there is always an optimum moment to make a move away from the concrete. This will depend on much, so there is always the possibility of more boxes

Generate more data

Alternatively, we can begin to collect more data by another means. We can skip the part where we actually make the boxes and work out, theoretically, what the volumes of the boxes in between would be. We can represent these values on our large-scale graph or we can move to a paper- or computer-based graph. This is a move to a more abstract idea where instead of boxes we are using points. I know you didn't need me to tell you that, but I am advocating the idea that you might make this distinction for your students so that they notice this transition. A graphing app is perfect here.

Enter the spreadsheet – an extraordinary tool for teaching and learning mathematics. Clearly you can enter the data here and plot a graph. You can also have it quickly set up so that whenever you add a new value the point appears on the graph. The real boon here though is that you can set up the spreadsheet to do the calculations for you. Column 1 has the size of the square, column 2 has a formula that uses the square size to generate the width, column 3 does the same for height, and column 4 multiplies the three together for the volume. The little black cross on the bottom right hand corner does the rest and we can now generate points in great volume and great speed. Again, this is no small, insignificant step. So many ideas are coming together to help solve this problem and it all points to the deduction of the cubic model that describes the situation.

I suppose that what I am confessing here is that, over the years, I have learned to 'stop and smell the roses' a bit more with this task. Actually, that may be true in general. It is part of recognising the difference between 'walking up and down these streets' for the first time and being a regular. Oh dear, serious metaphor fatigue creeping in here. It is easy to forget the difference though.

Obviously, for those that are ready, the next step to an optimisation exercise is there for the taking, but I hope I have been convincing that the exercise in itself and variations on it can be accessible at all kinds of levels and it would be a shame if this kind of activity, in the heart of all those intersections, is only seen for the first time when students start doing calculus. It seems to me like an experience students should have regularly and go a little deeper each time. (Please note I resisted a return to the Avenue Rene Descartes metaphor.)

For those who want to dial this all up a notch, I'd like to suggest the Maxcone problem. Again, I suspect many will have seen it and in that case I urge you to consider what you can get out of the spreadsheet exercise here because the algebraic model is pretty tasty and takes some doing. Here we go. You are given a circular piece of paper with a radius of 10 cm. If you cut a sector out of this circle with angle 'x', then the resulting sector can be folded up to make the curved surface area of a cone. What angle 'x' will result in the cone with the biggest volume? Play along here and have a go at answering intuitively first. Then think about all the possible variations there are here. How does the height of the cone vary with the angle? How does the base of the cone vary with the angle? What would a spreadsheet look like that could generate the volume from the angle? What does the model look like? Enjoy.

Now I'd like you to think about where you might put the Maxbox activity on the great Venn diagram of mathematical ideas. Actually, where are all the places you could put the different versions of it? I have singled out Maxbox as an example of a multifaceted activity, but there are of course many. Maybe even most. It has pride of place in my lessons to look forward to because it has so many of the ingredients I like in a good task. The one I'd like to mention briefly in summary is the ability to approach it from different angles. I particularly enjoy making use of a spreadsheet and the mathematics of designing/programming a spreadsheet to do the heavy lifting for us (although of course, secretly, the programming might be the heavy lifting). Have a go at this with the Maxcone and maybe get a taste of why this numerical computer-based approach might have an edge on the algebra. In closing I think that Maxbox is a good example for me of a task that I tired of out of overexposure, but that it came back with a serious second wind and more when I considered the different things it might be and all the places I could put it on my Venn diagram. I'd stick with the Big Breakfast Venn for the playground though!

From the box to the classroom

Thoughts and themes

- Classic tasks can be overused or maligned but often contain all kinds of gems. This is why they are classic.
- Think about using classic tasks in different ways to get a fresh look at them.

- How often do we demonstrate the interaction between otherwise discrete-seeming mathematical ideas?
- How often can a task invite really quite different approaches?
- As with other chapters, think about the value of bridges from concrete to pictorial to abstract.

Task to try

- Try the Maxbox activity as described here.
- Recognise that considerations here are less about what age your students are and more on how far you take it.
- Try variations on the activity that involve making shapes from limited resources.
- Try the Maxcone.
- I highly recommend the Big Breakfast Venn.

17 Dancing vectors

What's in the box?

Imagine a class of 16 year olds performing a dance routine to Donna Summer's 'Hot Stuff'. In a mathematics classroom. "Honest boss, this is really purposeful". This chapter is about conceptual analogy based on my experience of teaching about displacement vectors in the context of dancing! True story. It starts us thinking about important parallels between mathematics and movement and how to help students take a step up to more sophisticated ideas.

As any of us develop specialties in life, I am sure we have all developed these sharp radars for the moments and observations that allude to our specialties. I know that is true of teaching. We see and are drawn to references everywhere. There will be a passage in popular book that stands out to you, like when Lisbeth Salander, the girl with the dragon tattoo, sits on the beach and tries to find an exception to Fermat's last theorem, and you will nod appreciatively and maybe want to draw people's attention to it. Any article in the news, a dinner-time conversation or a movie might be punctuated for us by a lovely reference that stands out. Mathematicians may drool over things like Simon Singh's expose of the *Simpsons*, whose writers are all mathophiles and whose episodes are littered with mathematical easter eggs for our pleasure. It's great. I nearly fell out of my seat when the children's movie *Despicable Me* scripted a villain by the name of Vector. Clearly very proud of his name, he was frustrated by the world's lack of understanding of its significance. He took any opportunity to explain with great gusto that it was because he had *"magnitude and direction!"* It should have been met with great appreciation but, alas, usually fell flat. I appreciated it at least. The concept of a vector is one that most will not deal with in their daily lives and one that involves a good deal of previous understanding to get our heads around. These sophisticated ideas can be really next level for many students. For those that will choose maths and science and already have the appreciation, these are exciting times! For others this is when the abstraction of mathematics risks alienating a few more. As I have discussed throughout the book, the balance of these moments is the ongoing challenge.

DOI: 10.4324/9781003266501-17

As you will have deduced from the title, I am offering a chance to meet this particular challenge with another dance.

I think I got these chapters in the wrong order and am certain to be accused of crying wolf. As if to justify this accusation, I will now promise that, this time, there really is dancing. It is not *Saturday Night Fever*, but it is dancing. It might be proper dad dancing, but it is still dancing. There are some key moments that have contributed to what has become an annual institution and rite of passage at my school, where we convince an entire year group of 16 year olds to dance in their maths lesson. Let's run through them.

First – I once read an article about the use of vectors and a form of vector notation as a means of writing choreography. I confess that I have not dug any deeper than this. I read the article and in the true spirit of the information age, I took my one article as justification for a school of thought. Terrible really. I am sure that there is a lot more to read on the topic, but I was quickly satisfied that I thought it might make a good analogy for the notion of a displacement vector and that possibly, a dance routine could be written in vectors.

Next – serendipitously, a clip of the scene from the movie *The Full Monty* crossed my path. I can imagine jaws hitting the floor with concern about what I am planning. Don't be daft. If you don't know the movie, that is probably good for me right now. The most innocent summary I can give is that a bunch of unemployed men agree to try and make some money putting on a 'dance' show. They can't dance. It's funny, but also quite moving (no pun intended). There is a scene, just after they have decided they are kidding themselves and give up where they are in different queues at the job centre waiting for their turn and Donna Summer's 'Hot Stuff' comes on the radio. With their new found sense of rhythm, they all start moving to the beat and subconsciously start the same dance routine. Their enthusiasm and determination is rekindled. Anyway, I saw the scene again and listened to hot stuff. It's too late, my mind has started something.

The final piece – I am booked to go to the ATM conference in Swansea (think I have mentioned this before) and I receive a communication from my friend and mentor Anne Watson that she will be running a double session workshop on the idea of 'Mathematics and Dance' and is interested in ideas and contributions from anyone attending. This is it, the stars are aligned. I'm going to be a choreographer. I am going to teach children about displacement vectors by making them learn and perform a dance routine, written in vectors, to the tune of 'Hot Stuff' from Donna Summer. This is truly peak delusion.

I am enjoying some self-absorbed nostalgia now. You know those scenes in cheesy Hollywood movies (which *The Full Monty* is not, by the way) where delusional people set out crazy goals like this and then there is a 2-minute montage of the next six months that tracks their progress through hilarious failure, despair, then resilience and ultimately triumph. This is how I am incorrectly remembering the next couple of weeks of me 'dad dancing' in my living room, experimenting with different moves and combinations and getting them to correspond to the music while my family laughs at me half with raw amusement and half with deep concern. But the triumphant moment is reached and the routine is written and practised. The only thing that remains is to convince students to do it!!! Oh and also to try and establish that it has some actual educational value. Of course.

This is going to be hard to describe in writing, but probably less painful than having to watch me do it. The whole routine is based on four moves only. Each move is defined as a vector and each occupies two beats of the song. The size of the moves is defined in terms of an 'imaginary' square grid on the floor. Here they are.

Move 'a' the jump

Stood straight, this move starts with a bend of the knees on the first beat and then a jump forward one space.

Move 'b' the slide

Stood straight, you move your right leg one space to the right on the first beat and slide your left leg along to meet it on the second.

Move 'c' the twist

From standing, simultaneously twist your torso to the left whilst moving your right foot diagonally to a position that is one space to the right and one forward on the first beat. On the second beat, you twist back to straight and bring your left foot to the same position.

Move 'd' the reach

Similar to move 'c', but this time, on the first beat you move your left foot diagonally (one space left and one forward) while twisting to the right. On the second beat you twist back straight and bring the right foot next to the left again, and point your right arm and index finger to the sky.

Haha - we are already having a laugh. I do hope you are trying this and enjoying the thought of raised eyebrows from anyone you live with as you do. I told you I was delusional.

Clearly, any of these moves can be reversed so we understand the meaning of '-a' etc, remembering that it is really only the position that matters. Now we

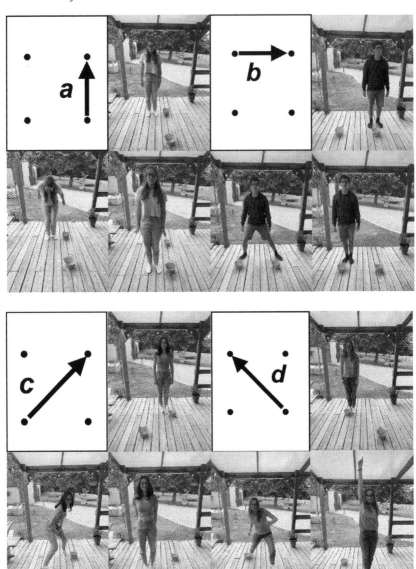

Figures 17.1 and 17.2 Dancing vectors – the moves. These images show the four moves in the dancing vectors routine.

can define the whole routine in terms of these vectors. The routine covers an introduction, verse and a chorus, and here they are below. Go on, put the tune on and have a go. You won't know unless you try!

Five went dancing

When these are all established, you can have a good run through the first two verse-and-chorus cycles. Then there is a guitar solo in the song which allows for a bit of a freestyle moment which has the condition that each of five groups that I have nominated end up in a certain position on the dance floor. Looking from above, this would be like the five dots that show 5 on typical dice. Each of the five groups has its own little routine which they have to work out and perform in formation with each other (shown in the bottom left of the diagram). They are given the routine as a vector map and a few minutes to practise. The group in the middle has some half vectors and end up where they started. The other groups all end up at the next dot along as it were. One group finishes where the group next to them started and they rotate clockwise around the room. At the end of this, we are ready for the grand performance!

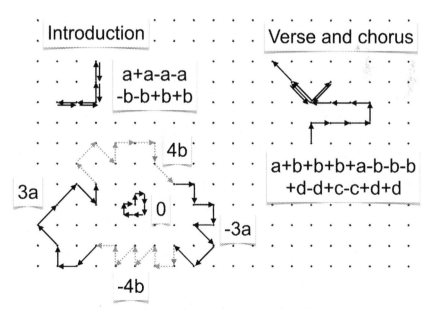

Figure 17.3 Dancing vectors – the routine. This image shows the routine as a combination of vectors a, b, c and d.

It seems certain that much of what you can do in a classroom (or ballroom) environment, depends on the established culture in that classroom and that school, mixed with a good sense of how to appeal to the teenage mind. I think I have developed a good awareness of these things in my setting (and that is important of course), but I was pretty nervous about this the first time and with each new year group this one always feels a bit out there. It always delivers though. I mean we always get good participation and have some fun and because of that we always build some great foundations for working with displacement vectors. Of course we also always end up with some classic footage to bring out at school assemblies and leaving dos! It is generally a really nice moment that can help to punctuate what can be a demanding period for 16 year olds. Amongst the things I appreciate is the spirit you can generate amongst the students to balance a bit of light hearted laughter with supportive help. The reluctant movers are cajoled and supported into taking part, the rhythmically challenged are offered help and leaders to follow and as we practise, the room is a lovely buzz of thinking, laughter, support and music. There is a small, welcome shift in the usual classroom hierarchy. All the while we are practising this key notion that a displacement vector represents, in this context, a dance move that has 'magnitude and direction!'

I have tried to be objective about this exercise over the years about its value above the not to be underestimated team building effect. The analogy is pretty simple. When dealing with combinations of displacement vectors, we might see it as limited ways in which we are allowed to move around a space. The dance moves make a great analogy for this. Often in a routine a person makes a lot of moves, expends a lot of energy and ends up where they started. Vulcan logic might ask us to explain the point. Not that I am saying that dancing justifies the existence of vectors, but rather that dance routines might be a viable analogy. Again, where possible, I like to point out when we are using analogies, as with metaphors, so that students develop an awareness of the role such tools have in developing knowledge and understanding. We are asking for an expression of how you might get from one point to another across a space when you are only allowed to move in certain ways. In the abstract, these are vectors that are described by their size and direction. In our analogy they are defined by dance moves that are essentially boiled down to size and direction. There is nothing more going on here than that.

What follows in the classroom is then a series of tasks that begin to bridge that gap. We start by still talking about dance moves and routines, but now we are on paper and the moves are more easily referred to as a, b, c and d. The routines are then functions of these vector moves. Subsequent questions introduce new moves that are simply expressed, and accepted as vectors that have size and direction. I am sure you can see where this goes as we make a transition from the dance analogy into an abstract context for vectors. We could pass via an alternative context and come back out to one. In any case, what we are paying attention to is the role played by context here as an analogy that facilitates the move to abstract.

This activity was specifically about vectors and, in that sense, one of the less obviously scalable activities in the book. That was bound to happen at some point, sorry. There is still, however, an underlying principle here that I think is scalable. Apart from anything else, it is a catalyst for us to think about parallels between movement and mathematics. Many have done some very interesting things in this field that goes way beyond my suggestion here. Certainly mathematics and dance is no new idea. The element I think that we can take from this activity to younger students is the option of using what is effectively algebraic notation to describe movements so that those movements can be written down. As such this seems to be potentially fertile ground for explorations of algebra. The moves a, b, c and d don't have to be vector quantities; they could be scalar quantities, and then any activity becomes a lot like exploring algebraic concepts with Cuisenaire rods. Moves could be defined in ways that might mean there are interesting equivalents and combinations. We could be collecting like terms, switching between sums and products and working with algebraic manipulation in general. The principle is units of movement being given algebraic notation. The addition of routines and music gives a convincing context and a good element of memorable fun.

As for my delusion. I am now the hero at the end of the Hollywood montage. I have brought mathematical power and enlightenment to people through their feet. A world unlocked, a barrier broken, cheers of intellectual progress at the triumphant crescendo. In reality I am more likely a parallel to Vector the villain who keeps going on about magnitude and direction. Hundreds of students and teachers can no longer listen to Donna Summer or watch *The Full Monty* without wincing in pain as the memories of this ritual humiliation come flooding back. Hopefully somewhere in the middle. I dare you to have a go.

From the box to the classroom

Thoughts and themes

- Thinking about useful parallels between mathematics and movement and simply opening that door.

- Particularly, dance moves might be a good analogy for a displacement vector.
- For many who have enjoyed maths, the move into more sophisticated concepts is a welcome change of pace. For many others, there is an even greater need to help conceptually. Either way, there can be something for everyone.

Task to try

- Try the dancing vectors as it is described above.
- Try scaling it as suggested.
- Explore other links between mathematics and movement.
- Try creating your own dancing vectors routine.

18 Pleasure at the fairground

> ## What's in the box?
>
> Here I want to look at a more elaborate, large-scale activity that I do every year and definitely comes under the heading of fun and games. The fairground is a perfect context for playing with experimental probability and can happen on all kinds of scales at any age. It also raises legitimate questions about efficiency and value of time which I'll try to answer by writing about the wider benefits of letting our hair down a little as well as the value of experiences that we can feed off.

It is an odd sensation that writing this book appears to be generating the same emotional roller coaster of any given term. Before it started there was a flurry of excited planning and determined thinking so that the method and purpose was all clear for what was to come. It then started with the same adrenaline-fuelled enthusiasm. As we got further into term, I was getting tired and working hard to get things done well and now, as we get towards the end it begins to feel a lot like the end of term. You seem to get an extra reserve of energy to push you through and really go for it and that high allows for just one more high octane activity! A real highlight of the calendar, this activity essentially involves our grade 9 (13/14 year olds) running a fairground for our Grade 5 (9/10 year olds) and is packed with thinking, creativity, performance and fun. There is a real danger that this might be seen as frivolous end-of-term space-filling, but it really isn't, I promise.

A quick bit of background first, of course. As a teenager I lived and went to school in Sydney, Australia, for a while. This was ace for many reasons. The outdoor lifestyle is a huge part of life and is really accessible. As a result I played a lot of sport, including getting into golf. I know many consider it a good walk spoiled, but I love the combination of sport, psychology and fresh air. Northbridge Golf Club was a low-key club that was happy for teenagers like me to hack up the course. Its location, however, was second to none, curling around the edges of one of the beautiful inlets of Sydney Harbour. Yes, I lost a few balls in the water, but if you have to watch your tee shot sail into the water, it might as well be beautiful Sydney Harbour. Anyway, this new pastime hinged a lot around the idea of a handicap. For non-players, a typical round of golf is

DOI: 10.4324/9781003266501-18

designed to be completed in 72 strikes of the ball (this varies, but 72 is typical) over 18 different holes. If you typically take 85 shots, then your handicap would be 13, because you 'typically' take 13 shots more than you are supposed to. Trust me, for amateurs, 13 is awesome. This allows you to play and compete against people that are better or worse than you. For example, if you play against someone with a handicap of 5 (really good) then they are allowed 77 shots to your 85. If they take 77 shots but you manage in 84, then you win. It is a clever system and there are many variations on games and scoring that take this into account to make it so we can all play against each other at the same game. I think this is something quite unique about golf as compared to other sports. The aim is to encourage and enable amateurs and beginners to take part. Nice. This is good food for thought about school too, but I'll not digress there just now.

The real focus here is on the question about how we arrive at someone's handicap? This is a question riddled with notions of mathematics, statistics and knowledge. When you play an 'official' round of golf, you have to play with another member who will sign your scorecard to vouch for its accuracy. A club might have a system where once you have submitted five of these scorecards they can be used to calculate your handicap and any subsequent score cards that are submitted will give rise to incremental changes. I don't play anymore, but believe it might be the case that some countries have national agreements for this process. (I am reliably informed by my Dad, after proofreading, that systems have evolved and become more international.)

The catch is that if you have an official round (let's say you play in a competition one morning), you have to submit your card, even if you didn't like it. If on the other hand, you are playing with a friend who is a member, not in a competition, you can choose if you submit the card or not. So, this introduces some elements of strategy. First you have to decide if you want your handicap to be lower or higher. Of course, lower indicates that you are a better golfer, so there may be elements of pride and status at play here. Higher though, works in your favour for competitions! Whilst we could get into this all day, what I really want to get into here is the accuracy of such results based on experimental data. How good is Jim at golf? Well, let's take his next 10 rounds and average the score. If Jim has the ability to pick and choose which 10 to give you, then surely this is problematic. He might feel that there were some days where his play was not representative of him for various reasons, but this is surely fallacious right? At this age, I think I can face up to the confession that my best ever rounds of golf happened when I was playing alone. *"Hmmm"*, I should hear you say. Was Jim really good and honest about counting his shots on those days? Of course, I was never able to submit those for my handicap. The point here is that what Jim thinks is representative of him is irrelevant. What he actually did is what counts. Again, I find myself thinking about how this plays out in a school context.

This makes me think about the notion of the outlier in statistics. Imagine a golfer who plays a good steady round of golf, bar one hole where they put three successive balls into Sydney Harbour (yes, if it sounds personal it is because it is) and had a complete disaster. What and where is the logic in allowing him to write it off as an outlier? Food for thought, right? The context here is probability from experimental data, and this is what the fairground is all about.

Let me give a clear outline of the project so that everything that follows can be put into this context. Students will work in groups. I am aware of the pros and cons of group work. I make the groups and have actually spoken to some students about this in advance. The result might be some pairs, some 3s and the occasional 4. Each group is charged with designing, building and testing a fairground game that G5 students will come and play. There are some simple rules.

- Grade 5 are given tokens.
- Each game costs one token to play.
- If the player loses the game, the game owner keeps the token.
- If the player wins the game, then they get their token back, plus one more (so the owner loses a token).
- Whatever the game involves, this fundamental rule of play must apply.
- Although this last rule may seem odd, it has become apparently necessary. There are to be no prizes/sweets given out to encourage people to play your game! No edible incentives are allowed.

The goal of the gamemakers is to suck all the money they can out of grade 5. The goal of grade 5 is to have fun and make their money last as long as they can. As such, the gamemakers have to keep the following in mind.

- Their game must be designed so that a player loses more often than they win. I set a target of designing a game that has the probability of winning at around a third.
- The game must be actually winnable or no one will play it. If you stand and watch 10 people before you all lose, you might think it is not worth it and choose not to play.
- The game has to be appealing to the audience. It has to look like fun and pull people towards it.
- At the same time, it can't take too long for people to play, otherwise you won't get enough transactions, even if your game is well designed.
- Part of this means not getting over complicated.

Typically, I will be prepared for our first lesson on the fairground with three screwed-up balls of paper and an empty cardboard box on the other side of the room. I'll tell the class that this is a sample game and that I have to get two out of three of the bits of paper in the box to win. Typically, I manage. This is either a bizarre skill, crazy luck or an indication of serious procrastination over the years. Then I'll ask them if they think I can do it again and stand somewhere else, hoping that someone will observe that I have changed the rules and need to be consistent or it's not fair. It is a game, so someone always does. Once we have established that I am a paper thrower extraordinaire, we agree to let everyone in the room have a go. After a few people have had a go and we have had some good *"oohs"* and *"aahs"*, I'll ask the group how many wins and losses we have had just to expose the fact that they don't know anymore because no one has been keeping track. So now we keep track. When everyone has had a go, we will look at our tally chart and see what we think of our game and how close we have come to the target of the probability of winning being one-third. Depending on my mood (terrible but honest) I have either set up the first game as too hard or too easy so that it will need adjustment. Then we take suggestions for adjustment. Get a bigger box, stand closer, throw it backwards, etc etc etc. All the way through we have been having discussions about the consistency of the exercise and the weight of the evidence. *"If 2 people out of 6 trials won, does this mean our game is good?"* *"Do I need to get a large range of people to play my game or can one person do all the testing?"* The fact that everyone is watching and waiting for their turn makes for a captive audience who are happy to have these little conversations along the way. At the end, we have collected some experimental data on a couple of versions of the game and made clear both the process of how to design and test a game as well as looking for the red flags and considerations that come up along the way.

I have done this with older students where we focus on the notion of conditional probability. Does the person get better at throwing with each turn because they have found their range? As such, are these independent events and so on? This is just a quick note to nod to more complex versions of these ideas.

In the next lesson, depending on the year, I might do something similar only this time the game is not experimental, but it is theoretical. For example, we might play the classic from Chevalier de Mere. The player throws four ordinary dice. They win if none of the dice shows a 6; otherwise they lose. Think about it for a moment. This is really quick to obtain some experimental data with, but clearly there is a theoretical calculation we can do to establish the probability of winning. I'll leave it with you. The goal is to establish the important and sometimes subtle difference between an 'experimental' game and a 'theoretical' one.

This is a key idea in applications of probability. When can a probability be calculated completely independently of experimental data? Again, I'll leave it with you.

This introduces the possibility of the game that students design being a theoretical game which brings advantages and appeals to some students. I have sometimes made suggestions to certain groups that they might prefer this. It all brings a nice bit of variety to the fairground.

A strict time schedule follows and to stop this running away from me, I always plan this in advance so the date for the visiting students is set and preparation time is limited. To get their game owners licence to trade, each group has to give me a description of their game, an estimation of the probability of winning and evidence of the test data to support it. For once, it is students from my class that go home with something to make instead of certain other unnamed subjects who seem to commandeer disproportionate amounts of students' independent time with their projects. No chip on my shoulder there. Games are made, games are tested, there is noise, there is mess, there is urgency, there is purpose.

Yes, if I am honest, the control freak in me struggles a little here with the messiness, but it is good for me. I also confess that I could teach students about how to work with the notion of relative frequency and experimental probability in less time. For me, the task offers something more though and a more concrete and memorable experience that makes it worth it. It is a lovely moment when students in grade 9, making the game, remember coming to the fairground when they were in grade 5. I don't know if any of this would stand up in court. You decide. As ever there are variations on a theme here for you to work with as you see fit in your setting. I have considered, but never dared to, tie this in with a school fair.

Let me tell you about some of the games we have seen.

It's not hard to imagine that there are a thousand variations on the paper toss game and most of them end up fairly successful. I particularly enjoyed the one that introduced a moving fan to divert the path of the paper on the way to the basket, emulating a popular phone app. We see all kinds of projectiles and obstacles to bring appeal to the game, but they all have the same key principle.

Various emulations of angry birds are always a crowd pleaser, not to mention a maths teacher pleaser. These can get quite elaborate!

Not a million miles away are the games that involve getting a ring over an object. My absolute favourite of these was when three boys turned up in grass skirts, danced the hula while players tried to throw real hula hoops over them. Others made different shapes to throw rings over with harder shapes being worth more points and a certain points total required with three rings to win.

A good old fashioned coin shove, where a coin is placed halfway over the edge of the table and shoved with the base of the hand towards a target in the middle. Again, a points total was required to win.

We have seen some elaborate plays on a marble run or crazy golf that all depends on the ball going in the hole.

Amongst all these there is a smattering of theoretical probability games designed with a pack of cards, some dice or roulette wheel to give us a casino feel and give the players some food for thought as they try to work out their chances.

One of the games that stood out for me and gave rise to a flurry of activity was an innocent looking game called 'Shoot Bieber' in which there was a large cardboard cut-out of a certain singer and a Nerf gun. I was confused as those testing the game appeared to be standing at point blank range in front of the target. I thought, *"Hmmm, this lot may have missed the point in favour of some sinister ritual"*. I was pleasantly surprised to learn that the 6-barrel Nerf gun was not fully loaded and players were allowed to decide if they wanted to spin the barrel or not in between two shots. This was a good one and warrants a brief little aside, as this has become another activity all on its own.

Nerf gun roulette

I'll confess to being slightly uncomfortable with this context, especially as I can conjure disturbing images of Christopher Walken in the Deer Hunter far too quickly and certainly don't let anyone put the Nerf gun at close range against their head. I like to think I worry just about the right amount about this to say enough things to students to make sure we are all taking this lightly and I hope I pay enough attention to the sensitivities. It is mostly pretty funny when I line up a student against the door and shoot a Nerf gun at them. It is probably funnier when I let them shoot at me. Just imagine me, a grown adult, going through airport security with a Nerf gun showing up on the scanner in my hand luggage. They must be used to it because no one ever says anything, but I always sweat a little like I am in the movies. Overactive imagination.

There are some great questions about the probability of getting the Nerf bullet when there is only one in there and what difference it makes when you spin the barrel between tries. I was pleased with this game and the opportunities it gave us for exploring probability in other classes, not related to the fairground. As the way we used it evolved, so, of course, did Nerf guns, so one year I asked students to bring in Nerf guns they had at home. This was disturbing. It was like an organised crime amnesty, as Nerf guns of all shapes and sizes turned up, including one semi-automatic looking job that had 5 different barrels, each with 6 slots. This was gold for our exploration! Imagine each barrel with a different amount of bullets in it and spinning the barrels and then the barrel and working out the chances of getting a bullet in three shots. Anyway, I just wanted to share some potential here. Even as I write, it still makes me a bit uncomfortable, thinking about horrible things involving schools and guns, so I understand if you object or don't like it. You don't have to shoot each other though, you can always shoot a can of a ledge. Do with it what you will, but don't be surprised to find your class can produce a plastic arsenal at the drop of a hat.

So you get it, there are lots of games and yes, it can sometimes be a challenge to make sure that the emphasis is on simplicity and reliable design and testing instead of elaborate construction and outlandish aesthetics. A little bit of the latter and even a costume and little performance really make it, but the game is the main event.

Fair day

Fair day arrives pretty quickly and I usually book a slot right after lunch so that students can come and set up their games during lunch and be ready for customers. I give each team a float of 20 counters which they have to give me back at the end and a data sheet to record what happens. Enthusiastic grade 5 students arrive, each with a pocket full of counters, also 20, and their eyes wide with the potential fun awaiting. They are making choices about which one they want to do first and which ones they think they can win. The stall holders are making their final preparations and getting their 'patter' ready to encourage the clients. Instructions are written on boards and I am playing a fairground organ! Sorry, that went a bit far. I am playing a Spotify playlist of a fairground organ.

Like the calm before a kick off, there is a moment where I speak to the room (I am not alone, the grade 5 teachers have come with their classes) and make sure that everyone is clear about the rules and then the games begin. It's wonderful in so many ways. It's wonderful to see what happens to older students when they are given some responsibility for younger students. It's great to see such industry in the room and students enjoying playing their roles whilst dealing with the reality of something they have only considered in theory. It can be surprisingly hard work. It's awesome to see students watching and thinking and weighing up their options. Naturally some of the games are instantly more appealing and they get the longest queues. If they are good then their queues stay long. Not too long though, because no one wants to spend their afternoon in a queue and this directly benefits the other games. It is true that some games end up being more popular than others. Some are too hard, some take too long, some are less appealing, but everyone gets customers and this is really all part of the exercise.

An hour goes by in a flash and the quiet is welcome when grade 5 slope away with their spoils. Some are in profit, some are spent and they will go back to their classrooms, count their money and compare experiences. There is lots of potential with that data. See an example table in Figure 18.1. What questions can we ask? How much of this spreadsheet can we usefully ask students to make themselves? What analysis is there to do? Can we average the probabilities? Is that fair?

My lot have to clear up, then they have to count their money and check that it tallies with the records they have kept. They don't always! Then, the next time we are together, we collate the data and do our own analysis. What was the relative frequency of winning each game? How did the number of plays compare? Then, the question on everyone's lips: who made the most money and why? Invariably the winning team had a good combination of a game that is simple but appealing, quick to play and designed well to leave just enough of a chance but clearly be weighted in their favour.

I think the rest is there for you to think about. It is elaborate, but this book isn't a description of my everyday; it is about things I do that I look forward to most. Some of those are simple and quick, and occasionally I make room for something that requires a bit more, if I feel it is worth it for reasons I have explained here and throughout the book. This is one that some will read and say *"Oh yes I want to do that"* and others will say *"Never in a million years"*, and that is all 'fair' enough. Each of these chapters seems to end with a statement about how I hope you have seen some possibility for engaging, concrete and fruitful activity for your classes. It goes with saying really, but I really do. I have taken so much inspiration from hearing about what others do. Variations on this can span a huge age range. As I mentioned, I have used something like this as a context for exploring conditional probability – is the probability of the third throw succeeding better than the first? – and can often be found throwing paper rings over bottles and encouraging others to do it so we can collect data on a large Venn diagram. I have learned at teacher workshops that this is an everyone thing, not just a student thing. It feels like we could get to some binomial probability pretty quickly here too. If this book gets a sequel, I'll tell you about playing with the glass bridge from Squid Game. If you don't know what I mean, you are probably better off.

It feels like we may have peaked here with this end of term frivolity. We should not forget to return our focus to how significant the notion of experimental data is to knowledge in general, but there is time to build on that down the line. We also know that all terms are longer than they seem and, despite all the effort and energy expended on this activity, there are a couple of important lessons still left before the end of term. We are nearly there.

Game Name	How many people won your game?	How many people lost your game?	How many counters did you have left at the end?	How many counters should you have had?	Probability of winning your game	Profit made in Practice	Profit made in Theory
Super Shooter Slay	26	54	57	48	0.33	37	28
Rocket launcher	19	30	35	31	0.39	15	11
Splat the Villain	12	45	56	53	0.21	36	33
The Conquest	5	5	20	20	0.50	0	0
Spin the wheel game	14	46	52	52	0.23	32	32
Ring pole	6	15	34	29	0.29	14	9
The mini-golf game	20	28	25	28	0.42	5	8
Basketball Game	18	35	40	37	0.34	20	17
The skill shooting	7	19	30	32	0.27	10	12
Kill the Monster	23	21	18	18	0.52	-2	-2
Do you wanna throw balls at a snowman?	28	30	13	22	0.48	-7	2
Pie Face	18	75	77	77	0.19	57	57
Deuce it before you lose it	8	25	39	37	0.24	19	17
The Spinner Game	4	7	21	23	0.36	1	3
Plinko board	26	69	69	63	0.27	49	43
Target Practice	5	16	36	31	0.24	16	11

Figure 18.1 Fairground stats. These are some results from my recent fairground. What questions can we ask? What analysis can we do?

From the box to the classroom

Thoughts and themes

- Experimental probabilities depend on experimental data, which usually requires an experiment.
- In the fairground exercise we really do have 'skin in the game' and the advantages that come with that.
- Elaborate activity might be the reserve of rare moments but is worth it occasionally and can bring so many wider benefits.

Task to try

- Try any version to any extent of any part of the fairground activity, even if you just throw some paper balls in your classroom.
- Consider other experiments that you can use to collect data for experimental data.

19   Impossible diagrams

What's in the box?

Ok, so not as visually appealing as the wonderful work of MC Escher and others, but still a great way to explore and practice ideas. I can sketch anything I like in maths but that doesn't mean it can exist in reality. These activities are about another way of looking at problems kind of in reverse and the associated reasoning that is required. This task encourages students to dig around their mathematical armoury and use it to make arguments.

For various reasons, I went to 8 different schools in three different countries between the ages of 3 and 18. No, I wasn't expelled from any of them, and I am hurt that you might have thought that. We were just a fairly nomadic family. It was a fine range of different schools too. Mostly state schools, but when we moved to Sydney because of Dad's job, my sisters and I went to private school. I went to two of those and even they were wildly different with one being at the very traditional end of the scale and the other much more to the liberal end. The latter was where I finished school and was very 'right on'. Lots of long hair, guitars and '90s-style flower power. We raised money for Amnesty International with our school concerts and were all budding eco-warriors, presumably exhibiting a good degree of hypocritical behaviour simultaneously. Although I was up and down with mathematics at school, I do think back to certain memories that point to where I ended up as a teacher, and this is one of them. During a typical lunchtime, sat out on the grass and swapping stories, a young eco-warrior shares that they have read that an area of rainforest the size of Wales is being destroyed every second. Astonished noises come from the group as we count seconds in our head and imagine Wales-size lights going out on the planet, and the despair is palpable. Well, except me. I am doing some maths, trying to work out, if that were true, how long it would take for all the rainforest to be gone. Of course, an important and often unacknowledged reality here is that very few people actually know the area of Wales, or the area of rainforest, but that doesn't stop many of us from pressing ahead with our associated assumptions. We fall easily victim to such numerical fallacy.

A quick google and a few sums tell us that the area of Wales fits approximately 25,000 times in the surface area of the whole planet. Even if we ignore

DOI: 10.4324/9781003266501-19

the fact that about 71% of this is water, we learn that, at this rate, an area of rainforest the size of . . . the whole planet . . . would be gone in around 7 hours. This is all such food for thought again. The fact was almost certainly 'misquoted' from something that was probably alarming enough. I think there are some good questions about how much it matters. The aim of the quote is to communicate a sense of alarm, which it did successfully, and only a few bother with the calculations. What people hear is, wow, rainforest is disappearing at an alarming rate, but few will take the time to make sense of the rate. This speaks to things I have read in many places, but particularly from John Allen Paulos, whose books I thoroughly enjoy (try *Innumeracy* and *A Mathematician Reads the Newspaper*). He often talks about our inability to deal with big numbers. That once they get past a certain size we often don't differentiate between numbers that are actually vastly different. He cites a survey that counted the frequency with which millions and billions were incorrectly stated the wrong way round. Suffice to say, in the spirit of the point here, the frequency was alarming.

This then gives rise to plenty of need to help students to get better at this so that they are better able to examine critically the information they are presented with. This is a huge area and areas of rainforest the size of Wales (Maybe they meant an actual whale?) are but the tip of the iceberg – and the iceberg is melting, by the way, at an alarming rate and contributing to a corresponding rise in sea levels. I am sure you are following. Whilst all of this can be done in the deeply meaningful contexts I have alluded to here, I think it speaks to a fundamental principle of mathematics and examining the possibility of statements that are given. At one end we have the idea of *reductio ad absurdum* where, for example, we might prove that the square root of 2 is irrational by assuming it is rational and expressing it as a fraction. By exploring what that would mean, we arrive at repeating nonsense and effectively show that this is impossible, much as I wanted to do with the factoid about Wales, and that, as such, it must be irrational. At the other end we might examine the ease with which we can draw and label a mathematical diagram that makes no sense and cannot exist. This chapter is more about the latter and activities where students are presented with mathematical scenarios and asked to decide whether they can be true or not. In its various guises, this is about 'impossible shapes'.

When I remember to, I like to introduce such activities with a reference to some of MC Escher's amazing art that plays with our perceptions of reality. Clearly we could dwell on much of Escher's work and probably should another time. Here though I am talking about the well-known drawings of impossible buildings where water appears to be going in a loop, but always flowing down. There are buildings where staircases seem to go on forever, and there is a good reference to the Penrose stairs in Christopher Nolan's *Inception*, which is a nice link too. It is just another important idea to recognise that the 'sketch' has the potential for the creation of things and ideas that can't exist in reality. I would imagine that most teachers have experienced this accidentally when making worksheets and generating examples a little too quickly (and this is not a judge-ment at all – we all know the circumstances). A simple example might be a tri-angle you have drawn that you label with sides 7, 3 and 10 as you rely on your mind's random number generator that works overtime. You can draw it, you can add the labels, but it can't exist. I suspect that some of the versions I have done of this stem from having had that accidental experience and enjoying the expla-nation the student offered me when they told me!

Here are some examples. Look at the sketches in Figure 9.1 with a few to decide whether the shapes could exist in reality or not. As you do so, pay atten-tion to the arguments and reasoning you use. Pay attention to the questions you asked and what you wrote down. Think about what you are doing so you can imagine what your students might be doing too.

I started to write 'at the risk of sounding like a broken record', and then I realised that this is chapter 19 and the risk passed some time ago. I like to

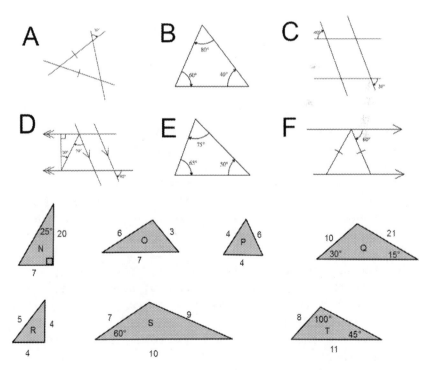

Figure 19.1 Impossible diagrams. Can the shapes in these diagrams exist in reality?

think of it as more of an album by an artist whose songs all have an instantly recognisable DNA but each of which offers something different. There I go with delusions of artistry again. Teaching epistemology requires an explicit focus on reasoning, deductive, inductive, abductive and the construction of arguments and counter arguments that become a Socratic dialogue aimed at making all participants wiser. Ah what a wonderful vision of debate. Social media works out a bit differently. Drawing attention to these features and the differences in types of reasoning is a really important part of understanding knowledge and different areas of knowledge. For example, if you were to sketch a square and label the sides *a, a, a and 2a* and ask people what shape it is, what kind of reasoning would you expect people to use? All this points to the idea that construction of sound logical arguments in this context is a key part of the exercise. This is maths; you should be able to demonstrate to me if these shapes are possible or not.

In many ways, the task and the diagrams offered above, tell us what we need to know I think. Once you have tried a few and then tried to think of designing your own, I think the validity of such an exercise becomes self-evident. It is another context for practice that also builds in an opportunity to develop argumentative skills. I also think the principle is broadly applicable to all kinds of mathematical ideas. We could do this with angle rules, properties of shapes, area and perimeter and trigonometry. Geometry offers lots of obvious ones because they involve sketches, but we can go beyond. For example . . .

The integers 2, 3, 4, 5 and x have a mean average of 30. Does x exist?

This is just a starter, but I think that if you choose your numbers carefully, you might want to provoke a reasoned response about why it must exist as an alternative to finding the value of x which is also of course a very convincing argument. As ever, it is about what kind of thinking you might want to elicit or what options you want to build on for different approaches that lead to reasoning. The above is not posted as an example to use with your class, but rather a provocation to think about the kinds of questions you could ask on this theme. I hope that we have you thinking!

As we are near the end of term here, I am happy that this chapter is a little shorter, at least to read! I could have started with it as one of the more profound ideas that permeates mathematical thinking everywhere. It is such a key feature of 'doing mathematics' to offer and test explanations and arguments for conclusions that we reach. It can, on the one hand, seem like the ultimate level of thinking, but it should be a feature of doing mathematics from the outset. I wonder if you checked my calculations on Wales and the rainforest!

From the box to the classroom

Thoughts and themes

- There is a difference between what we can sketch and what can exist in reality!
- Asking students to provide arguments for why any given sketch can exist or not offers an alternative thought process and encourages good reasoning.

Task to try

- Try the impossible diagrams as shown above.
- Try making some more like the ones in the diagram so as to think about what the focus might be when students are trying to argue about it.
- Try making some impossible diagrams in another context.

20 Cubism

What's in the box?

And finally. Experienced during my teacher training year, here is an activity I have used every year since that gets right to the heart of mathematical generalisation and proof but starts with a lovely playful element. A perfect mathematical recipe! In describing this activity I invite you to think about the potential and the value in mathematical classroom manipulatives.

If you are still reading at chapter 20, then I feel safe telling you about some of my chequered history with mathematics. We were a reasonably nomadic family and when I was 12, Dad came home and told us he had accepted a job in Sydney, Australia! This was pretty exciting on lots of levels, but worked out a bit less exciting on the maths front for me. I arrived in time for end-of-year exams (what with different seasons and all) where it was clearly established that I was quite some way behind the Australian curve in terms of mathematics. This resulted in me being signed up with a maths tutor over the long, hot Australian summer holiday, which you can imagine, like most 12 year olds, I was ecstatic about. I went once a week and was set an hour of maths a day to do for the other days – more joy. The first visit to my tutor is the bit I remember the most. It was the most humiliating! I turned up with Dad at this lady's house and was invited to sit at a table in the living room where there appeared to be several members of this lady's extended family as well. There was idle small talk going on between all these people while my tutor gave me a puzzle to complete. It was a wooden, shape-based puzzle, you know, of the kind I now buy for people with young children. She told me she wanted to watch me try to solve it so she could learn some things about the way I think. Apparently everyone else in the room shared this curiosity about my thinking capacity. For this fairly typically self-conscious 12-year-old who had recently acquired dunce status in mathematics, it was a truly excruciating moment. As I write I am still incredulous and suspecting that my memory has embellished this a little, otherwise it couldn't possibly be true. If I have, it is only to make clear the way I felt! I am also aware that you might be expecting a happy ending here at the hands of some pedagogical revelation and so I should put you out of your misery straight away. I remember nothing else

DOI: 10.4324/9781003266501-20

from the maths I did that summer. I should tell you though that whatever happened that summer, it worked, and my dunce status was retracted fairly soon afterwards. I am sure there are some cautionary tales wrapped up in here somewhere, and maybe I'll get there in some other book because I only mentioned it here so I could start talking about classroom manipulatives. My tutor felt there was something to learn about me from watching me with that puzzle and at the time it meant nothing to me. Now, at this distance, I am prepared to give her the benefit of the doubt, although inviting her family still seems a bit unnecessary!

Watching students with virtual manipulatives and the tasks that can go with them is indeed a great way to learn about them and how they think as well as an excellent way to encourage mathematical behaviour – who knew? I have mentioned my primary colleagues and, in particular, Simon, before. Simon has co-authored a fabulous book for the ATM (whose conference was the scene of the dancing vectors and the rice and more of course) about Cuisenaire rods which I highly recommend. It is full of wonderful tasks and associated thinking. My favourite might be the 'Hundred face', where students are asked to make a face out of Cuisenaire rods that makes a total of 100 units. So much thinking and behaviour is wrapped up in that simple little task. Try it. I'll not give the rest away. Simon has also written for ATM about pattern blocks, which are an equally wonderful source for exploration. He and I went to a 'mathematics for the public' event and ran a couple of stalls for visitors, one of which was pattern blocks. I took two of my daughters that day and they spent an entire morning simply exploring pattern blocks. In the age of the tablet, apps and the internet, this was such an incredible revelation. It crosses over some with work we have done on Islamic tile design, which was the stall I was running that morning. Having already mentioned two books that specialise in these manipulatives, there is probably no need to tell you that this is a world that warrants further investigation.

For my part, I am a disciple of the ubiquitous multilink cube. These are coloured plastic cubes that can be attached to each other. I have never had a classroom without a big box of these at the ready. You will recall I am sure that in the opening chapter about 'what is in the box', these wonderful cubes took centre stage, so it feels only right that the final chapter should revolve around these too. In between I have used them in chapter 7 about loci as we move from people to being the points to pen and paper; the cubes are a nice interim stage on a manageable scale. I used them in chapter 5 as a means of exploring the number of ways four people could stand in a queue. In chapter 8 I used them to approximate a pie chart or make a bar chart or pictogram where each person was a cube. Also here they are an excellent resource for looking at those box plots on a smaller scale and identifying medians and quartiles etc and the shape of distributions. In chapter 15 they are essential for marking the points on our distance time graph, and I am very surprised if someone doesn't use them for the fairground. Ubiquitous. For this last chapter I want to focus on using these cubes to look at sequences. We can look at all kinds of sequences with growing patterns made out of cubes but, to start with I want to talk about a simple linear sequence. I was first asked this question by Tony on my PGCSE course and have since asked it to countless teachers and students all over the world. (Yes, I travel with my cubes alongside my Nerf gun.) Given a supply of these cubes, please make a visual representation of the sequence that begins 1, 5, 9, 13. I'll follow this up by saying that despite having asked this question many times before, no class has ever failed to deliver at least one new answer to this question that I have never seen. This is important because it lets students know straight away that they have to think beyond their first assertion that there is one correct answer that involves making four lines of different lengths. Please try this yourselves. Please push yourself to keep looking for new ones and, if you do this with a class, be prepared to go through what seems like an odd moment where everyone in the room thinks you've lost it a bit, because you keep pushing. It is really worth it when the creativity kicks in, often spurred on by one student breaking out of the shackles! Then eventually, oddly enough, it can be difficult to stop them. Below are a few typical results that come out from this activity.

This is a tricky one for the control freaks like me because you get all sorts. I try to set it up as a kind of 'exhibition' where each model is being exhibited for the rest of the class and will often ask students to look at each other's. This can be messy though, and we run out of cubes quite quickly, so I am quite proud of this little tech trick where I open a Google Drive folder on my screen and take photos with my phone directly into the folder. This means that as I wander around taking photos of the exhibits, they appear on the screen at the front. Simple but nice, and it means we can record what they have done and use the cubes again. Then I'll often ask students to classify the exhibits into different groups. This will typically involve recognising that some students used the number of cubes that correspond to the term and some didn't. There are lots of interesting ways to make the visual representation that way too, we are just recognising that this is a different classification. There are those that have made four separate things, one for each term, and those that have made one object that represents all of the terms. Amongst these there are those that grow systematically (i.e. each new term is some kind of systematic enlargement of the previous term) and those that don't. There are those that are colour coded where the four that are added each time are a different colour, for example. Each is, of course, a perfectly valid representation, but the justifications that are offered for them set them apart. This is definitely one part where we learn a bit about the students and the way they think. They also learn this about each other, and, more importantly, we all

Figure 20.1 The sequence 1, 5, 9, 13. The images show different visual representations of this sequence made out of multilink cubes.

get to see the justifications and merits of each other's work rather than play a game of guess what I, the teacher, want you to make.

Now, picking on one of the examples (one of the ones I wanted them to make, if I am honest), I'll run through some typical questions about how many it would take to make the next pattern and how many it would take to make the tenth and the hundredth. This is a good conversation and an opportunity to let students spot and correct problems with answers and methods here. They are also quite likely to generalise for you too and there are more ways to do this as well. Some might recall something like "The 4-times table shifted up by 1" and others might talk about the number of times you add 4 for each step. We can dwell on which responses draw on the shapes we made and which ones just draw on the number sequence and so we recognise, once again, that the cubes are possibly a concrete or pictorial step that can help us into the abstraction. I am sure you can imagine various ways this conversation and task can develop and will have your own preferences, but the upshot here is that the development of a generalisation for the number of cubes needed for any given term is highly desirable mathematical behaviour and offers students a different experience from being taught a formula and shown how to apply it. This is the art of using logical deduction to piece together bits of existing knowledge to make and test new knowledge claims. This is the process that I hope has been modelled for students regularly in classes so that they are able and allowed to do it themselves too. If the discussion about experts and novices has value then, for me, it has to go back and look at this amazing mathematical Venn diagram we spoke of in chapter 16 and recognise that it contains myriad subsets and the potential to define new ones with different properties. In any one of these subsets a student might enter as a novice but be able to behave as an expert within that subset quite quickly and then leave the subset for another and repeat. It is clearly a valuable thought process, but expertise has to be considered relative for it to be a useful model.

Moving on, I like this question, *"OK class, if we pooled all of our cubes together, how many terms of this sequence do you think we could make?"* I might have to repeat and add some explanation to the question to help people understand, but eventually, the minds start whirring. The eyes start scanning the classroom and estimating cube numbers and trying to frame the problem. The guesses will come and then others will refine their guesses based on the other guesses. Interestingly enough, this happens with teachers too. I can usually rely on a dry humoured and skillful work avoider to say *"We don't know, Mr Noble"*, and I do have a good deal of respect for this answer. It is probably the most correct or at least the best reasoned. This is a difficult question to answer intuitively. *"OK"*, I'll say *"Let's just see how many you can make"* and I'll point to a table in the corner and say *"You make the first five"* and point to another and give them the task of the next five and so on until someone figures that they got a raw deal! OK, it's a little contrived, but I like these little moments if they come off. Then we spend 5 minutes making lengths of 4, 8 and 12 cubes so that we can get as many terms as we can and arrange them next to each other on the floor.

I would assume that this is where you know what is going to happen next, but from experience of teachers on workshops, I'd say it's worth me continuing. So we have this arrangement of 18 terms of the sequence (that's all we could build) and I'll say *"So how many cubes do you think we have here, then?"* My dry guy will start to count and we'll laugh and agree that, although we know we could, we would all rather not. Someone will point out that it looks a bit like a triangle so perhaps we could estimate that way - nice thought and estimate we could and do, but recognise that it is an estimate because the shape is not an exact triangle. It's a great thought though. *"Could we arrange the lines of cubes into another shape?"* There is thinking and fingers on lips and virtual 'moving'. This might be followed by suggestions and one of those will be that we can take half the triangle and turn it around so it makes a rectangle and as we do so, there are audible gasps. I can hear cynical spluttering from some

Figure 20.2 The first 14 terms. The image shows the first 14 terms of the sequence 1, 5, 9 and 13 as lengths of cubes so that they form a rectangle.

readers and I get it. As described in a book, this all sounds like a dodgy recipe and also a lot like the *"guess what I want you to say"* I mentioned earlier. Try it though; I know that not all students make the critical points, but everyone watches it happen and some contribute to it and many are genuinely moved to 'gasp' by this neatness. You might also set something up in smaller groups that lets more students be active in this. We are not quite finished though. We need to recognise that the length of the rectangle is the first term plus the last term and that width is half the number of terms and this, like the first bit, can be handled in a variety of ways so I'll leave it with you. I have just tried to share with you the kind of thing that happens when we do this. I can see that no two groups will be the same and it depends on all the usual variables, but this is here on my list of 20 lessons to look forward to because it seldom disappoints. More significantly, it is another concrete experience that bridges that gap to abstraction and really helps what comes next. We can always come back to the cubes.

Different ways to sum

You might be able to go back to some of the original models to look for other ways to sum. It is good to go back and point to these different classified exhibits that have this property. This is really good fun. Think about nested 'Ls' or 'Ws' and how these might be put together to make shapes that we could use to sum the number of cubes. There is more to be done with this.

Pattern blocks

Now imagine a similar activity with pattern blocks, where students are given the freedom to create sequences with pattern blocks. What is lovely about this is that they can be interlocked sequences with the number of each kind of (colour/

shape) block being its own sequence. The separate sequences sum to the overall sequence. Lovely.

Painted cube

In chapter 16 I discover new life in a much maligned piece of coursework. I have done so with this painted cube too. For those that don't know it, here it is in a nutshell. If I build a 3 × 3 × 3 cube out of multilink cubes and then dip it in a pot of paint, how many of the smaller cubes will have three faces painted? How many will have two, one or zero faces painted? You can imagine that we might then ask the same question about a different shape and explore related generalisations. It is still wonderful, branches out into quadratic sequences and offers lots of wonderful moments where we connect algebra to the physical object. There is nothing quite like building the cube using different colours to help explore it.

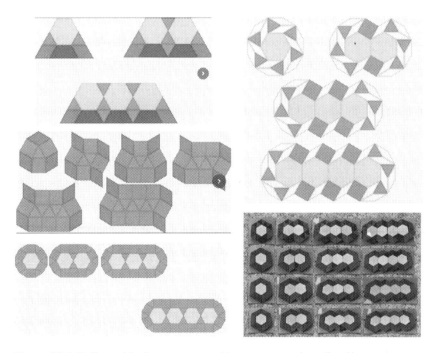

Figure 20.3 Pattern block sequences. How can we describe the sequences below, and can we break them down into separate sequences for each type of pattern block?

Exponential decay

Try this. Out of four tables and some piles of books, I created a little area where I could empty my box of cubes like throwing a bucket of water on a floor you are cleaning. The cubes have only one face with a protruding circle that is used to attach them to another cube. I ask students to take out all the cubes whose one protruding face was pointing up and join them together in a straight line. Now do it again and place the new line next to the first line, on the right. Now again, and again until you have no cubes left. What sequence models this lovely decaying graph you have just created? If you are anything like me (and I know there are at least some of you) this might take a bit more thought than you imagined.

I am pleased with the symmetry of finishing back where I started with my Swiss Army multilink cubes. The goal was to extol their virtues wrapped up in a chapter about sequences, sums and generalisation and related activities that are a highlight for me and my students. As ever, they are there for you to interrogate, explore, disagree, reject, reform or whatever you like. I am happy if it made you think and provoked some thought about similar activity. The classroom manipulative, as we have said, is a vast area of mathematics education about which much has been written and tried and shared and researched. I can't cover all of that in this book, but I also couldn't write a book about lessons to look forward to that didn't include any classroom manipulatives and these cubes are one of my non-negotiables. I am still sceptical about what happened in that suburban Sydney house that day, but not at all about the value of things you can play with in mathematics classes.

From the box to the classroom

Thoughts and themes

- The value of the classroom manipulative in its role as bridge from concrete to abstract and as a tool to promote mathematical behaviour.
- The sequences task as an example of students behaving mathematically to put together knowledge they have to make new knowledge.

Task to try

- Try the activity as described, making visual representations of a given sequence and following it through as far as you want to nth terms and sums.

- Try different ways to sum sequences by making shapes out of the terms.
- Try growing patterns with other manipulatives like Cuisenaire rods or pattern blocks.
- Try the painted cube task and let students build some of the cubes.
- Have a go at that exponential decay task before you give it to students!

Back to the staffroom - an epilogue

The staffroom is a funny old place, at least in the schools I have worked in. Aside from all the stuff associated with the dynamic amongst the people in it, I mean more about the different moods it catches you in. It can be a safe haven or an oasis, but sometimes it feels like a green room where you get nervous about what is about to happen because so much can depend on you and the things you do. For some it is like the big brother diary room or confession or a place to let off steam about what happens in our classrooms - goodness knows we all need a bit of that. At other times it can be a quiet place for reflection about what just happened. Like most rooms in a school it has many different faces. At least this one comes with tea!

I have a clear memory of retreating to the staffroom once during teacher training after a lesson that had been spectacularly awful. An early attempt at teaching algebra no less. Whilst I desperately wanted to escape inside, the safety was uncomfortably mixed with the upheaval of reflecting on what had just happened, how it happened and what I needed to learn from it. It was a pretty horrible moment on the steep learning curve. As time has gone on I have learned to be more philosophical about this moment - and yes, it still happens. It is just a part of the teacher's lot. In the beginning of this book as I recounted trying to explain to my friend Ben why I didn't just do the same thing every year, I acknowledged the huge amount of variables that are simply not possible to control. It is a pipe dream to imagine that everything you do or try or change or repeat will go exactly as you might hope. The reflection is endless and part of what makes the job appealing. I am wary of peoples' derision of their younger selves, but one thing I would go back and tell that desolate dude in the staffroom is that he was about to enter a profession he would likely never master and should expect a bumpy ride. *"Learn to enjoy it mate!"* Maybe I am just doing it wrong!

It seems natural then, that having written to you about 20 of my lessons to look forward to, I might retreat to my staffroom and reflect on what has just happened. I like the odd inspirational and reassuring quote from the internet, but stopped in my tracks recently when I read one that went something like this. *"The biggest reason people feel imposter syndrome is that they are, actually, imposters"*. Just going to leave that there and cry. Then I'll dust myself off and return to what I wrote about at the start, about what I wanted to do with this book. I just wanted to make a contribution. I have been teaching since 1999 and have just told you about 20 of my lessons I look forward to, how they might work and why I think they matter. I have tried where possible to generalise these tasks into types so they can be adapted or scaled or translated across the age and topic ranges so as to be as useful to as many as they can be. I have invited you to experience these tasks and notice what happens to you so you might adapt them to your own setting or make them better and hopefully, in one way or another, inspire you to design. I really hope you try some and I really hope you have enjoyed reading my accounts. I expect you have recognised a lot and just taken the time to dwell on it all. To finish, I'd like to share some of the things that I keep in my head as I re-teach and rethink.

Believe in possibility

I mean this in every sense. From the saccharine motivational end - I am a huge *Ted Lasso* fan (check him out if you don't know who I mean) - to the practical realities of trying to do something. I like to believe things are possible until proven impossible rather than the other way around. It means I experience failure, but it means I experience immense satisfaction from trying new things. Try stuff.

Value the old

This can't be overstated. For so many years so many people have developed so many wonderful classroom activities. Most of them are as good today as they were when they were first conceived of.

Revitalise

Sometimes old ideas just need a new twist. Maybe you have just done them a lot and need a change, maybe they need updating. Whatever it is, taking an old idea and working to see what new joy you might get from it is a great way to get stuck into task design.

Create

Creating gives me a huge amount of pleasure. We are not all the same; this is just my list. The whole process from conception to design to prototype to pilot to first draft to constant tweaking can be so wonderfully satisfying. I have spoken of my artist's delusion through the book. I firmly believe that teaching is part science and part art and try as often as possible to be in that intersection.

Exchange with people

In your department, in the staffroom, at conferences, online, at parties - OK maybe not. Telling people about what you did and hearing their questions is really productive. Listening to other people do that and asking the questions is even better. We are our best source of professional development.

Enjoy

With the best will in the world, teaching is such a multifaceted and demanding profession, I know we can't always enjoy it. This shouldn't stop us trying as much as possible though. Bouncing out of bed on those days, I am looking forward to what I am doing is much better than the alternative! I don't think I can expect my students to look forward to them if I don't.

In truth, at this end of the book, this all feels a bit self-indulgent. Telling stories of my experiences and of the ideas that have worked for me and where they came from has been hugely pleasurable. Such a lovely reflective exercise that I hope celebrates this most rewarding part of being a teacher. I hope I have made it clear through the book that I recognise my own shortcomings as a teacher and still have much to try and to learn. I am just sharing what I think I have to offer. The best possible outcome is that readers have a few more 'lessons to look forward to' and the enthusiasm to go off and create more.

Thanks for reading.

Appendix 1

The school of mathematical behaviour

The following is really important in terms of understanding the bigger picture of what I write about here in this book. I felt it was better here at the end, reserved for those that wanted answers to questions about how these activities fit into the whole scheme of my teaching. I felt the introduction was long enough and that it was likely to mean more once you have read about the activities.

I have stated that, when working with teachers, it has been a consistent goal to 'do some mathematics' together, and this has often involved working on activities like the ones in this book so that we might notice what happens to us when we do them and use this, with our experience, to dwell on what happens to our students. All this so that we can better understand what their experience is like and their associated needs. This experience has been broadly appreciated by teachers and, I hope, reinvigorated people to think about their teaching. Despite this, and not at all surprisingly, there are often cries of *"How do you find time to do all these activities with students?"* and *"How do you make sure you cover the curriculum?"* and similar questions. At the same time, the massive web of teachers and academics online, in books and at conferences quite rightly debate about things like 'explicit instruction' and 'discovery learning' and lots of things in between. These are all good discussions, even if the limits of the medium for them, and binary definitions are sometimes exposed. I love that there is so much to read about and am grateful to all those that write. Naturally, people want to ask questions about this too. I will share some answers to these excellent questions.

I hope it has been clear throughout my writing that I have no delusions of myself as some kind of super teacher that has it all sewn up and is now serving it up to the rest of you. I mostly just ask teachers to think about the various goals that they and their schools have written down, the nature of mathematics and to notice how these things come together in their classrooms. I offer up some mathematical experiences to help us do that. That's it.

Beyond that, I am constrained by the same realities, frustrations and dilemmas as teachers appear to be the world over. I have syllabi to 'cover'; administrators to please; students with many more concerns than mathematics; parents who want you to find the perfect balance between keeping their children happy, confident and achieving; governors; parents and students who need exam results; oh and a family and a life and a mortgage and so on. I have a huge interest in the wider goals of a school and its community, but am sympathetic to the consequences of being spread too thinly. Schools, from my experience, are a hotbed for good intentions meeting strained resources. How much of any of this am I, a classroom teacher, expected to try and control? I read about plausible alternative models that try to address this and I see pros and cons in most. My response is, perhaps disappointingly, to be rather pragmatic about it all. I try only to control the variables I can, and only as far as I can. I accept that much of my professional life is a compromise and, most importantly, that I am human and flawed.

Like most, we have schemes of work that are largely geared towards the external assessments they will lead to. We are a small department of three, which gives us some useful flexibility to adjust as and when it suits us. Our schemes are almost certainly not revolutionary but do, hopefully, demonstrate good sequencing, thoughtful linking of mathematical ideas and the scope for activities to drive, to some extent, the direction, all in the knowledge that they are flexible enough to re-organise to account for this.

Now, I also wrote a book about some of my favourite lessons. I can't imagine that a book about my 20 worst lessons would be as interesting. Although, saying it out loud makes me think it might be! At the same time, I get a huge amount of satisfaction from lessons where I carefully explain a concept to students using my whiteboard and some good examples that allow for good questions and answers. I know my students really appreciate these lessons and I value them every bit as much. I see most of the classes I teach around three times a week for an hour and, as a rule of thumb, I might plan to spend one hour with an activity like ones in this book, one with more formal, didactic teaching and a third that is focussed on practice while I am there to support. It is not always in that order and sometimes that ratio might spread over a longer period. Some of the activities in this book are also exciting contexts for practice which is a great notion. Read about Colin Foster's 'Mathematical Etudes'. The worst thing that could happen is that you could read the book and imagine that I am arguing that we should *"Just give them the raw materials and let the magic happen by itself"* or that *"All my lessons are like this and I just go where the class takes me"*. Everything in here depends on me being a teacher.

I am loath to write down the term 'discovery learning' (again!) because it seems to have become such a dirty, polarising, ill-defined notion, very much synonymous with my first quote above. As such, I would be upset if anyone thought that this book was arguing the case for this poorly defined 'discovery learning'. (I have to stop saying it.) No, this book is about some of my lessons that promote and encourage mathematical behaviour. The idea that exploration is a natural part of mathematics or that two premises can be put together logically to prove a conclusion. Conjecturing and trying to add reason that justifies or discounts those conjectures. Encouraging the notion that any given mathematical scenario could be met with *"What could I do?"* as opposed to *"What am I supposed to do?"* I once read someone describing the difference between what they saw as mathematics and what they saw as robotics. I quite liked that distinction. In all of that behaviour, there is, of course, much to be discovered, but I hope the difference between what I suggest and the aforementioned badly defined term is clear. I teach a lot of ideas explicitly but believe that once armed with some knowledge, students can be expected to behave mathematically with that knowledge at different levels and stages. It's a cycle. I have read and listened to great arguments for all kinds of principles of teaching and I like to think I employ lots of them over a period of time. The activities in this book are a key element that I think feeds and feeds off the others (I should definitely have used the term 'symbiotic'). Ultimately how they work and when they fit is a function of the individual teacher, their students and their bigger picture. I rarely read a reasoned argument about teaching that I think has no merit. I hope others will be as open reading this. If this book subscribes to a school of thought, then it is the school of behaving mathematically. Most, if not all, of the teachers and academics I read seem to agree on the importance of this, even if they agree less on the way in which such behaviour can be taught and learned. I would suggest that many of the teachers I have worked with have used the activities as I present them, but that many others have changed them to better fit the way they work. I would expect nothing less.

Appendix 2

Theory of knowledge

I have mentioned the teaching of theory of knowledge on a number of occasions through the book and thought some readers might find it useful to know more about this and how I think it has impacted my thinking. There is a great risk that, in doing so, I will come across as the amateur fledgling wannabe philosopher that I am. Hey ho.

Theory of knowledge, or epistemology, is a key branch of philosophy that essentially deals with the notion of knowledge, what it is, and how we produce and acquire it. All wrapped up in this, of course, are the important concepts of truth and certainty. Just as many countries have a compulsory philosophical element to their 16–18 year old curriculum, IB (International Baccalaureate) diploma students are all required to complete a 100-hour course in Theory of Knowledge alongside all the other elements. There are written assessments that ask students to write responses to questions about problems of knowledge and the significance of the different ways in which it is produced in different areas of knowledge. Students will learn about cognitive bias and explore the role of perspective where multiple truths might exist. They will learn about deductive, inductive and abductive reasoning (I had to look the last one up too! – Look on YouTube at 'crash course philosophy') and then at the holy trinity of thesis, antithesis and synthesis. They will explore scope and methodologies across the arts, history, the natural and human sciences and of course, mathematics while examining the difference in the nature of knowledge based on where it comes from, how it was produced and its position on a scale between subjective and objective. I'll stop now because there is a detailed guide and no need for me to paraphrase it all. The honourable intention is that this is the thread that pulls all the 6 subjects they study together. In practice it is pretty challenging, but a lot of fun.

To the point. A number of things about this have been very good for me. Firstly, it has made me spend much more time and thought on other subjects (areas of knowledge). This, in turn, has helped me to pay more attention to the different ways in which knowledge is produced. For example between the deductive logic that is common in mathematics and the inductive reasoning at the heart of much of the scientific method.

In chapter 1 I told the story of a mathematician and a scientist that are being held captive in a room. They are backs against the wall opposite the door from which they can escape. They are told that with each passing hour they will be allowed to travel half of the distance between themselves and the door. The mathematician's head drops as they dissolve into the despair that comes with knowing they will never escape. The scientist, by contrast, beams from ear to ear as they work out that after a few hours they will be close enough for all practical purposes. This is a provocative summary of the difference. Given that a student in school will, in different classes/circumstances be required to use both, it is reasonable to imagine that there are times when they might get confused about what reasoning is appropriate and when. They could be forgiven for getting it wrong. In history they learn that an argument will be considered when some good evidence is provided to support it. In the arts they will explore an artist's intent and possible alternative interpretations. It all sounds wonderful but is a very potent mix with huge potential for confusion. As such, I have found that being aware and explicit about the different types of justification being used to reach a conclusion has helped me to help students also be aware so that they might be conscious of the limits of that conclusion.

As individuals we reach conclusions that we turn into knowledge claims through a variety of methods. Our senses provide evidence – *"It looks like a square, I have seen squares before, I think it's a square"*. This is perfectly rational but could get you into trouble with the indestructible quadrilaterals. We use our intuition successfully all day long, so how are we supposed to know when we can't rely on it anymore? When is our intuition sufficiently informed to be useful? I see a pair of axes where one of my students might just see two intersecting lines. Who is right? How do we know? How do we mitigate these differences? What are the problems with language and how might they manifest themselves in a mathematics classroom? (I wonder who thought I was talking about two woodchopping implements in that earlier sentence.) All of these are ideas to do with knowledge and the knower that have helped me to understand important subtleties about conclusions students might rightly or unexpectedly or erroneously make when presented with a scenario that I am only seeing one way. I am certain (although we don't use this word often in theory of knowledge class) that having to think much more about all this has helped me to be more aware of how and why my students might construct knowledge, or make knowledge claims successfully or not. In turn, it has helped me to help them be aware. In the book I have pointed out that this might happen with quick observations that I say out loud, nothing much more than that. I think I was in my forties before I started to get my head around this, so I am just advocating a bit of drip-feeding for students.

More often than not, when a student makes a claim or a conjecture about something we are doing, it is the result of some kind of justification they have found. This is great. The influence that theory of knowledge has had on me is to help me be more aware and sympathetic to the different ways students do and are asked to do this so I can help them to do it successfully.

As I write, it feels like much of this is common knowledge and doesn't need to be put under a heading for people to understand it. All I am saying is that when I was asked to explicitly (or not, as the case may be) teach these ideas, it made me pay more attention to them.

References

At the start of the book, I wrote about 'originality and the lost bone' as an homage to how much of what teachers do relies and builds on what has gone before. I have borrowed very little from others in this book but recognise that all of it leans of the various sources of inspiration that have driven me. I have mentioned many through the book and thought it prudent to list them here in the order that they appear.

1089 and All That – David Acheson, 2010

The Big Bang Theory – 'The Raiders Minimization', Episode 4, Season 7, 2013

If the World Were a Village – David J. Smith and Shelagh Armstrong, 2003

Of All the People in All the World – Stans Café, 2007

Quote – "One death is a tragedy; a million is a statistic" (origin disputed)

The Billion Dollargram – David McCandless, Information Is Beautiful (updated June 2022)

The Wisdom of Crowds – James Surowiecki, 2005

Finding Nemo – Pixar Animation, 2003

Fermat's Last Theorem – Horizon BBC 2 Documentary, Simon Singh, 1996

Fermat Last Theorem – Simon Singh, 1997

100 Ways to Quarter the Cross – David Butler, 2016

Quarter the Cross – *Great Assessment Problems* – Dekker and Querelle, 2002

Number Search – Simon Gregg, 2019

Square of Squares – Pierre Claverie, 2015

Harry Potter and the Philosopher's Stone – Warner Bros Pictures, 2001

Anything You Want – Derek Sivers, 2015

Obvious to You. Amazing to Others – Derek Sivers, 2011

Bad Pharma – Ben Goldacre, 2013

Prime Club – Daniel Finkel

Yellow Constellation – Pierre Claverie, 2015

Gapminder.org – The Gapminder Foundation

Desmos

Mindstorms – Seymour Papert, 1993

GeoGebra

Maths Is the Hidden Secret to Understanding the World – Roger Antonsen, 2016

The Math Instinct – Keith Devlin, 2006

The Girl with the Dragon Tattoo - Stieg Larsson, 2011
Despicable Me - Illumination, Universal Pictures, 2010
The Full Monty - Redwave Films, 1997
The Deer Hunter - EMI, 1978
A Mathematician Reads the Newspaper - John Allen Paulos, 1995
Innumeracy - John Allen Paulos, 2011

Acknowledgements

I'll get straight to this. I said in the epilogue that I felt this has been a fairly self-indulgent exercise, even if the intention is a good one! For that, many people have put up with me and helped me. I must say thank you.

My family – It goes without saying that I depend so very much on the support of my family to do anything. In their case they have gone beyond the call. My wife, Li, is my rock, best friend and proofreader extraordinaire. My four amazing children have all been, and still are at the time of writing, guinea pigs in my classroom. As if that wasn't enough, they have had to take part in the debrief and reflection for my benefit too and pose for dancing vectors pictures. My parents and sisters mix a great brand of support with some diverse views on maths and education which has been really helpful!

Rich in S3 – It has been such an amazing experience to be in a department of three that have taught together in neighbouring rooms since 2006. Rich and I go back to 2004. We are close to having had every conversation there is to have about what we do, but still we can go on about it. Cricket and football too of course. Every chapter in this book is made up of bits of teachers everywhere and bits of Rich. Thanks mate.

Ollie in S2 – In between us is the enigmatic Ollie. Everyone needs an Ollie in their life, but I fear he is unique. He has been another enormous source of support and inspiration to me over the years. He will always stretch me to think deeper because he always asks the same of himself. I am forever grateful.

Tony – I had occasionally mentioned an interest in teaching and so, before Li and I headed off around the world in '97, Mum and Dad made me sign up to a PGCSE at Nottingham University to give me some chance of direction. There was no looking back after an amazing year in Nottingham under Tony Cotton's guidance. What a brilliant introduction to this career. Emulating Tony's depth, enthusiasm and skill has always been a goal.

Anne – I moved from Nottingham to Oxford where I was casually persuaded into a postgrad thing with Anne Watson at Oxford University. Anne has been a mentor for me ever since. No doubt as a source of inspiration too but probably more like the voice in my head that asks really good questions about my motives, my practice, my students and my assumptions. Anne's contribution to mathematics education is enormous and I am grateful for any of that I have been able to benefit from.

Maths teachers everywhere – I have been so lucky to have met many teachers from all over the world. I am often given to saying at the start of weekend workshops that I find the idea of being locked in a room full of maths teachers my ideal weekend. To those that were not understandably frightened off by this, I am very grateful for our exchanges, however long or short. To those out there in the ether who share their thoughts and ideas so willingly through blogs, resources and books I am also grateful. I hope I have, and can continue to, return the favours.

Bruce – Writing has been a great challenge, but it doesn't go anywhere without a publisher and Bruce Roberts at Routledge is giving me my first chance with this book. He has been very gentle, supportive and honest with me, and I am so grateful for this and this chance. Thanks Bruce.

David – My brother-in-law is a retired (in theory) publisher with oodles of experience and contacts and he has been a wonderful sounding board for me in recent years, for which I am very grateful.

Lizzie – My brilliant sister Elizabeth is a best-selling novelist who has been writing as long as I can remember. She too has been an awesome sounding board along the way. She once wrote in a good spirited exchange that I was *"coming for her brand"*. I don't think she understands what I am writing about!

My colleagues – I have had some incredible colleagues over the years. Everyone brings something to the school table. Lots are inspiring, lots are supportive and everyone cares so much about what we do. This is one of the most exciting things about teaching that also helps to get me out of bed in the morning.

Pierre – My good friend Pierre's dad was a maths teacher, so Pierre became an artist! Then, eventually, a primary school teacher. Pierre has grilled me endlessly about what I see and think about maths at school. This has resulted in a beautiful series of posters he made depicting some mathematical ideas we talked about. He always wants to talk about my book. That is a really good friend!

Benoit – My friend Ben, who I talk about in the introduction, is arguably the starting point for all this, right? This is certainly cause for acknowledgement. Ben and his family have had a really tough year, but he still comes over and asks good questions about it all. Thanks Ben, we'll always remember G.

Bring on the maths lessons!

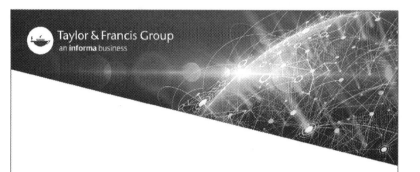

Taylor & Francis eBooks

www.taylorfrancis.com

A single destination for eBooks from Taylor & Francis
with increased functionality and an improved user
experience to meet the needs of our customers.

90,000+ eBooks of award-winning academic content in
Humanities, Social Science, Science, Technology, Engineering,
and Medical written by a global network of editors and authors.

TAYLOR & FRANCIS EBOOKS OFFERS:

A streamlined
experience for
our library
customers

A single point
of discovery
for all of our
eBook content

Improved
search and
discovery of
content at both
book and
chapter level

REQUEST A FREE TRIAL
support@taylorfrancis.com

 Routledge
Taylor & Francis Group

 CRC Press
Taylor & Francis Group

Printed in the United States
by Baker & Taylor Publisher Services